T0215667

Asynchronous Programming with SwiftUI and Combine

Functional Programming to Build UIs on Apple Platforms

Peter Friese

Apress®

Asynchronous Programming with SwiftUI and Combine: Functional Programming to Build UIs on Apple Platforms

Peter Friese
Hamburg, Germany

ISBN-13 (pbk): 978-1-4842-8571-8   ISBN-13 (electronic): 978-1-4842-8572-5
https://doi.org/10.1007/978-1-4842-8572-5

Managing Director, Apress Media LLC: Welmoed Spahr
Acquisitions Editor: Susan McDermott
Development Editor: James Markham
Coordinating Editor: Jessica Vakili

Distributed to the book trade worldwide by Springer Science+Business Media New York, 1 NY Plaza, New York, NY 10004. Phone 1-800-SPRINGER, fax (201) 348-4505, e-mail orders-ny@ springer-sbm.com, or visit www.springeronline.com. Apress Media, LLC is a California LLC and the sole member (owner) is Springer Science + Business Media Finance Inc (SSBM Finance Inc). SSBM Finance Inc is a **Delaware** corporation.

For information on translations, please e-mail booktranslations@springernature.com; for reprint, paperback, or audio rights, please e-mail bookpermissions@springernature.com.

Apress titles may be purchased in bulk for academic, corporate, or promotional use. eBook versions and licenses are also available for most titles. For more information, reference our Print and eBook Bulk Sales web page at http://www.apress.com/bulk-sales.

Any source code or other supplementary material referenced by the author in this book is available to readers on the Github repository: https://github.com/Apress/Asynchronous-Programming-with-SwiftUI-and-Combine. For more detailed information, please visit http://www.apress.com/source-code.

Printed on acid-free paper

For Anne

Table of Contents

About the Author xv

Foreword xvii

Preface xix

Acknowledgments xxi

About This Book.. xxiii

Part 1 1

Chapter 1: SwiftUI: A New Beginning 3

  Why a New UI Framework?.. 5

  SwiftUI Principles.. 7

    Declarative vs. Imperative 7

    State Management 8

    Composition over Inheritance.. 9

    Everything Is a View—Except That It Isn't....................................... 10

    UIs Are a Function of Their State 10

  A Quick Tour of SwiftUI.. 11

    Prerequisites 11

    Creating a New SwiftUI App.. 11

    Adding Some Interaction to Your App 19

Using SwiftUI's State Management to Keep UI and Model in Sync 25

Exercises..31

Summary..31

Chapter 2: Getting Started with SwiftUI 33

What We're Going to Build...34

Composing a View for Displaying a Book...36

Build the View with Static Data...40

Using the Preview to Make Sure Our View Works As Intended 51

Displaying a List of Books...53

Setting Up Data Binding..56

Adjusting the Preview Canvas..59

Making the Code Reusable 60

Refactoring the Code Using Extract Subview 60

Renaming ContentView 64

Keep Complexity in Check 65

Views and View Modifiers 65

Exercises..66

Tips and Tricks 66

Summary..67

Chapter 3: SwiftUI Building Blocks...69

Views 70

User Interface Views..74

Container Views...78

Layout Behavior...79

Views Are Just Descriptions of the UI..80

View Modifiers 83

Configuring Views..84

Applying View Modifiers to Child Views...87

Using View Modifiers to Register Action Handlers........................89

Summary...92

Chapter 4: State Management 93

Managing State in SwiftUI 94

Binding Value Types 95

Binding Objects...98

ObservableObject..99

@StateObject 99

When to Use 101

@ObservedObject 101

When to Use 103

@EnvironmentObject 103

When to Use 106

Summary...106

Chapter 5: Displaying Data in Lists..107

Getting Started with Lists in SwiftUI 107

Using Other SwiftUI Views Inside List Rows 109

Building Custom List Rows..111

More Complex List Rows 114

Dynamic Lists..117

Displaying a List of Elements 117

Using List Bindings to Allow Modifying List Items....................121

Asynchronously Fetching Data 123

Pull-to-Refresh 126

Searching 130

Styling 134

    List Styles 135

    Headers and Footers 137

    List Cells 139

    Separators 140

Actions 143

    Swipe-to-Delete 144

    Moving and Deleting Items Using EditMode 145

    Swipe Actions 147

Managing Focus in Lists 154

    How to Manage Focus in SwiftUI 154

    How to Manage Focus in Lists 156

    Handling the Enter Key 158

    What About MVVM? 159

    Eliminating Empty Elements 163

Summary 165

Chapter 6: Building Input Forms 167

Building Simple Forms 168

Showing Data in a Form 179

Make It Editable 182

Drill-Down Navigation 184

Input Validation 191

    Using .onChange(of:) 192

    Using a View Model to Handle Form Validation 193

    Synchronizing a Local Source of Truth with the Global Source of
    Truth by Using @Binding and @ObservableObject 196

    Using Combine to Perform Form Validation 202

Summary 204

Part 2 205

Chapter 7: Getting Started with Combine 207

What Is Functional Reactive Programming? 207

Publishers 209

Subscribers 211

Operators 213

Composing Operators 215

Combining Publishers 220

Summary..223

Chapter 8: Driving UI State with Combine 225

Input Validation Using Combine 226

    The Sign-Up Form View 227

    The View Model 229

    Validating the Username 232

    Displaying Validation Messages 234

    Encapsulating Combine Pipelines in Computed Properties.......................236

    Validating the Password 238

    Putting It All Together 241

Exercises..243

Summary..244

Chapter 9: Networking with Combine...247

Fetching Data Using URLSession 248

Using Combine to Fetch Data...252

    Destructuring Tuples Using Key Paths..254

    Mapping Data 254

    Fetching Data Using Combine, Simplified...255

Connecting to the UI..256

Handling Multithreading..262

Optimizing Network Access 263

    Finding the Root Cause..264

    Using the share Operator to Share a Publisher 266

    Using debounce to Further Optimize the UX...............................269

    Using removeDuplicates to Avoid Sending the Same Request Twice..........270

Bringing It All Together..271

Exercises..273

Summary...274

Chapter 10: Error Handling in Combine 275

Error Handling Strategies..276

    Ignoring the Error 276

    Retrying (with Exponential Backoff) 276

    Showing an Error Message 277

    Replacing the Entire View with an Error View 277

    Showing an Inline Error Message...278

Typical Error Conditions and How to Handle Them 278

    Implementing a Fallible Network API...279

    Calling the API and Handling Errors..282

    Handling Device/Network Offline Errors......................................286

    Handling Validation Errors 289

    Handling Response Parsing Errors 293

    Handling Internal Server Errors 298

Summary...305

Chapter 11: Implementing Custom Combine Operators 307

What Is a Combine Operator? 307

Implementing Custom Operators 309

Implementing a Retry Operator with a Delay.......................................311

Conditionally Retrying..313

Implementing a Retry Operator for Exponential Backoff.....................314

Summary...316

Chapter 12: Wrapping Existing APIs in Combine 317

A Case Study..317

Using Combine to Access Firestore..321

    Using View Models and Published Properties 322

    Using Combine to Wrap APIs 325

Creating Your Own Publishers...327

    Using PassthroughSubject to Wrap Snapshot Listeners....................328

    Using Future to Implement One-Time Fetching from Firestore 332

Summary...335

Chapter 13: Combine Schedulers and SwiftUI 337

What Is a Scheduler 338

Types of Schedulers 340

Default Behavior...341

Switching Schedulers 344

    Controlling Upstream Publishers Using subscribe(on:) 346

    Controlling Downstream Subscribers Using receive(on:) 349

    Other Operators That Influence Scheduling.......................................351

Performing Asynchronous Work..353

Integrating with Other APIs 354

    URLSession 355

    Firebase 356

Summary 358

Part 3 361

Chapter 14: Getting Started with async/await 363

Synchronous Programming with Functions 367

Asynchronous Programming with Closures 371

Asynchronous Programming with async/await 377

    Defining and Calling Asynchronous Functions 377

    Calling Asynchronous Functions in Parallel 381

Summary 383

Chapter 15: Using async/await in SwiftUI 385

Fetching Data Asynchronously Using URLSession 386

Calling Asynchronous Code 387

The Task View Modifier 388

Calling Asynchronous Code When the User Taps a Button 390

Using Pull-to-Refresh to Update Views Asynchronously 390

Searchable Views and async/await 391

Updating the UI from the Main Thread 394

Summary 402

Chapter 16: Bringing It All Together: SwiftUI, async/await, and Combine 405

Fetching Data Using Combine 406

Fetching Data Using async/await 407

Is This the End of Combine? 409

Connecting the UI…..410

…to a Combine Pipeline..410

…to an async/await Method 413

Calling Asynchronous Code from Combine 415

Summary...420

Index...**423**

About the Author

 **Peter Friese** is a software engineer with over 30 years of experience in building software for a wide range of platforms—from Windows, J2EE, the Web, Android, to iOS and the Mac. He works as a Senior Developer Advocate on the Firebase team at Google, where he is in charge of making sure iOS developer have a great experience using the Firebase SDK on iOS and Apple's other platforms.

Peter writes about SwiftUI, Swift, and Firebase development on his blog, peterfriese.dev, and can be found on Twitter as @peterfriese.

Foreword

I've been developing iOS apps for a while and started learning SwiftUI almost as soon as it was released back in 2019. I remember that I couldn't wait to start using it because it just seemed so much more intuitive for me than UIKit.

There wasn't much SwiftUI documentation at first and those of us who jumped straight in had to figure out a lot of things for ourselves. So I started sharing what I learned while building apps with SwiftUI on a blog.

Just a few months later, the SwiftUI team at Apple reached out to me to join them in working on the framework. It was an invaluable experience and it gave me a great perspective on the inner workings of SwiftUI and the decisions behind the APIs. Sure, SwiftUI is not perfect and still needs time to mature, but it's already making many developers happier and more excited about building apps for Apple platforms. A lot of thought goes into making SwiftUI APIs as simple and as streamlined as they are, so that we can get the right behavior for the platform by default.

I left Apple in April 2022 and joined Nil Coalescing as a cofounder and a software engineer. Though I'm a little sad that I don't get to contribute to the SwiftUI framework directly anymore, I'm really happy that I'm now able to use the APIs I helped to develop and to share my SwiftUI knowledge with other iOS developers.

Seeing how much Apple is betting on SwiftUI by introducing new frameworks that require using it like *WidgetKit* and *Swift Charts,* I believe it has a great potential. It's also nice to see how many more developers are starting to use SwiftUI and how much more great SwiftUI-related content is now available both from Apple and from the community.

I believe that *Asynchronous Programming with SwiftUI and Combine* is a valuable addition to your book collection if you are going to work with SwiftUI. I like its unique focus on calling asynchronous APIs from SwiftUI applications, since it's usually a major part of a real-world project. And Peter Friese is certainly the right person to talk about it given his work as a Developer Advocate for Firebase where he gets to experiment a lot with the Firebase asynchronous APIs and teach how to use them with SwiftUI. This book is full of practical examples using both Combine and Swift async/await APIs and will serve as a great foundation for developing SwiftUI apps with networking or local asynchronous data processing.

Natalia Panferova

Author of *Integrating SwiftUI into UIKit Apps*

and Founder of *Nil Coalescing* (https://nilcoalescing.com/about/)

Preface

I started developing for iPhone OS (as it was called back then) in 2009. I had just upgraded from an iPhone 3 to an iPhone 3GS, and I was super excited to kick the tires and build my first app—using Xcode and Objective-C!

I already had practice using a variety of other IDEs, languages, and operating systems: starting out with GW-BASIC on MS-DOS, to Visual Basic and Delphi on Windows, to Java with Jbuilder, Websphere Application Developer, and Eclipse (for building J2EE and Spring applications for enterprise customers).

But using Xcode and Objective-C was a bit of a shock. All the other IDEs that I'd used before were a lot more powerful (e.g., they all offered refactoring support), and Objective-C with all its square brackets looked a bit strange to me.

Looking back at all the years of building software, Delphi was one of the most productive environments I've used to build software. It combined a mature, object-oriented language (Object Pascal) and a powerful IDE that allowed developers to quickly put together UIs for Windows apps. Plus, the tagline "Rapid Application Development" certainly had a ring to it.

But Xcode and Objective-C were the future, so I buckled up and continued my journey to learn how to use them.

Fast forward ten years—I had just watched WWDC 2019 and was thrilled by SwiftUI and its ease of use. Building UIs with SwiftUI felt so snappy, and reminded me of Delphi in many ways. I started thinking about how amazing it would be to combine SwiftUI with a framework that makes building backend systems easier.

When the Firebase team at Google was looking for a person to join their Developer Relations team to specifically focus on the iOS developer ecosystem, I realized the opportunity this meant for me: bring together a language I love (Swift), a UI toolkit that enables developers to quickly build great-looking UIs (SwiftUI), and an SDK that makes developers more efficient by removing the need to run and operate your own backend system (Firebase). With all these tools, I could help people build better apps, faster.

On day one after joining the Firebase DevRel team as a Developer Advocate, I started building demos to showcase the features of the Firebase iOS SDK. And I quickly learned that writing demos using SwiftUI was so much easier than using UIKit. This ease of use meant that I could focus on what I actually wanted to teach: how to use the Firebase SDK and its APIs.

SwiftUI's declarative approach to building UIs is a lot more opinionated about how your code should be structured when building UIs programmatically, making it a lot easier for other developers to understand what your code is supposed to do.

And thanks to using a state management model that is based on functional reactive programming, SwiftUI and Combine make it a lot easier to build UIs that are in sync with the underlying data model and other parts of your app all of the time. I'm pretty sure we all know of apps for which this is not the case and can attest to the terrible UX this means.

The goal of this book is to introduce you to building applications with SwiftUI, Combine, and async/await. I also aim to provide some guidance that helps you architect apps that reap the benefits of using declarative and functional reactive approaches for building UI-heavy applications that interface with asynchronous backend systems, such as Firebase.

Thanks for buying this book! I hope it turns out to be useful for you, and I would love to hear from you. You can tweet me (I am @peterfriese on Twitter), or leave a comment on the GitHub repo[1] of this book.

---

[1] https://github.com/peterfriese/SwiftUI-Combine-Book/issues

Acknowledgments

Writing a book is a cross-functional effort, and the result of contributions from many different people, and this book is no different.

First and foremost, I must thank Todd Kerpelman for believing in me and giving me the opportunity to join the Firebase Developer Relations team and become the resident iOS expert.

Additionally, I'd like to thank the many people who provided feedback, encouragement, guidance, and technical expertise for the topics covered in this book, including Heiko Behrens, Paul Beusterien, Bas Broek, Marina Coelho, David East, Rosário Fernandes, Todd Kerpelman, Shai Mishali, Rachel Myers, Laurence Moroney, Natalia Panferova, Donny Wals, and Ryan Wilson. The conversations with you were invaluable input to this book and helped inform my thinking about SwiftUI, Combine, asynchronous programming, and how to present these topics in a written form.

This book simply wouldn't have been possible without the various teams at Apress/Springer who guided me through the process and helped shape this book into what it is now. I am particularly grateful to Aaron Schwarz for convincing me to write this book in the first place, Clement Wilson for helping me stay on track, and Jessica Vakili for shaping the content into great teaching material.

I also owe a huge debt of gratitude to all the reviewers who provided feedback along the way, including Tunde Adegoroye, Paul Beusterien, Marcus Ficner, Adam Fordyce, Dominik Hauser, Rachel Saunders, Florian Schweizer, and Ryan Wilson. They did an amazing job at finding inconsistencies, typos, grammatical issues, and coding errors that the compiler didn't spot. Any remaining errors and mistakes are entirely mine.

ACKNOWLEDGMENTS

If you spot any, I would be grateful if you filed an issue[1] on this book's GitHub repository, so I can fix them for any future editions.

Finally, my deepest thanks go to my wife Anne and my sons Sören, Lennart, and Jonas. You endured the time I put into creating this book and its companion code, and my focus when writing it. Your encouragement and company is what kept me going—I couldn't have done this without you!

---

[1] https://github.com/peterfriese/Asynchronous-Programming-with-SwiftUI-and-Combine/issues

About This Book

Asynchronous Programming with SwiftUI and Combine was written to provide a practical guide to building UIs using the latest APIs and toolkits available from Apple. It begins by introducing SwiftUI as a modern and easy-to-use framework for building reactive UIs in a declarative way. After covering the basic concepts you need to understand to build efficient user interfaces in SwiftUI, it then dives into functional reactive programming and how you can use Combine to solve many of the challenges developers face when building UI-heavy applications that interact with asynchronous backend services. Finally, the book covers Swift's new structured concurrency features, how they relate to Combine, and when you should use one or the other.

Who Should Read This Book

Asynchronous Programming with SwiftUI and Combine is for anyone who builds applications with SwiftUI.

If you have some SwiftUI experience, and would like to better understand how its state management works, and how you can build your apps more efficiently using view models and Combine, then this book is probably for you.

How This Book Is Organized

This book is organized into three main parts, each covering a different aspect of building reactive UIs on Apple's platforms.

Part 1 covers SwiftUI and its state management. You will learn how to build user interfaces with SwiftUI's declarative approach, and how SwiftUI's reactive state management makes it easier to write apps that keep their application state in sync even across multiple screens.

- Chapter 1 explains why SwiftUI is an important building block in Apple's strategy for making app development easier. It also provides a quick introduction of some of the key concepts this book will cover in more detail in the following chapters.

- Chapter 2 walks you through building a simple application from scratch. In this chapter, you will learn some key SwiftUI concepts, as well as some useful techniques for keeping your code maintainable.

- Chapter 3 dives deeper into key SwiftUI concepts such as views, view modifiers, and layout behavior.

- Chapter 4 covers one of the center pieces of SwiftUI: state management. It explains the different ways for managing state in SwiftUI apps and provides practical examples for when to use which approach.

- Chapter 5 provides an in-depth look at one of the most common types of UI: lists. SwiftUI provides a very flexible and powerful API for building List views, and this chapter will be your guide for navigating it.

- Chapter 6 explains how to build another very popular type of UI: (input) forms.

Part 2 focuses on Combine, Apple's reactive framework. You will learn how Combine works and how to use it for both UIs and code that interfaces with the backend.

- Chapter 7 provides an introduction to functional reactive programming and Combine's key concepts. You will lean what publishers, subscribers, and operators are, and how you can use them to process events over time.

- Chapter 8 explains how to use Combine to implement complex UIs. You will learn how to use multiple Combine pipelines to drive the UI state of an input form with several input fields.

- Chapter 9 shows you how to use Combine to access the network. You will then learn how to integrate this with the pipelines you built in the previous chapters to build a more complex input validation pipeline.

- Chapter 10 covers the important topic of error handling and will equip you with a number of progressively more powerful strategies for handling errors and looping in the user for error mitigation in a meaningful way.

- Chapter 11 picks up where Chapter 10 left off and will demonstrate how to build a custom Combine operator for implementing incremental backoff—an error-handling strategy that is useful especially for accessing networked resources.

- Chapter 12 teaches you how to wrap existing APIs in Combine so you can use them in Combine pipelines. As a case study, this chapter will wrap some of Firebase's asynchronous APIs to demonstrate two common strategies for wrapping APIs in Combine.

- Chapter 13 explains what schedulers are and how they will help you write multithreaded code in a declarative way.

The third and final part covers Swift's new structured concurrency (better known as async/await), how it relates to Combine, and how you can use it to build apps that feel snappy but are able to interface with asynchronous APIs such as URLSession and other asynchronous APIs such as Firebase.

- Chapter 14 provides an introduction to asynchronous programming, covering traditional ways (using closures) and async/await.

- Chapter 15 explains how to use Swift's new concurrency APIs with SwiftUI, specifically covering the custom view modifiers (such as task, refreshable, and searchable) that have been added for this task.[1]

- When Apple released Swift's new structured concurrency model, people were confused about whether or not they should continue using Combine in their apps, or make the switch to async/await. Chapter 16 focuses on this and provides some guidance for when to use which (spoiler: it depends on your use case).

About the Code

You can find the code for this book in the book's GitHub repository at https://github.com/peterfriese/Asynchronous-Programming-with-SwiftUI-and-Combine.

All sample projects can be compiled with the latest stable version of Xcode (at the time of this writing, Xcode version 14) and run on the latest released version of iOS (at the time of this writing, iOS 16).

---

[1] Please forgive the pun.

Great care was taken to make sure the sample code compiles with the latest versions of Xcode and iOS. Should you run into any issues, or find any mistakes, please file an issue on the issue tracker[2] of this book's repository:

- For any typos or mistakes in the book itself, please use the *typos* issue template.

- For any issues with the code, please use the *code* issue template.

You're also very welcome to send PRs to fix any issues in the code. If you do so, I will make sure to mention you in any future version of the book.

---

[2]https://github.com/peterfriese/Asynchronous-Programming-with-SwiftUI-and-Combine/issues/

Part 1

CHAPTER 1

SwiftUI: A New Beginning

Every year at the Worldwide Developers Conference (WWDC), Apple introduces new features and capabilities to their platforms and operating systems. The event is met with great anticipation, as it means developers will finally be able to get their hands on the new APIs and frameworks Apple engineers have been working on for the past year, and incorporate them into their own apps.

To enable developers to make use of the new features, Apple provides new APIs, SDKs to use them, and often new tooling, such as Xcode.

While all those new features Apple has launched at WWDC throughout the years have been exciting and often breathtaking, sometimes they ship an update of extraordinary significance.

> *Every once in a while, a revolutionary product comes along that changes everything.*
>
> —*Steve Jobs, 2007*

Obviously, the unveiling of the original iPhone in 2007 was such a moment.

© Peter Friese 2023
P. Friese, *Asynchronous Programming with SwiftUI and Combine*,
https://doi.org/10.1007/978-1-4842-8572-5_1

The release of the Swift programming language in 2014 was another moment of significance. Swift made software development much easier and a lot more approachable for developers who might have been scared away by Objective-C and its rather special syntax and Smalltalk-esque call semantics. It's no exaggeration to say that Swift and Swift Playgrounds brought more developers to Apple's platforms than ever before. Swift Playgrounds—an interactive programming environment geared toward explorative and playful interaction with Swift—has positioned Swift as a great language for anyone who is looking for a low-barrier way to explore and learn programming. Swift and Swift Playgrounds have democratized software development. And the results of this bold move are visible each year at WWDC, when Tim Cook takes the stage to announce how many apps are on the App Store and which percentage of those use Swift. At WWDC 2021, Susan Prescott (VP of Developer Relations) unveiled that "the majority of the top 1000 apps on the App Store are built using Swift."[1]

The release of SwiftUI in 2019 was another such moment. When Josh Shaffer stepped out onto the stage to announce SwiftUI,[2] people were stunned by its ease of use and the speed at which it was possible to build UIs from scratch. But also, and maybe even more importantly, people were thrilled by the fact that SwiftUI included a native way to manage application state—something notoriously complicated. Apple even went so far as to implement their own version of RxSwift: Combine—a functional reactive framework centered around the idea that applications can be seen as a piece of software that transforms events over time.

To better understand what all of this means and why exactly Apple chose to implement a new UI toolkit, let's dive a little deeper.

---

[1] WWDC 2021 Keynote—https://youtu.be/OTD96VTfOXs?t=5800
[2] WWDC 2019 Keynote—https://youtu.be/psL_5RIBqnY?t=7782

Why a New UI Framework?

Why implement a new UI toolkit, if there are already UIKit and AppKit, you might ask, and you'd be forgiven for doing so. After all, implementing a UI toolkit is no small feat, much less bringing it to production quality, shipping it, and asking an entire community of app developers to adopt it.

Here are some of the driving factors that might have influenced Apple's decision.

First and foremost, we have to acknowledge that Apple positions SwiftUI as a cross-platform UI toolkit. The introduction on the SwiftUI landing page[3] specifically mentions that *"SwiftUI helps you build great looking apps across all Apple platforms with the power of Swift — and surprisingly little code. You can bring even better experiences to everyone, on any Apple device, using just one set of tools and APIs."* Apple now has no less than five consumer-facing platforms (iOS, iPadOS, watchOS, tvOS, and macOS), and as anyone who has tried to ensure feature parity across platforms will be able to tell you, supporting more than just one platform is becoming increasingly burdensome for developers. By providing a unified way to reason about and build UIs for as many of these platforms as possible, Apple is relieving developers of this burden. It should be noted, however, that SwiftUI is not trying to fit a "write once, run everywhere" paradigm—on the contrary, it does have platform-specific parts. But it's much easier to learn one UI toolkit and use it across all those platforms than having to learn a new paradigm for each individual platform.

Secondly, SwiftUI aligns with Apple's investment in helping developers to write better software and reduce the number of potential bugs in the apps on the App Store. Apps with fewer bugs tend to get better ratings on the App Store—and consequently return a higher revenue.

---

[3] https://developer.apple.com/xcode/swiftui/

The Swift language contains many features that make it easier to write bug-free software. Its language designers and compiler engineers have been working hard on eliminating potential causes for bugs, such as

- Null dereferencing

- Type mismatches

- Incomplete decision trees

- ...and more

SwiftUI has two major attributes that help increase software quality:

1. It has built-in state management, an aspect of UI development that is notoriously challenging. SwiftUI's state management makes it easier to build UIs that reflect the state of the app at all times—even across multiple screens.

2. It is centered around a domain-specific language (DSL[4]) that makes it easier to describe the UI, eliminating any issues that might be caused by incorrectly instantiating and structuring UIs, and making it easier to write and reason about UIs.

And lastly, SwiftUI makes software development more approachable. It is not without reason that we've seen a lot more web developers and designers start building UIs in SwiftUI. Putting together a working prototype in SwiftUI has become increasingly feasible and has helped to improve the collaboration between UI designers and developers. Xcode's preview canvas for SwiftUI has dramatically shortened turnaround times and provides developers and designers with instant feedback to the

---

[4] Specifically, a so-called internal DSL. See *DSL Engineering: Designing, Implementing and Using Domain-Specific Languages* by Markus Voelter to learn more about DSLs.

changes they make. This instant feedback has enabled more students and beginners to get started with app development and achieving results within minutes rather than hours or even days.

SwiftUI Principles

Before we take the first steps in SwiftUI, it is worth taking a look at some of its key properties.

Declarative vs. Imperative

Traditionally, there have been two main ways how developers build UIs:

1. Using visual tools (such as *Interface Builder*) to lay out the UI elements, and then connecting their app's code to the UI elements

2. Programmatically laying out the UI elements

In the past couple of years, there has been an increasing number of UI toolkits that follow a declarative approach to building UIs. These toolkits make use of so-called internal or external domain-specific languages (DSLs) to let developers specify the structure of the UI. Examples for such toolkits are Angular[5], React[6] and JetPack Compose[7].

In an imperative world, you need to implement everything yourself: layout, behavior, data binding. In contrast, a declarative approach allows you to simply tell the framework what to do, and it will take care of the specifics for you. It's a bit like cooking a meal by yourself (imperative) or going to a restaurant, where you place your order and receive a nicely cooked meal in return (declarative).

---

[5] https://angular.io/guide/glossary#domain-specific-language-dsl
[6] https://reactjs.org/
[7] https://developer.android.com/jetpack/compose

State Management

Managing state is one of the major challenges when writing an application. It's quite simple when your app only has one screen, but as the number of screens increases, so does the complexity of keeping all parts of the UI and the underlying data model in sync.

It becomes even more of a challenge in apps that share data with a backend and synchronize data via the Internet. Not to mention the challenges you will face when writing a multiuser app that needs to ensure the data is up to date and in sync for all users who simultaneously work on the same piece of data (e.g., a shared document in Google Docs, or a task lists in a to-do list application).

Probably all of us have used an app that, despite the fact you updated your address in a detail dialog, didn't reflect that change of address in the shopping basket. Excruciating!

Data binding is not an entirely new concept on Apple's platforms—Cocoa Bindings[8] on macOS has been around for a number of years now, providing developers with the basic tools to map data between UI elements and the underlying data model. Despite developers clamoring for a data-binding framework for iOS, Apple never provided one—so far. Left to their own devices, developers had to come up with their own, homegrown solutions, and it didn't take long for the community to come up with iOS-specific implementations of functional reactive frameworks such as RxSwift[9] or ReactiveSwift[10].

---

[8] https://bit.ly/3PBVoOZ
[9] https://github.com/ReactiveX/RxSwift
[10] https://github.com/ReactiveCocoa/ReactiveSwift

With SwiftUI, Apple finally acknowledged the need for a native framework for keeping your data model and UI in sync. SwiftUI comes with a number of tools to help you build UIs that reflect the state of your model at all times, and keep in sync across your entire app.

Most importantly, SwiftUI combines well with Combine, Apple's own implementation of a reactive framework, making it possible to express the flow of data in your apps as a stream of events over time that are transformed by business rules and logic operators to meet the requirements of the app.

Composition over Inheritance

In contrast to UIKit and many other UI frameworks, SwiftUI encourages developers to compose their UIs by piecing together many small UI components. Developers who come to SwiftUI from UIKit will find this rather surprising, as they've learned to minimize the number of UI elements—in particular in scrolling views such as `UITableView` or `UICollectionView` to optimize their app's performance.

The reason for this is that SwiftUI is a DSL that describes the look of a UI, rather than prescribing the UI primitives it is made up of. The SwiftUI team has encouraged developers to make liberal use of views to compose their UIs right from the onset—in their first-ever public presentation of SwiftUI on the WWDC 2019 stage, Jacob Xiao, SwiftUI Engineer, says "and with SwiftUI, views are really lightweight so you don't have to worry about creating extra views to better encapsulate or separate your logic."[11]

---

[11] WWDC 2019 Session 204, Introducing SwiftUI: Building Your First App, time code 11:56 (https://bit.ly/3FSaz3k)

Everything Is a View—Except That It Isn't

Once you start building UIs in SwiftUI, you will quickly notice that all the UI elements are called *Views*—even a screen is considered a *View*! It is tempting to think that all those views are equivalent to UIView (or the respective subclass). SwiftUI might in fact choose to render some parts of your UI using one of UIView's subclasses. However, it is worth noting that when SwiftUI talks about *Views*, it doesn't refer to the specific instances of a UI element on the screen, but rather a *description* of that element.

In fact, it might have been easier if the SwiftUI team had decided to say *"everything is a view description"*—but of course, that's not as catchy.

UIs Are a Function of Their State

One of the biggest challenges in building UIs is making sure the UI reflects the state of the underlying data model at all times. Previously, developers had to use a variety of tools and mechanisms to ensure any changes to the model are reflected in the UI, and vice versa. A variety of architectural patterns for dealing with this challenge have been devised: MVC (Model View Controller), MVVM (Model, View, ViewModel), MVP (Model View Presenter), VIPER (View, Interactor, Presenter, Entity, and Routing), etc. With SwiftUI, Apple decided to bake state management right into the framework. In SwiftUI, the UI is a function of the model's state. This is worth keeping in mind.

In SwiftUI, the UI is a function of the model's state

To update the UI, you no longer directly manipulate the individual UI components. Instead, you bind the UI elements to underlying models. Every time you change an attribute on the model, SwiftUI will refresh the UI elements that are bound to this attribute, making sure the UI and model are always in sync.

This also means it becomes very difficult to accidentally forget to update parts of the UI: all parts of the UI that are bound to an underlying model will be updated automatically by SwiftUI for you.

A Quick Tour of SwiftUI

To get a better understanding of SwiftUI and how it works, let's build the traditional "Hello World" sample application. But instead of just displaying "Hello World," we will use SwiftUI's built-in state management capabilities to greet you by name.

By following this little tutorial, you will learn how to

- Create a new SwiftUI project in Xcode

- Use the code editor and the *Attributes* inspector to make two-way changes to the UI

- Use SwiftUI's simple state management capabilities to ensure UI and model are kept in sync

Prerequisites

To follow this tutorial (and all others in this book), you will need the following:

- A recent version of Xcode (14 or higher)

- A Mac running macOS Monterey

Creating a New SwiftUI App

1. Launch Xcode and click *Create a new Xcode project.*

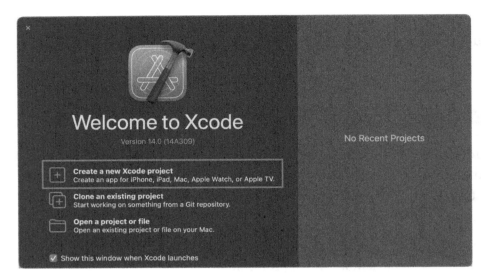

Figure 1-1. *Creating a new project in Xcode*

    2.   Make sure to select the *iOS* section, and then choose the *App* template.

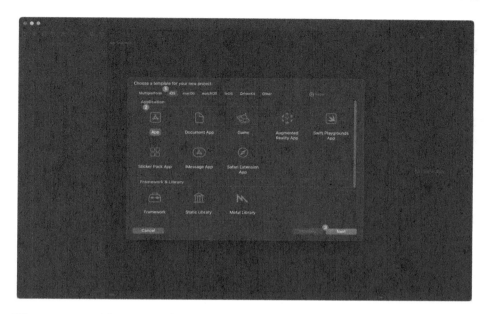

Figure 1-2. *Choosing the iOS App template*

3. Provide a name for your project (I chose `Hello`
    `SwiftUI`), and make sure the following options
    are set:

    – Interface: *SwiftUI*

    – Life Cycle: *SwiftUI App*

    – Language: *Swift*

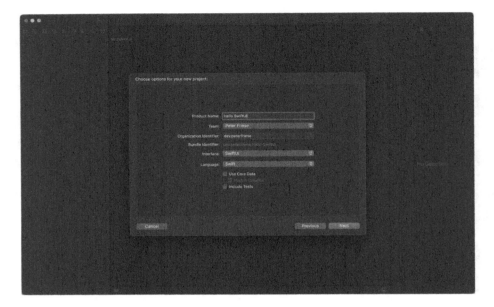

Figure 1-3. *Setting the project name and other project options*

For now, you can leave the *Include Tests* option unchecked.

4. Click Next and choose where to store your project.
    You can leave the *Create Git repository on my Mac*
    option checked, or turn it off if you like.

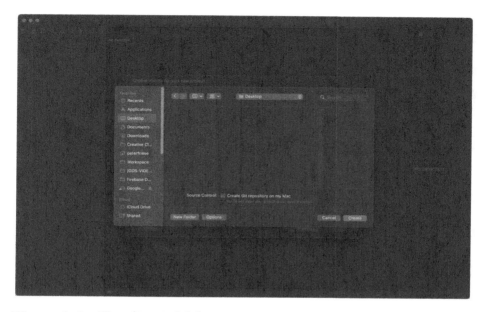

Figure 1-4. *Choosing a folder to save the project to*

Xcode will create the project for you, and you should find yourself in the editor for ContentView.swift:

Figure 1-5. *Xcode source editor and preview canvas*

To the right of the editor, you will find the *Canvas*, which will display a preview of your UI. If it shows a message saying "Preview paused", click the Resume button or press `Option` + `Command` + `P`. After a short moment, you will see a preview of your UI:

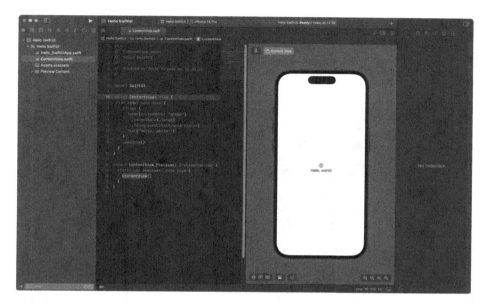

Figure 1-6. *Xcode editor and UI preview*

Let's make a few changes to get a feeling for SwiftUI's two-way tooling:

- In the code editor, update the text of the greeting so it says your name instead of world. So for me, "Hello, world!" becomes "Hello Peter!".

- Observe how the preview is updated immediately with every single keystroke you make—without requiring you to compile and relaunch the app on your phone or Simulator.

Let's now change how the text looks:

- Make sure the cursor is still on line 16 (the line that says Text("Hello, (your name)").

- In the *Attributes* inspector (on the right-hand side of the Xcode window), open the *Color* drop-down menu and choose a different color.

17

– Observe how, as you make changes, Xcode immediately reflects this change in both the preview canvas and the code editor.

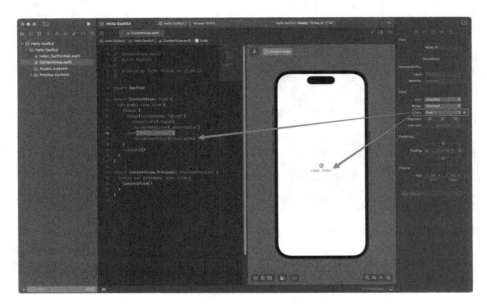

Figure 1-7. *The updated text color is reflected in the editor as well as the preview canvas*

Let's make one more change before we move on:

– In the source code editor, `Command + Click` the `Text` view.

– In the pop-up, choose *Show SwiftUI Inspector.*

– Xcode will display the inspector in a pop-up window.

– Change the font from *Inherited* to *Title.*

– Observe how Xcode updates the source code and the preview simultaneously.

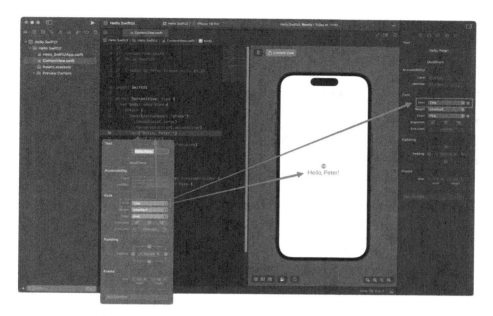

Figure 1-8. *Updating the font using the SwiftUI Inspector*

Congrats, you have just experienced Xcode's two-way editing tools for SwiftUI! Note that you can use any of them at any time. The SwiftUI Inspector is a great tool for exploring the attributes and capabilities of SwiftUI's views. Once you get more acquainted with the individual SwiftUI views, you might find it more efficient to use the source code editor and its code completion to modify the views directly.

The modifications you've applied to the Text view are called *View Modifiers*, and we'll talk about them in more depth in Chapter 3.

Adding Some Interaction to Your App

Let's add some interactivity to your app—and learn how to use the *Xcode Library* along the way!

- Make sure you're still in the source code editor and that the preview pane is still visible.

- Make the elements in the canvas selectable by clicking on the small icon with a mouse pointer on it.

Figure 1-9. *Making the elements on the canvas selectable*

- Click the + icon in the Xcode toolbar (right above the preview pane), or hit *Command+Shift+L* to open the *Library* window.

- Make sure the *Views library* is selected (the leftmost icon).

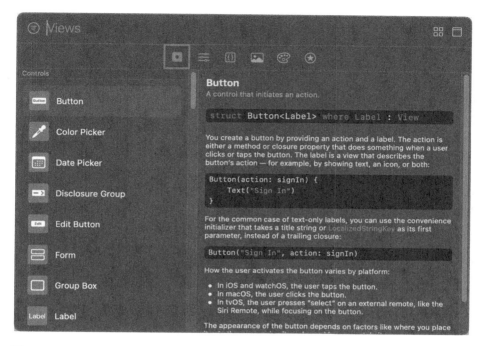

Figure 1-10. *The Views library*

- Find the *Button* view and drag it out of the library and into the preview canvas, right below the *Hello, (your name)* text.

- Notice how Xcode will highlight the drop location as you drag the button view around on the preview canvas.

Figure 1-11. *Dragging a button underneath the text view on the preview canvas*

Once you drop the Button into the code editor, Xcode will automatically update the source—it should now look like this:

```
struct ContentView: View {
  var body: some View {
    VStack {
      Image(systemName: "globe")
        .imageScale(.large)
        .foregroundColor(.accentColor)
      Text("Hello, Peter!")
        .font(.title)
        .foregroundColor(Color.pink)
```

```
        Button("Button") {
          Action
        }
      }
      .padding()
    }
}
```

Notice how both Action and Content are colored slightly different—this indicates these two pieces of text are an *editor placeholder*. You can navigate between those placeholders by pressing the *Tab* key on your keyboard.

- Click the Action placeholder and press *Enter* to replace it with the following text: { print("Hello") }.

- Click the Content placeholder (or press the *Tab* key), and replace it with the following text: Text("Tap me").

The source code of your ContentView should now look like this:

```
struct ContentView: View {
  var body: some View {
    VStack {
      Image(systemName: "globe")
        .imageScale(.large)
        .foregroundColor(.accentColor)
      Text("Hello, Peter!")
        .font(.title)
        .foregroundColor(Color.pink)
```

```
Button("Tap me") {
    print("Hello")
  }
}
.padding()
      }
   }
}
```

To see the result of your work so far in action, we need to run the app on the Simulator:[12]

- Drop down the Destination menu in the Xcode toolbar (or press *CTRL + Shift + 0*), and select one of the iOS Simulators.

- Click the *Run* button (or press *CMD+R*).

- Open the *Debug Console* (*View* ➤ *Debug Area* ➤ *Activate Console*, or press the *Command+Shift*+C keys.

- Once the app has started up in the Simulator, tap the *Tap me* button.

- You should see the text *"Hello"* appear in the debug output.

---

[12] In previous versions of Xcode, it used to be possible to run the application in *Live Preview* in order to see the debug output. This is no longer possible, as this feature has been turned off by Apple in Xcode 13: https://bit.ly/3hmRKMc

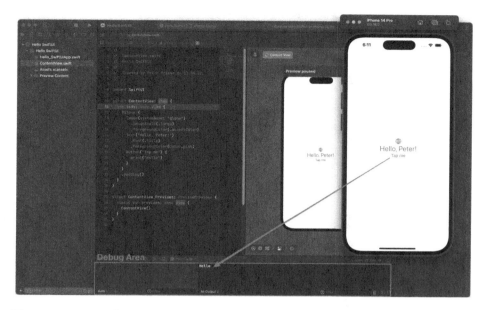

Figure 1-12. *The app running on the Simulator, with some output in the Debug Console*

Using SwiftUI's State Management to Keep UI and Model in Sync

To whet your appetite for more SwiftUI, as a final step in this chapter, let's make use of SwiftUI's state management to update the greeting whenever the user enters their name.

Here is the UI we want to achieve.

Figure 1-13. *Automatically updating greeting*

Let's first update the existing UI:

— Remove the `Button` from the source code—we don't need it anymore, as we'll be updating the UI whenever the user enters a text.

— Open the *Library* (using either the + button or by pressing *Command+Shift+L*).

– Find the *Text Field* view (by typing *Text* into the library's search field).

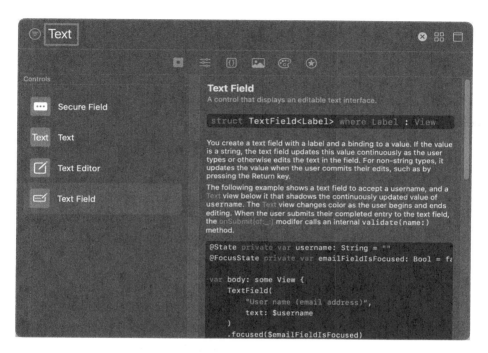

Figure 1-14. *Filtering the list of views*

– Drag the *Text Field* view into the preview canvas, right above the label which reads *Hello, Peter!*.

The ContentView source code should now look like this:

```
struct ContentView: View {
  var body: some View {
    VStack {
      Image(systemName: "globe")
        .imageScale(.large)
        .foregroundColor(.accentColor)
```

```
        TextField("Placeholder", text: Value)
        Text("Hello, Peter!")
    }
    .padding()
  }
}
```

Again, *Placeholder* and *Value* are highlighted to indicate these are just editor placeholders:

- Replace the *"Placeholder"* text with "Enter your name here".

- Just above the line starting with var body, insert the following text: @State var name = "". This will define an empty instance variable named *name* and tell SwiftUI to handle its state for you[13].

- Replace the *Value* editor placeholder with $name—this will tell SwiftUI to bind the *name* variable to the *TextField*. Whenever the user enters some text, the value of the *name* variable will be updated. Vice versa, if the value of the variable is changed, SwiftUI will update the TextField instance and display the updated value. You have now essentially set up a two-way binding[14].

- Change the content of the Text view to "Hello, \(name)!". This is called *string interpolation*—Swift will replace \(name) with the current value of the name variable.

---

[13] Don't worry if you're not familiar with @State—we will be discussing in Chapter 4
[14] Again, this is something we'll be covering in Chapter 4.

To make the input field a bit more pleasing to the eye, let's add some padding and a border:

- Make sure the TextField is selected by placing the cursor somewhere within the line starting with TextField.

- In the *SwiftUI Inspector*, click into the small circle at the right edge of the *Padding* section. This will add some padding around the text field.

- At the bottom of the *SwiftUI Inspector*, place the cursor within the input field labelled *Add Modifier*.

- Type *border*, and then click the *Border* drop-down menu item to add a border to your TextField. You can choose a color of your liking.

- Finally, add some padding around the border by typing *padding* into the *Add Modifier* field once more. Click the *Padding* drop-down menu item to insert the padding.

Your code should now look like this:[15]

```
struct ContentView: View {
  @State var name = ""
  var body: some View {
    VStack {
      Image(systemName: "globe")
        .imageScale(.large)
        .foregroundColor(.accentColor)
```

---

[15] You might see some of the values you just inserted be highlighted. This means they're placeholders. If that's the case, click on the placeholders and then press the *Enter* key to commit the value. You can use the *Tab* key to cycle through all the placeholders in your file.

```
    TextField("Enter your name here", text:$name)
      .padding(.all)
      .border(Color.pink, width: 1)
      .padding(.all)
    Text("Hello, \(name)!")
      .font(.title)
      .foregroundColor(Color.pink)
  }
  .padding()
}
}
```

To see your code in action, click the *Live* button on the bottom toolbar of the preview canvas. After a short moment, you can start interacting with the live preview. Try typing your name and observe how the greeting is updated instantaneously with every single keystroke.

Figure 1-15. *Running the app in live preview*

To run the app on the iOS Simulator or a physical device, choose the device in the *run destination* dropdown in Xcode's title bar, and then press the *Run* button.

Congratulations! You've just implemented your first SwiftUI application driven by SwiftUI's powerful state management.

Exercises

- Add a button to reset the name variable to an empty string.

- When the name variable is empty, the greeting will read *Hello, !*, which looks a bit awkward. Using what you've learned in this chapter, can you try to think of a way to only show the comma if name contains at least one letter?

Summary

In this chapter, we looked at some of SwiftUI's specific properties and why Apple launched a completely new UI toolkit in the first place. We learned what the differences are between declarative vs. imperative UI frameworks, that SwiftUI favors composition over inheritance, and that everything is a view. We talked about SwiftUI's state management, and how this is the basis for SwiftUI's premise that the UI is a function of an app's state.

Next, you experienced first-hand how easy it is to build a SwiftUI application. You learned how to use Xcode's two-way tooling for building SwiftUI user interfaces, and started to develop an understanding of when to use the graphical tools, and when the source code editor might be more efficient.

Finally, you dipped your toes into using SwiftUI's state management, which hopefully got you excited about how much easier this is than having to wire up UI updates manually.

With this under your belt, it is now time to take a closer look at SwiftUI and some of its key UI elements.

CHAPTER 2

Getting Started with SwiftUI

In the previous chapter, you've learned about the basic principles of SwiftUI and some of the reasons why Apple implemented a new UI framework when they already had a number of UI toolkits that work perfectly fine. We also took a whirlwind tour of SwiftUI and the tooling Xcode provides for building SwiftUI apps.

In this chapter, we're going to dive deeper into using SwiftUI. The best way to learn is by doing, so we will be building a simple app that might turn out to be useful for you.

We will look at using simple SwiftUI views such as Text and Image and how to use stacks to build both simple and more complex UIs by composing simple UI elements into reusable views.

SwiftUI puts a strong focus[1] on building reusable UI components, so we will take some time to understand how this works and which tools Xcode provides to make this easy. Composing views and decomposing them into reusable components is a central concept of developing SwiftUI apps and will help you to write code that is easy to manage and maintain.

Later in this chapter, we will start looking at how to build List views, which are a staple in many iOS apps.

---

[1] Forgive the pun.

© Peter Friese 2023
P. Friese, *Asynchronous Programming with SwiftUI and Combine*,
https://doi.org/10.1007/978-1-4842-8572-5_2

Throughout the chapter, we will be working with *Views*, *View Modifiers*, and *Property Wrappers*. At the end of the chapter, you will have learned what these are and how they work together to make SwiftUI a magical experience.

What We're Going to Build

The sample app we're going to build in this chapter will display a list of books, including their title, author name, and the book cover.

To keep things simple, we will focus on the UI aspects and leave the data access layer for a later moment. So instead of fetching book data from a remote API, we'll define a static array of books and retrieve the book covers from the app's asset catalog.

Drawing on what you've learned in Chapter 1, we'll start by putting together a view for displaying a book's cover, its title, author, and some other details.

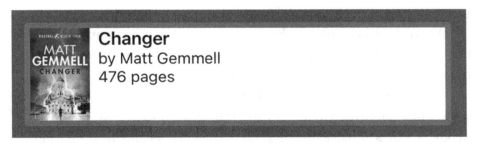

Figure 2-1. *A view for displaying details about a book*

In the next step, we will use this custom view inside a list view to display multiple books as a list.

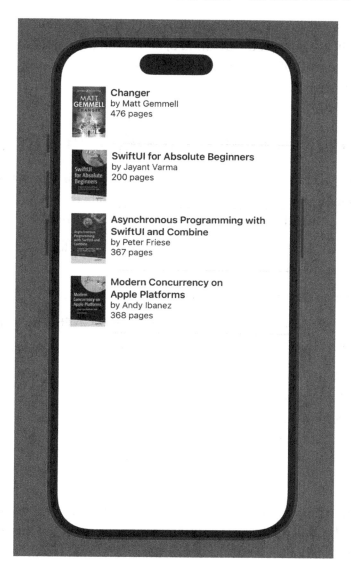

Figure 2-2. *The app we're going to build in this chapter*

Finally, we will refactor the code to make it more reusable. In this step, you will learn about the *pyramid of doom* and how to avoid it by composing your UI of many small, use case–specific components.

Let's get started!

Composing a View for Displaying a Book

To help you get started, I've prepared a starter project for this chapter that already contains some book covers and a simple data model for books.

Clone the GitHub repository that accompanies this book[2]

- Navigate into the folder for the starter project for this chapter

- Open the project in Xcode.

In the project's Model folder, you will find Book.swift, which contains the Book struct that defines the data model for this app.

```
struct Book {
  var title: String
  var author: String
  var isbn: String
  var pages: Int
}
```

The same file contains an extension on Book with a few computed properties that will make it easier to determine the names of the cover images for each book.

---

[2] https://github.com/peterfriese/SwiftUI-Combine-Book

```
extension Book {
  var smallCoverImageName: String { return "\(isbn)-S" }
  var mediumCoverImageName: String { return "\(isbn)-M" }
  var largeCoverImageName: String { return "\(isbn)-L" }
}
```

And finally, there is a global constant sampleBooks that contains a collection of sample books—this allows us to display some demo data without having to fetch data from an API.

```
extension Book {
  static let sampleBooks = [
    Book(title: "Changer", author: "Matt Gemmell", isbn:
    "9781916265202", pages: 476),
    Book(title: "SwiftUI for Absolute Beginners", author:
    "Jayant Varma", isbn: "9781484255155", pages: 200),
    Book(title: "Asynchronous Programming with SwiftUI and
    Combine", author: "Peter Friese", isbn: "9781484285718",
    pages: 367),
    Book(title: "Modern Concurrency on Apple Platforms",
    author: "Andy Ibanez", isbn: "9781484286944", pages: 368)
  ]
}
```

The app's asset catalog contains cover images for the books defined in sampleBooks—as you can see, they're provided in three different sizes: small, medium, and large.

Figure 2-3. *The asset catalog contains cover images for the books in the sample array*

The app's entry point is defined in `BookShelfApp.swift`—this is where you instantiate the main view your users will see when they launch the app.

```swift
import SwiftUI

@main
struct BookShelfApp: App {
  var body: some Scene {
    WindowGroup {
      ContentView()
    }
  }
}
```

This main view, `ContentView`, can be found in `ContentView.swift`, and this is where we will spend most of our time for the rest of this chapter.

```swift
import SwiftUI

struct ContentView: View {
  var body: some View {
    Text("Hello, world!")
  }
}

struct ContentView_Previews: PreviewProvider {
  static var previews: some View {
    ContentView()
  }
}
```

Whenever you create a new SwiftUI view using Xcode, it will create a file looking similar to this one, so it's worth taking a closer look at the anatomy of a SwiftUI `View`.

The preceding code snippet creates a new struct named `ContentView`, which conforms to the `View` protocol. The name of the view is `ContentView`, so it can be instantiated like this: `ContentView()`.

Inside the view, you will notice one property, named `body`. The type of the property is `some View`. If you've developed in Swift before, you might be wondering what's the meaning of `some`. The short answer is that this denotes a so-called *opaque return type*, which indicates that body returns a value of type View.

`body` has a significant role in SwiftUI—inside, you will define how the view looks like. In this code snippet, the view contains just a simple `Text` view that displays "Hello, world", but later in this chapter, you will learn how to compose more complex layouts by assembling several views inside the body property.

The second structure in this source code file is named `ContentView_Previews` and conforms to `PreviewProvider`. This is a special construct SwiftUI uses to display a preview of your view in the Preview Canvas on the right side of the Xcode window. Later on in this chapter, you will learn how to modify the preview to display your view in light mode and dark mode.

Build the View with Static Data

Now that we've got a basic understanding of what SwiftUI views are, it is time to look at another very important aspect of views: composability.

SwiftUI views can be made up of other views. It's hard to overstate this, but it essentially means that you can build arbitrarily complex UIs from SwiftUI views, just by composing individual primitive views into larger, more complex ones.

SwiftUI makes this possible by providing a handful of container components (`HStack`, `VStack`, and `ZStack`), a component that dynamically takes up space between other components (`Spacer`), and an easy and straightforward way to nest views inside other views.

To give you a better idea of what this means and how it works in action, let's take a look at building a view for displaying book details.

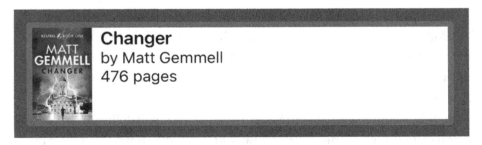

Figure 2-4. *A view for displaying book details*

Along the way, you will learn several different ways for building SwiftUI views using the tooling Xcode provides.

Let's first display the title of a book by making the following changes in the code editor:

- Change the label of the Text view from "Hello world" to "Asynchronous Programming with SwiftUI and Combine".

- Change the font of the text by adding .font(.headline) to the Text view.

The code should now look like this:

```
struct ContentView: View {
  var body: some View {
    Text("Asynchronous Programming with SwiftUI and Combine")
      .font(.headline)
  }
}
```

To display the author, add another Text view just beneath the book title. Instead of coding this manually, let's use Xcode's graphical tooling to make sure we get the layout right.

- Make sure the preview is active. If the preview canvas is not visible, select *Editor* ➤ *Canvas* from the main menu (or press CMD + Option + Enter). In case Xcode has stopped the preview, you can restart it by clicking on the *Resume preview* button or pressing CMD + Option + P.

- Make sure the canvas is in *selectable* mode by clicking on the mouse pointer icon at the bottom of the preview canvas

Figure 2-5. *Canvas in selectable mode*

– Open Xcode's *Library* by clicking the + button in the toolbar (or by pressing CMD+Shift+L).

– In the *Library* window, type *text* to find the Text view.

– Drag the Text view element from the *Library* window into the preview canvas. *Don't let go of the mouse button yet!*

– As you drag the Text view around the preview canvas, you will notice Xcode highlights the current drop position to indicate where the element will be placed if you let go.

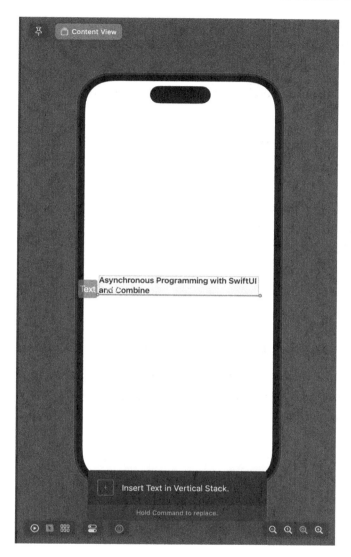

Figure 2-6. *Inserting a new Text view below an existing view*

- Drop the new Text view just below the text *Asynchronous Programming with SwiftUI and Combine.*

- Notice how Xcode's two-way tooling automatically updates the source code.

```
struct ContentView: View {
  var body: some View {
  VStack {
      Text("Asynchronous Programming with SwiftUI and Combine")
        .font(.headline)
      Text("Placeholder")
    }
  }
}
```

- Replace the placeholder text with "by Peter Friese"

- While the cursor is still on the same line, use the *Attributes Inspector* to change the font of this Text to *Subheadline.*

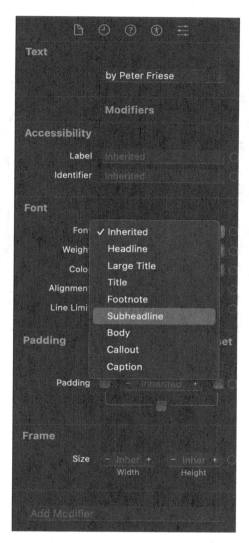

Figure 2-7. *Attribute Inspector*

Xcode updates the source code accordingly and refreshes the preview.

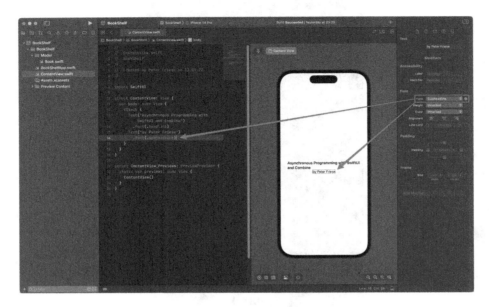

Figure 2-8. *Updated UI*

In case the preview doesn't refresh, click the *Refresh* button at the top of the preview pane, or press *CMD+Option+P*.

```swift
import SwiftUI

struct ContentView: View {
  var body: some View {
    VStack {
      Text("Asynchronous Programming with SwiftUI and Combine")
        .font(.headline)
      Text("by Peter Friese")
        .font(.subheadline)
    }
  }
}
```

```
struct ContentView_Previews: PreviewProvider {
  static var previews: some View {
    ContentView()
  }
}
```

Notice how Xcode automatically inserted a VStack container to nest the two Text views inside a vertical stack.

Use the code editor to insert another Text view to display the number of pages:

```
import SwiftUI

struct ContentView: View {
  var body: some View {
    VStack {
      Text("Asynchronous Programming with SwiftUI and Combine")
        .font(.headline)
      Text("by Peter Friese")
        .font(.subheadline)
      Text("451 pages")
        .font(.subheadline)
    }
  }
}

struct ContentView_Previews: PreviewProvider {
  static var previews: some View {
    ContentView()
  }
}
```

To match our desired layout, let's update the alignment of the text views inside the vertical stack.

- In the code editor, select the VStack, and then use the *Attributes Inspector* to left align the text views.

- This will change the alignment attribute of the VStack to .leading.

To insert an image to the left of the two Text views, we'll need to nest the VStack and an Image view inside a horizontal stack. Instead of using drag'n'drop, this time we'll use the code editor.

- In the code editor, CMD+click the VStack and select *Embed in HStack.*

- Inside the HStack, just before the VStack, insert an Image view: Image("9781484285718-M"). This will fetch the image named *9781484285718-M* from the asset catalog.

Your code should now look like this:

```
struct ContentView: View {
  var body: some View {
    HStack(alignment: .top) {
      Image("9781484285718-M")
      VStack(alignment: .leading) {
        Text("Asynchronous Programming with SwiftUI and Combine")
          .font(.headline)
        Text("by Peter Friese")
          .font(.subheadline)
        Text("451 pages")
          .font(.subheadline)
```

```
        }
      }
    }
}
```

However, as you'll notice, the image is much too large, so we need to scale it down a bit.

- Open the library (by pressing the + button or hitting CMD+Shift+L), tap the dials icon to switch to the *Modifiers* library, and type *resi* to find the *Image Resizable* modifier.

- Grab the modifier, drag it out of the library, and drop it on the book cover in the preview. The image will now occupy the entire height of the preview.

- We're not done yet. Open the library again, type *aspect*, and drag the *Aspect Ratio* modifier onto the cover image.

- In the code editor, change the contentMode value from .fill to .fit.

- Finally, find the *Frame* modifier in the library and drag it onto the image.

- Using the code editor, remove the width attribute (up to and including the comma), and set the height attribute to 90.

- Use the *Attribute Inspector* to set the alignment of the HStack to .top, so that the image and the book title align nicely.

Your code should now look like this:

```
import SwiftUI

struct ContentView: View {
  var body: some View {
    HStack(alignment: .top) {
      Image("9781484285718-M")
        .resizable()
        .aspectRatio(contentMode: .fit)
        .frame(height: 90)
      VStack(alignment: .leading) {
        Text("Asynchronous Programming with SwiftUI and Combine")
          .font(.headline)
        Text("by Peter Friese")
          .font(.subheadline)
        Text("451 pages")
          .font(.subheadline)
      }
    }
  }
}

struct ContentView_Previews: PreviewProvider {
  static var previews: some View {
    ContentView()
  }
}
```

Using the Preview to Make Sure Our View Works As Intended

Until now, the preview window showed the view inside a device frame, which makes it hard to tell how much space it takes up. As the preview canvas is just a SwiftUI view, we can easily fix that.

- In the code editor, select the ContentView() line in the preview provider (line 31)

- In the Attribute Inspector, find the *Layout* attribute in the *Preview* section and set it to *Size that fits*

The device frame will disappear, and the preview will now allocate the exact space required for the view. You'll notice that the view actually consumes less space than we intended:

Figure 2-9. *Preview of the book details view being too narrow*

To fix this, we need to insert a Spacer view at the right of the view. This is a transparent view that expands to consume as much space as possible in the layout orientation of the surrounding container. You can think of it as a spring that pushes your view apart.

- The easiest way to add a spacer to our layout is to use the code editor and add Spacer() after the closing brace of the VStack containing the Text views.

The code should now look like this:

```
import SwiftUI

struct ContentView: View {
  var body: some View {
    HStack(alignment: .top) {
      Image("9781484285718-M")
        .resizable()
        .aspectRatio(contentMode: .fit)
        .frame(height: 90)
      VStack(alignment: .leading) {
        Text("Asynchronous Programming with SwiftUI and Combine")
          .font(.headline)
        Text("by Peter Friese")
          .font(.subheadline)
        Text("451 pages")
          .font(.subheadline)
      }
      Spacer()
    }
  }
}

struct ContentView_Previews: PreviewProvider {
  static var previews: some View {
    ContentView()
      .previewLayout(.sizeThatFits)

  }
}
```

In the preview, we can see the view now takes up the entire width of the device[3].

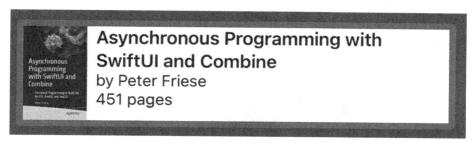

Figure 2-10. *Preview of the book details view with the correct width*

Displaying a List of Books

Now that we've got a view for displaying book details, let's turn this into a list of books. As you will see in a moment, this turns out to be surprisingly simple, and Xcode facilitates the process of doing so.

- In the code editor, *CMD+Click* the outer HStack of the book view.

- Select *Embed in List* from the pop-up menu.

Xcode wraps the view inside a list that iterates over a half open range from 0 to 5 (excluding), which results in five instances of the book view displayed in a vertically scrolling list. In a moment, we will connect the List view to our array of sample books to display something more meaningful than the same book repeated over and over again.

But before we do that, I'd like to draw your attention to the layout of the text views. As you can see, the book title is no longer top-aligned with the book cover. Looking at the source code, you might notice that the HStack

---

[3] Note that this only works when the preview is in selectable mode. In live mode, Xcode will display the entire device frame.

that surrounded the `Image` view and the `VStack` disappeared when we asked Xcode to wrap the `HStack` in a `List`. While you might argue that this is a bug in Xcode's editor, this is actually by design, as a `List` view contains an implicit `HStack`. However, as there is no way we can modify this implicit `HStack`, we'll have to manually reinsert the same `HStack` we used before.

Figure 2-11. *Broken layout after wrapping the view inside a List*

There are three ways to fix this:

1. Wrap the original HStack(alignment: .top) in another HStack **before** wrapping the additional HStack in a List view.

2. Manually wrap the inner views of the book view in HStack(alignment: .top) { ... }.

3. Instead of making use of Xcode's help, wrap the book view in a List view manually.

Which one you choose is largely a matter of personal preference, and you'll quickly become well versed in choosing the most efficient way to building your UIs with SwiftUI once you become more familiar with the API and Xcode's quirks.

For now, let's manually insert HStack(alignment: .top) { right after the List view, as well as a closing } in the line after the Spacer().

Let's also append .listStyle(.plain) to the closing curly brace of the List view to display the list as a plain list view.

Your code should now look like this:[4]

```
struct ContentView: View {
  var body: some View {
    List(0 ..< 5) { item in
      HStack(alignment: .top) {
        Image("9781484285718-M")
          .resizable()
          .aspectRatio(contentMode: .fit)
          .frame(height: 90)
```

---

[4]Xcode 14 automatically re-indents your code when you type a closing curly brace, but you also trigger this manually: select the code you want to format (or press CMD + A to select the entire file), and then press Control + i (for indent) to re-indent the code.

```
            VStack(alignment: .leading) {
              Text("Asynchronous Programming with SwiftUI and Combine")
                .font(.headline)
              Text("by Peter Friese")
                .font(.subheadline)
              Text("367 pages")
                .font(.subheadline)
            }
            Spacer()
          }
        }
        .listStyle(.plain)
      }
    }
```

Setting Up Data Binding

Of course, displaying five identical copies of the same book is not what
we wanted to achieve. Instead, let's connect the view to the collection of
sample books defined in Book.swift.[5]

SwiftUI's List view is capable of displaying elements from a
RandomAccessCollection. Conveniently, Swift arrays conform to this
protocol, which means we can provide an array of Book to the book
list view.

Before we can connect the List view to the collection of sample books
defined in Book.swift, we need to declare a property on ContentView that
holds a reference to the sampleBooks array.

---

[5] This file is contained in the *starter* version of the code for this chapter you can
download from the GitHub repository for this book: https://github.com/
peterfriese/Asynchronous-Programming-with-SwiftUI-and-Combine

- Add `var books: [Book]` to the top of `ContentView`.

- Fix the compiler errors by updating the call to `ContentView()` both in the preview and in `BookShelfApp` to `ContentView(books: sampleBooks)`.

We can now connect the `List` view to this new property. First of all, let's replace the closed range `0..<5` with a reference to the books property.

- Change `List(1..<5)` to `List(books)`.

- Rename the closure parameter `item` to `book`.

The compiler will complain that `Book` is not `Identifiable`. This is because `List` needs to be able to identify the elements it displays in order to display them in a deterministic order. If the elements weren't uniquely identifiable, the list rows would jump all over the place whenever there is an update to the data collection.

Follow these steps to ensure `Book` conforms to the `Identifiable` protocol:

- In `Book.swift`, change `struct Book {` to `struct Book: Identifiable {`.

- Add `var id = UUID().uuidString` to the Book's attributes.

This should fix the compile errors. You might have to compile the code again (press `CMD+B`).

In the next step, we'll connect the individual UI elements to the respective attributes of the `Book` structure.

- To display the book cover specified in the current `Book` instance, change `Image("9781484285718-M")` to `Image(book.mediumCoverImageName)`.

- For the title change the hard-coded strings to `book.title`.

–   For the author and number of pages, we can make use of string interpolation. Replace "by Peter Friese" with "by \(book.author)" and "367 pages" with "\(book.pages) pages".

Finally, let's change the preview configuration to make sure the list view will be displayed in a device frame. To do so, just delete the line previewLayout(.sizeThaFits).

Your code should now look like this:

```swift
import SwiftUI

struct ContentView: View {
  var books: [Book]
  var body: some View {
    List(books) { book in
      HStack(alignment: .top) {
        Image(book.mediumCoverImageName)
          .resizable()
          .aspectRatio(contentMode: .fit)
          .frame(height: 90)
        VStack(alignment: .leading) {
          Text(book.title)
            .font(.headline)
          Text("by \(book.author)")
            .font(.subheadline)
          Text("\(book.pages) pages")
            .font(.subheadline)
        }
        Spacer()
      }
      .listStyle(.plain)
    }
  }
}
```

Adjusting the Preview Canvas

To monitor whether the UI looks great in both light mode and dark mode, use the *Variants* button in the preview canvas toolbar, and select the *Color Scheme Variants* option. The preview canvas will now show the UI in both light and dark mode.

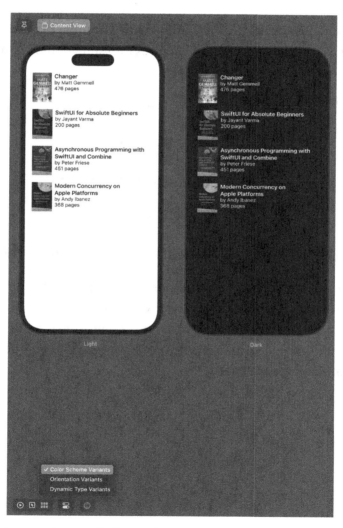

Figure 2-12. *previewing light and dark mode side by side*

Making the Code Reusable

Before we can finish this chapter and move on to the next topic, we need to talk about a critical issue: the *pyramid of doom*.

The ease with which views can be composed in this way can quickly lead to deeply nested code that's difficult to navigate—hence the term "pyramid of doom."

The good news is that SwiftUI comes with a number of mechanisms that allow us to decompose view structures into smaller blocks, making our code easier to read and maintain:

- – Extract Subview

- – Extract to Method

- – Extract to Property

Throughout the book, we'll use several of these techniques, but for now, we'll use the most popular one, *Extract Subview*.

Refactoring the Code Using Extract Subview

Probably the most important technique to manage complexity in SwiftUI views is to extract reusable parts of your view hierarchy into subviews.

Obviously, the book view in our sample application is a prime candidate for this refactoring—if you recall, we even started out by building this as a separate view.

Here's how you apply the *Extract Subview* refactoring:

- Make sure the *Preview Canvas* is visible. Otherwise, SwiftUI refactorings aren't active.[6]

- In the code editor, `CMD` + `click` the `HStack` that contains the list row making up the book view.

- In the context menu, select *Extract Subview.*

Figure 2-13. *Using the Extract to Subview refactoring*

Xcode extracts the entire view structure into a new view at the bottom of the current source code file, naming it `ExtractedView`.

---

[6] In case the preview canvas is not visible, press `CMD+Option+Enter` to show it.

You will notice that there is a compile error in the extracted view: *"Cannot find 'book' in scope"*—this is because the Book instance in this view displays isn't in scope.

To fix this, we'll have to define a new property in the new view:

- Inside BookRowView, declare a new property named book of type Book.

```
struct BookRowView: View {
  var book: Book
  var body: some View {
    ...
  }
}
```

The compile error will disappear, but there will be a new one instead— at the call site, the compiler tells us that there is a missing argument for the book parameter.

To fix this, add the current book instance to the ExtractedView() call.

Since ExtractedView is not a great name for our view, let's rename it to BookRowView. To do so, put the cursor somewhere inside the symbol name ExtractedView, and then bring up the *Code Actions* context menu using the CMD + Shift + A key binding.

Once you choose the Rename refactoring, Xcode will show all occurrences of the selected symbol. Type the new name (BookRowView) and hit Enter to apply your changes.

The code should now look like this:

```
import SwiftUI
struct ContentView: View {
  var books: [Book]
  var body: some View {
    List(books) { book in
      BookRowView(book: book)
```

```
    }
    .listStyle(.plain)
  }
}

struct ContentView_Previews: PreviewProvider {
  static var previews: some View {
    ContentView(books: Book.sampleBooks)
  }
}

struct BookRowView: View {
  var book: Book
  var body: some View {
    HStack(alignment: .top) {
      Image(book.mediumCoverImageName)
        .resizable()
        .aspectRatio(contentMode: .fit)
        .frame(height: 90)
      VStack(alignment: .leading) {
        Text(book.title)
          .font(.headline)
        Text("by \(book.author)")
          .font(.subheadline)
        Text("\(book.pages) pages")
          .font(.subheadline)
      }
      Spacer()
    }
  }
}
```

With this, the *Extract Subview* refactoring is basically complete, but there are two optional steps you might want to consider:

1. Marking the extracted subview as `private`. This is useful if you're not going to use this view in any other context.

2. If you *are* going to use the extract subview elsewhere, move it to a separate file. To do so, create a new *SwiftUI View* file using Xcode's *New File* dialog, and then choose `BookRowView` as the file name. This makes sure that the new file contains a preview provider named `BookRowView_Previews`. It also contains a view name `BookRowView`, which you can just replace with the `BookRowView` implementation we extracted in the preceding steps[7].

Renaming ContentView

Once you start adding new features and screens to your app, it might feel a bit odd that one of your screens is still named `ContentView`, so you should rename this and choose a name that reflects the functionality of the screen more closely.

To do so, place the cursor on the name `ContentView`, and choose *Refactor* ➤ *Rename* from the editor context menu. Xcode will fold your code and show a preview of how the refactored code will look like. Just start typing the new name (e.g., `BooksListView`), and hit *Enter* when you're done.

---

[7] Unfortunately, there is no *Extract to File* refactoring in Xcode.

Keep Complexity in Check

Decomposing nested view structures into smaller components is a SwiftUI best practice, and Apple themselves actively encourage this in their WWDC videos[8] and developer documentation.[9] When building UIs with SwiftUI, keep the techniques I showed you in mind and remember to refactor your code as soon as you recognize it's starting to get out of hand.

Views and View Modifiers

Let's pause here for a moment and recap what we've just learned so far.

Views are the core building blocks of SwiftUI—each view defines a piece of the UI.

Views can be **composed** into new view, resulting in more feature-rich and complex UIs. A composition might be as simple as putting an image next to a text label, but things can easily become more complex.

Instead of positioning UI elements using absolute coordinates, SwiftUI promotes using a system of vertical and horizontal **stacks and spacers** to lay out UI elements.

Most views **hug** their content (e.g., Text), whereas others **push out** to consume all available space (such as Spacer).

There are two main ways to **configure** views:

1. The main properties of a view can be configured using constructor arguments (e.g., the text displayed on a Text view, or the alignment of a HStack).

2. Secondary properties of a view are configured using *View Modifiers.*

---

[8] For example, in WWDC 21 Session "Demystify SwiftUI),
https://developer.apple.com/videos/play/wwdc2021/10022
[9] https://developer.apple.com/documentation/swiftui/

65

View Modifiers are functions that you call on SwiftUI views (e.g., Text("hello").font(.headline)). Most of these allow you to specify the look of a view (e.g., by setting the font, foreground and background colors, frame size, etc.). As we will see in the next chapters, there are also view modifiers that allow you to register closures that are called upon certain events (such as a button tap).

Exercises

1. Add another Text view to display the ISBN of each book on the same line that displays the number of pages.

2. Align the page number text to the left, and the ISBN to the right of the view.

Tips and Tricks

If you're not sure how a certain view works or how it can be configured, you can use the *Library* to learn how to use the view. Drag a view from the *Library* into the preview canvas (or the code editor) to get an initial implementation. Or, drag a modifier from the library and drop it onto a view to see how to use it. After you've done this a couple of times, you'll understand how the individual views and view modifiers work, and can then use the code editor to enter the code manually (or using code completion).

Summary

In this chapter, you learned how to use simple SwiftUI views to incrementally build an application for displaying information from a data model in a list view.

We looked at composing a cell for displaying a book's cover, title, and other details using Image and Text views, and you used HStack, VStack, and Spacer to lay out the UI elements.

Using Xcode's two-way tooling, you experienced firsthand how to quickly put together a UI by making use of the *Library*, the *Preview Canvas*, the code editor, and its context menus.

Finally, you used Xcode's refactorings to organize the code into reusable components, making it easier to read and maintain.

If you're coming from UIKit and are used to building your views programmatically, the ease with which you can build the equivalent of a UITableView with a custom cell should be a pleasant surprise. This is not all, though—as you will see in the next chapters, SwiftUI's state handling makes it a lot easier to make sure all parts of your app reflect the current state of your data model—no more running out of sync!

This chapter provided a good overview of how to build UIs with SwiftUI, but we've barely scratched the surface. In the next chapters, we will dive deeper in to the individual topics to get a better understanding of how (and why) SwiftUI works and how to build better apps thanks to its reactive state management system.

CHAPTER 3

SwiftUI Building Blocks

In the previous chapter, you learned how to use SwiftUI to build a simple UI and how to use Xcode's refactoring tools to keep your code nicely organized and reusable. You also used SwiftUI's state management system which keeps your app's views and its data model in sync all the time.

Now that you've used SwiftUI's key components, like *views, view modifiers*, and *property wrappers*, let's take a closer look and understand how they work.

In this chapter, we will look at SwiftUI's building blocks, learn how they work, and how they allow developers to efficiently build UIs. Specifically,

- You will learn what views *really* are and how they help you describe your UI declaratively

- We will talk about different kinds of views in SwiftUI—user interface views and container views

- We will also look at view modifiers and their role in configuring views

© Peter Friese 2023
P. Friese, *Asynchronous Programming with SwiftUI and Combine*,
https://doi.org/10.1007/978-1-4842-8572-5_3

By the end of the chapter, you will have a more profound understanding of how SwiftUI works and how the individual concepts play together to make SwiftUI an easy-to-use DSL[1] for building UIs.

Views

SwiftUI follows a declarative approach for describing UIs. Instead of manually instantiating the elements of your UI, such as buttons, labels, lists, and so on, you declare how you want your UI to look like. Views are the most basic components for building UIs in SwiftUI. To define the UI of your application, you create a lightweight description of your user interface, making use of SwiftUI's built-in views. By doing so, you compose your own views, which you can then use in your app.

In addition to using these views in your own app, you can make them reusable by extracting them into s Swift package. This enables you to use them in your other apps, or share them with other developers on your team. You can even make them available to other developers by uploading them to GitHub and registering them with the Swift Package Index.[2]

In Chapters 1 and 2, you have already used the following techniques for building reusable SwiftUI components:

- You used some of SwiftUI's built-in views (such as `Text` and `Image`) to create simple UIs (such as the *Hello World* sample in Chapter 1).

- In Chapter 2, you created a reusable view (`BookRowView`) for displaying details about books, and then reused it inside a `List` view.

---

[1] Domain-specific language
[2] `https://swiftpackageindex.com/`

Let's look at the basic anatomy of a SwiftUI view. When you create a new SwiftUI file in Xcode, you will end up with a piece of code like the following:

```
import SwiftUI

struct ContentView: View {
  var body: some View {
    VStack {
      Image(systemName: "globe")
        .imageScale(.large)
        .foregroundColor(.accentColor)
      Text("Hello, world!")
    }
    .padding()
  }
}

struct ContentView_Previews: PreviewProvider {
  static var previews: some View {
    ContentView()
  }
}
```

The PreviewProvider is responsible for displaying the view in Xcode's preview canvas.

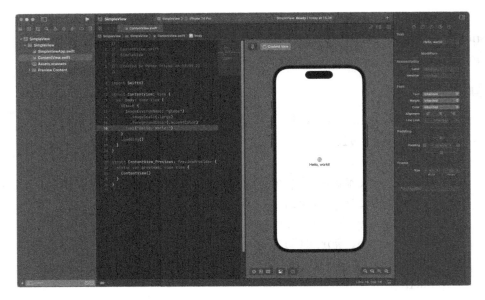

Figure 3-1. *A simple view in Xcode's preview canvas*

Leaving the `PreviewProvider` aside for a moment, let's focus on a simplified version of `ContentView`:

```
struct ContentView: View {
  var body: some View {
    Text("Hello, world!")
  }
}
```

This short snippet defines a simple view, named `ContentView`, that contains a `Text` view which displays *Hello World*.

Despite being such a short code snippet, we can learn a lot about the power of SwiftUI from it.

SwiftUI views are structs that need to conform to the `View` protocol. Looking at the source code for the `View` protocol, we can see that conformers need to implement a computed property named body that returns a *single* `View`:

```
@available(iOS 13.0, macOS 10.15, tvOS 13.0, watchOS 6.0, *)
public protocol View {
  associatedtype Body : View
  @ViewBuilder @MainActor var body: Self.Body { get }
}
```

Our simple Hello World snippet contains a computed body property that returns a simple Text view, so it meets the requirements of the View protocol.

To implement more complex views, such as a label with a leading icon, we can make use of SwiftUI's container views, such as Group, HStack, or VStack. Container views allow us to group child views and arrange them in a specific layout, for example, horizontally or vertically. The following code snippet uses a VStack to arrange an Image and a Text vertically:

```
struct ContentView: View {
  var body: some View {
    VStack {
      Image(systemName: "globe")
        .imageScale(.large)
        .foregroundColor(.accentColor)
      Text("Hello, world!")
    }
    .padding()
  }
}
```

By using container views, we can meet the View protocol's requirement of returning a *single* View from the body computed property. We'll talk more about container views later in this chapter.

You might be wondering why the return type is some View, and not just View, and why the return type of body cannot be plainly View.

When composing views, like in the preceding example, the concrete return type depends on the types of the individual views and in which order we put them together. For example, the type of the view that we return from the body property in the preceding code snippet is `HStack<TupleView<(Image, ModifiedContent<Text, _PaddingLayout>)>>`. Changing the order of the views will result in a different type: putting the Image after the `Text` will change the result type to `HStack<TupleView< (ModifiedContent<Text, _PaddingLayout>, Image)>>`.

This obviously is a bit unwieldy, and this is where the some keyword comes in: it turns a type into a so-called *opaque type*. This means that the compiler still has access to the underlying concrete type (e.g., `HStack<TupleView<(Image, ModifiedContent<Text, _PaddingLayout>)>>`, but clients of the module don't[3]—they just see the protocol of the return value.

This means: by returning the result of a view's body as some `View`, the caller will only see a view and doesn't get any insight into how this view is structured. Consequently, we can refer to custom types by their regular type name (for the earlier code snippet: `ContentView`), instead of the concrete type of the view structure being returned from the body property (for the earlier code snippet: `HStack<TupleView<(Image, ModifiedContent<Text, _PaddingLayout>)>>`).

User Interface Views

SwiftUI comes with a broad range of views for most of the UI elements that are common in iOS, iPadOS, macOS, watchOS, and tvOS, such as `Text`, `Image`, `Button`, `TextField`, and more.

These views are the basic building blocks that you can use to compose the UI of your application. You can also use these building blocks to create

---

[3] See `https://docs.swift.org/swift-book/LanguageGuide/OpaqueTypes.html`

your own custom components, just like the List row for displaying the cover and title of a book that we created in Chapter 2.

Here is an overview of SwiftUI's user interface elements:

Text Input and Output

Text Output

Name	Description
Text	Displays one or more lines of read-only text
Label	Displays an image and read-only text

Text Input

Name	Description
TextField	Displays editable text
SecureField	Lets the user securely enter text
TextEditor	A control that can display and edit long-form text

Images

Images

Name	Description
Image	Displays an image
AsyncImage	Asynchronously downloads and displays an image

Controls and Indicators

Buttons

Name	Description
Button	A control that initiates an action
EditButton	A button that toggles the *edit mode* environment value

Links

Name	Description
Link	A control for navigating to a URL

Menus

Name	Description
Menu	A control for presenting a menu of actions

Value Inputs

Name	Description
Slider	A control for selecting a value from a bounded linear range of values
Stepper	A control that performs increment and decrement actions
Toggle	A control that toggles between on and off states

Pickers

Name	Description
Picker	A control for selecting from a set of mutually exclusive values
DatePicker	A control for selecting an absolute date
ColorPicker	A control used to select a color from the system color picker UI

Indicators

Name	Description
Gauge	A view that shows a value within a range
ProgressView	A view that shows the progress toward completion of a task

Shapes

Shapes

Name	Description
Shape	A 2D shape that you can use when drawing a view
InsettableShape	A shape type that is able to inset itself to produce another shape
Rectangle	A rectangular shape aligned inside the frame of the view containing it
RoundedRectangle	A rectangular shape with rounded corners, aligned inside the frame of the view containing it

(continued)

Name	Description
Circle	A circle centered on the frame of the view containing it
Ellipse	An ellipse aligned inside the frame of the view containing it
Capsule	A capsule shape aligned inside the frame of the view containing it
Path	The outline of a 2D shape

Container Views

Most user interfaces are more complex than just a simple Text or Image in the center of a screen. In fact, the majority of user interfaces are constructed from several individual views. Instead of requiring developers to manually position views at an absolute or relative position on the screen, SwiftUI uses view containers[4] to make it easier to create complex layouts by grouping multiple views together and arranging them on screen.

SwiftUI has several categories of container views:

- Layout containers such as HStack, VStack, or ZStack allow us to lay out their child views horizontally, vertically, or by overlaying them on top of each other.

- Collection Containers, such as List, Form, Table, Group, or ScrollView provide built-in features like scrolling, swiping, filtering, and more.

---

[4]Apple calls them *view containers* and *container views* interchangeably in their own documentation: https://developer.apple.com/documentation/swiftui/ picking-container-views-for-your-content

– Presentation Containers (`NavigationView`, `NavigationStack`, `NavigationSplitView`, `TabView`, `Toolbar` and others) are intended to define the structure of your app's UI.

Since container views themselves are views, we can nest them, allowing us to build even complex user interfaces with ease.

On top of that, each view also has an overlay and a background, which can be accessed using the `overlay` and `background` view modifiers (more about view modifiers in the next section). This can be used to create some advanced layouts.

Layout Behavior

You will notice that some views seem to have a different layout behavior than others.

On a high level, the SwiftUI layout process works like this:

1. The parent view offers some size to its child view.

2. The child view then decides how much space it requires, taking into consideration its own size (the intrinsic size) and the space that the parent view offered (which the child view is free to ignore completely). It then returns this size to the parent view.

3. The parent view uses the size returned by the child to lay out the child view somewhere within the bound of the space it offered in step 1. It will respect the size that the child requested for itself.

SwiftUI uses two different strategies in step 2 when determining how much space a child view consumes:

Hugging

The view chooses the best size to fit its content, without consulting the size offered by its parent view. Text is an example of a view with this behavior: it will consume just as much space as the text requires, even if the container offers more space.

Expanding

The view tries to use up as much space as offered by its parent view. Color is an example for a view with this behavior: it will take up the entire space offered by the parent view.

Views Are Just Descriptions of the UI

In the very first presentation of SwiftUI at WWDC 2019,[5] Apple put a lot of emphasis on the fact that SwiftUI views are cheap to create. In fact, they encouraged[6] developers to make liberal use of views and to decompose views into subviews to keep the code for individual screens and views easy to read and maintain.

The reason for this is that SwiftUI views aren't views—instead, they are just *descriptions* of views.

Or, as Apple puts it in their SwiftUI documentation[7]: "[...] *with a declarative approach, you create a lightweight description of your user*

---

[5] See https://developer.apple.com/videos/play/wwdc2019/204/?time=1020

[6] "Behind the scenes, SwiftUI aggressively collapses your view hierarchy into an efficient data structure for rendering. Because of this, we make liberal use of small single-purpose views in SwiftUI, and you should too. What I want you to take away from the last couple slides is that views in SwiftUI are incredibly lightweight. As Jacob said, you should never hesitate to refactor your SwiftUI code because extracting a subview has virtually no runtime overhead."

[7] https://developer.apple.com/documentation/swiftui/declaring-a-custom-view

interface by declaring views in a hierarchy that mirrors the desired layout of your interface. SwiftUI then manages drawing and updating these views in response to events like user input or state changes."

To demonstrate this, let's take a look at a simple view and the resulting view hierarchy that will be rendered on screen.

```
struct ContentView: View {
  @State var text = ""

  var body: some View {
    List {
      Label("Hello World", systemImage: "globe")
      HStack {
        Image(systemName: "globe")
          .imageScale(.large)
          .foregroundColor(.accentColor)
        Text("Hello, world!")
      }
      TextField("TextField", text: $text)
    }
  }
}
```

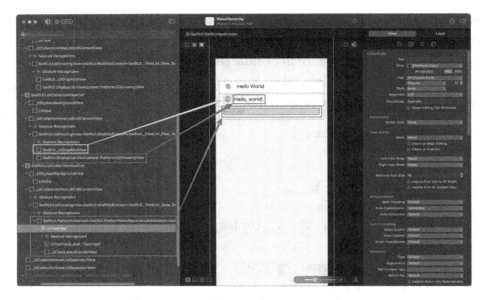

Figure 3-2. *View hierarchy of the code snippet above running on iOS (using the Reveal app)*

Note how the TextField view is mapped to a UITextField, whereas the Text view is mapped to a SwiftUI.DisplayList.ViewUpdater. Platform.CGDrawingView.

This is also one of the key reasons why SwiftUI can be used to define cross-platform UIs. As a view merely is a description of the UI, SwiftUI can use different primitives to render the UI on different platforms. Let's look at another example to understand this. Here is the same code as earlier, but running on tvOS. Note how the view hierarchy shows UI controls native to tvOS.

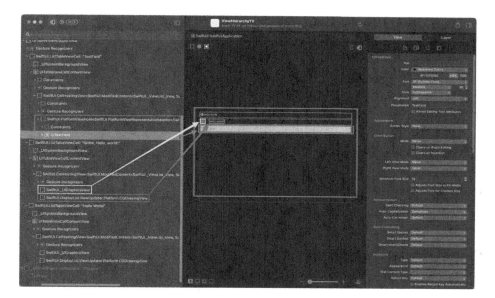

Figure 3-3. *View hierarchy of the same code snippet running on tvOS (using the Reveal app)*

When creating UIs in SwiftUI, you should always keep in mind that views are just a description of the UI, not the actual UI elements themselves. Also keep in mind that SwiftUI may call your views several times throughout the rendering process—this is why you should not perform any expensive processing or computations inside the initializers of your views.

View Modifiers

View modifiers are another key concept in SwiftUI—they allow us to customize the appearance and behavior of our app's views. For example, you can use view modifiers to

- Style your views

- Respond to events (like the user tapping on a button)

- Configure secondary views (like swipe actions, context menus, or toolbars)

View modifiers are Swift methods that can be called on any SwiftUI View. They are implemented as extensions on the View protocol, which means you can call them on any View—both built-in views like Text or Image and also on your own custom views.

Let's take a closer look to understand how they work.

Configuring Views

To modify the appearance or behavior of a view, just call one of SwiftUI's built-in view modifiers on the view instance. For example, here is how you can change the foreground color of a Text view to red:

```
Text("Hello World")
  .foregroundColor(.red)
```

By calling a modifier on a view, the modifier will create a new view that wraps the original view, and replaces it in the view hierarchy. For example, the type of the modified Text view will be ModifiedContent<Text, _PaddingLayout>.

You can apply multiple view modifiers to the same view to change multiple aspects of its appearance. For example, to change the font of the text in addition to its foreground color, just call the font view modifier:

```
Text("Hello, world!")
  .foregroundColor(.red)
  .font(.title)
```

It is worth pointing out that the order in which view modifiers are added to a view is significant. In the following code snippet, the view modifiers on the Text view are applied in a different order, resulting in a different output:

```
struct ContentView: View {
  var body: some View {
    HStack(spacing: 20) {
      // left
      Text("Hello, world!")
        .background(.red)
        .padding()

      Divider()

      // right
      Text("Hello, world!")
        .padding()
        .background(.red)
    }
    .frame(maxHeight: 50)
  }
}
```

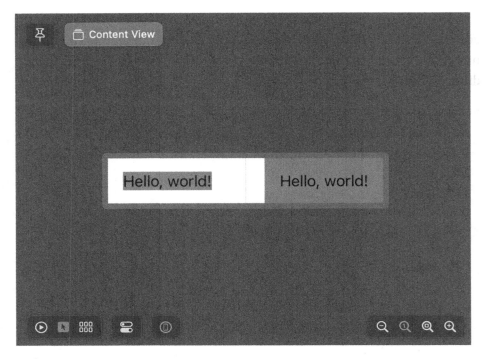

Figure 3-4. *The order in which you apply view modifiers has an impact on the view's appearance*

In the first example, the background color is applied to the Text view before applying the padding. This results in just the text being underlaid with the red background.

In the second code snippet, the padding is applied first. As mentioned earlier, applying a view modifier results in an altered version of the view taking the position of the original view. This means that the padded version of the Text view is now taking the position of the original Text view. Applying the background view modifier to this modified version of the view results in the entire, padded, background being filled with the red background color.

Applying View Modifiers to Child Views

View modifiers work on the view they are applied to. For example, in the previous code snippets, we applied the background view modifier to a Text view.

However, most view modifiers also impact the children of the view they are applied to. Consider the following code snippet, which applies the same monospace font to all labels inside the VStack:

```
VStack(alignment: .leading) {
  Text("Hello, World!")
  Text("How are you today?")
}
.font(.system(.body, design: .monospaced))
```

This is useful when you want to configure the appearance of several views at once. By applying the respective view modifier to a shared container view of the views you want to configure, you change the appearance of all contained views at once.

There are also a few view modifiers that propagate their value up the view hierarchy, for example, navigationTitle:

```
NavigationStack {
  HStack {
    Text("Hello, World!")
      .navigationTitle("Inner title")
  }
  .navigationTitle("Outer title")
}
```

Figure 3-5. *Setting the navigation title on a child view*

In this case, the inner `navigationTitle` takes precedence—
you can try this for yourself by commenting out the line that says
`.navigationTitle("Inner title")`—as a result, the title of the screen will
change to "Outer title".

Using View Modifiers to Register Action Handlers

So far, most of the view modifiers we've looked at modify how a view looks
like. These view modifiers usually take parameters of type `String`, `Int`,
`Color`, `Font`, or any of Swift's other types.

In addition to being able to declare the look of a view, we also need
to be able to specify what happens when the user taps on a button, enters
text into an input field, or performs other actions. To enable this, SwiftUI
also allows us to register closures for specific events, such as when a view
appears or disappears, when the user taps on a button or menu item,
triggers a swipe action in a `List` view, and more.

For example, here is how you can register a closure that gets called
whenever the user taps a button:

```
Button("Tap me", action: {
  self.message = "You tapped me!"
})
```

Thanks to Swift's trailing closure syntax, we can further
condense this to

```
Button("Tap me") {
  self.message = "You tapped me!"
}
```

Similar to view modifiers that affect the look of a view, these action
handler view modifiers can be applied to a container view and will
consequently be applied to all child views. The following example shows
an input form with two `TextField` views, allowing the user to enter

their first and last name. Whenever the user makes a change to one of the TextFields, the code updates the dirty property. We achieve this by applying the onChange(of:perform:) view modifier to the respective TextField, which allows us to specify which model property to watch for changes. Similarly, we apply the onSubmit view modifier and register a closure to call the save method on the view model to save the data to disk.

```
import SwiftUI

private class PersonViewModel: ObservableObject {
  @Published var firstName = ""
  @Published var lastName = ""

  func save() {
    print("Save to disk")
  }
}

struct ClosuresDemoView: View {
  @State var message = ""
  @State var dirty = false
  @StateObject private var viewModel = PersonViewModel()

  var body: some View {
    Form {
      Section("\(self.dirty ? "* " : "")Input fields") {
        TextField("First name", text: $viewModel.firstName)
          .onChange(of: viewModel.firstName) { newValue in
            self.dirty = true
          }
          .onSubmit {
            viewModel.save()
          }

        TextField("Last name", text: $viewModel.lastName)
```

```
            .onChange(of: viewModel.lastName) { newValue in
              self.dirty = true
            }
            .onSubmit {
              viewModel.save()
            }
          }
        }
      }
    }
```

Since both of these onSubmit closures do the same, we can refactor
the previous code and move the onSubmit view modifiers to the enclosing
Section:

```
struct ClosuresDemoView: View {
  @State var message = ""
  @State var dirty = false
  @StateObject private var viewModel = PersonViewModel()

  var body: some View {
    Form {
      Section("\(self.dirty ? "* " : "")Input fields") {
        TextField("First name", text: $viewModel.firstName)
          .onChange(of: viewModel.firstName) { newValue in
            self.dirty = true
          }

        TextField("Last name", text: $viewModel.lastName)
          .onChange(of: viewModel.lastName) { newValue in
            self.dirty = true
          }
      }
```

```
        .onSubmit {
          viewModel.save()
        }
      }
    }
  }
}
```

Summary

SwiftUI is a flexible internal DSL for building UIs, and in this chapter, you learned more about its basic building blocks:

> **SwiftUI views are just a description of the UI**, so we can make liberal use of them to construct our UI—just keep in mind to not perform any long-running or memory-intensive operations in a `View`'s initializer.

> **Views can be composed to create more complex views**, and we looked at some of SwiftUI's container views, such as `HStack`, `VStack`, and `ZStack`, that make this possible.

> **View modifiers can be used to customize views**— we can use them to modify a view's look and feel, such as the foreground color or the font of a `Label`. But we can also register closures that get called when certain events occur (e.g., when a view appears, or the user hits enter to submit a form).

With this knowledge under your belt, it is now time to dive into the important topic of state management. In the next chapter, you will learn how SwiftUI makes use of a functional reactive approach to ensure that the UI is always in sync with the underlying data model.

CHAPTER 4

State Management

SwiftUI is different from many other UI toolkits you might have worked with before: you cannot manipulate the UI views directly. Any changes you see on screen are determined by the state of the application's data model and its transitions. You might have heard "in SwiftUI, the view is a function of the application's state."

What does this mean, and why is this such a big deal?

Imperative UI toolkits suffer from one very big flaw: they allow developers to update model and view independently. This often results in inconsistent states and partial updates. You've probably used apps before that exhibit this behavior. For example, you make a change in a details screen, but this change isn't reflected on the main screen.[1]

The designers of SwiftUI decided to choose a different approach: a view in SwiftUI is either static, or it displays information that is driven by a model element. It is impossible to manipulate a SwiftUI view directly. The data that determines the state of the UI is called *Source of Truth* and there can only be one source of truth for each UI element.

This results in deterministic states and consistent user interfaces.

SwiftUI provides a number of ways to manage state in your application. In this chapter, we're going to learn about the different techniques and discuss their benefits and when to use them.

---

[1] You're laughing, but I use *several* apps (and websites) that have this exact behaviour.

© Peter Friese 2023
P. Friese, *Asynchronous Programming with SwiftUI and Combine*,
https://doi.org/10.1007/978-1-4842-8572-5_4

To give you a better understanding of this complex topic, we're going to look at a few real-world scenarios and discuss the state management patterns you can use in each scenario.

Managing State in SwiftUI

SwiftUI views are structs, which means they are value types. One of the major reasons for choosing value types for defining the UI of your app is that when copying a value type, you can be sure no other part of the app is changing the data under the covers.[2] As we will later see, the body of a view is a computed property, making it impossible for developers to accidentally modify a view directly.

However, updating the UI is a crucial feature for almost any app, so how can we build apps that dynamically update their UI?

SwiftUI provides two complementary tools that ensure you can freely manage and update your data model, while making sure the UI is always in sync with the data model.

Both mechanisms build upon *property wrappers*.

The first one helps you to define your data model in such a way that it is capable of publishing its state.

And secondly, SwiftUI manages the state of the UI for you in a memory area that only SwiftUI has control over.

SwiftUI therefore allows you to define your data model in an easy-to-build and reusable way. By making UI updates *unidirectional*, SwiftUI relieves you from the burden of having to make sure to always update the view and the model at the same time.

Let's first look at the different ways on how you can connect your data model to your app's user interface.

---

[2] See https://developer.apple.com/swift/blog/?id=10

SwiftUI provides several ways for storing and passing data around. Which one is most appropriate depends on which part of your app owns the data, whether you're working with value types or objects, and whether the view requires read/write access or read-only access to the data.

Binding Value Types

If the data you want to display in a view is an enum, struct, or a simple type, you can use either @State or @Binding to wrap the variable or bind to the variable directly.

If you just want to display the value of a variable, you can connect the variable to the view directly. For example:

```
let name = "Peter"
...
Text("Hello, \(name), how are you?")
```

This also works for complex types, like an address:

```
struct Address {
  let street: String
  let postCode: String
  let city: String
  let country: String
}

let appleHQ = Address(street: "One Infinite Loop",
                      postCode: "CA 95014",
                      city: "Cupertino",
                      country: "United States")
...

Text("Apple HQ: \(appleHQ.street)")
```

This approach works great in many situations, such as displaying attributes of a complex object in list view rows. However, structs are immutable when they're assigned to a `let` constant, so you cannot change their attributes after initialization. This means you cannot manipulate attributes of a struct from inside a SwiftUI view. In addition, plain structs and attributes do not offer a mechanism to publish changes, which means that SwiftUI cannot track any changes to simple variables or structs.

If you want SwiftUI to manage updating the UI to reflect changes in the underlying data, you need to use its state management property wrappers.

The first one we'll look at is `@State` which is also the easiest to use. Applying `@State` to a property allows the SwiftUI framework to manage the state of the property and respond to updates by redrawing dependent views. Conversely, any changes the user makes in the UI (for example by dragging a slider or entering text in a `TextField`) will be applied to the property.

The following code snippet shows a user interface for the infamous "Hello World" example: it defines a `name` variable that the user can change by typing in their name in the `TextField` view. As a result, the `Text` view will display a greeting with the user's name.

```
@State var name = "Peter"
...

TextField("Enter your name", text: $title)
Text("Hello \(title), nice to meet you!")
```

By prefixing the `name` variable with `@State`, SwiftUI creates a `Binding` for that variable, which can be accessed using the *projected value* using the $-prefixed version of the variable, `$name`. We use this Binding in the `TextField` view to allow the user to manipulate the underlying value. In the line below, we directly access the `name` property to display the greeting in a `Text` view.

We will take a closer look at how all of this works behind the scenes later in this chapter.

If your view needs access to data that is defined elsewhere (e.g., in a parent view), it doesn't own the data. In this case, you can use @Binding to connect the data to the view. This enables the view to read, write, and observe the data. We've already used bindings in the previous example: a TextField requires a Binding as its second parameter: TextField(_ title: StringProtocol, text: Binding<String>). In the example, we used @State to create a binding for the name variable and passed it to the TextField view.

A binding can refer to an @State variable or an @Observable object (more on this later).

Bindings are especially useful when assembling a view from several smaller, specialized views. They are an important tool to help create reusable views.

The following code sample shows how a parent view and a child view can share the same state by using @State in the parent view and @Binding in the child view:

```swift
struct ParentView: View {
  @State var favouriteNumber: Int = 42

  var body: some View {
    VStack {
      Text("Your favourite number is \(favouriteNumber)")
      ChildView(number: $favouriteNumber)
    }
  }
}

struct ChildView: View {
  @Binding var number: Int

  var body: some View {
    Stepper("\(number)", value: $number, in: 0...100)
  }
}
```

Both `@State` and `@Binding` are best suited for managing local UI state. For example, you can use `@State` to manage a Boolean property that determines whether a modal sheet is shown. `@Binding` in particular can also be used to connect views to individual attributes of more complex objects, as we will see later in this chapter.

However, you should avoid using `@State` or `@Binding` for complex objects that you want to persist on disk or send across the network. SwiftUI has more powerful tools to manage objects like these.

Since properties marked as `@State` are commonly used for handling local UI state, you should make them `private` to make sure they cannot accidentally be modified from the outside.

Binding Objects

If the data you want to use in a SwiftUI view lives in a reference type (i.e., a `class`), you should use one of `@StateObject`, `@ObservedObject`, or `@EnvironmentObject` to manage its state. You also need to conform the class to `ObservableObject`.

A class that conforms to `ObservableObject` acts as a publisher and notifies its subscribers about changes to its properties which are marked as `@Published`.

From the perspective of the consumer (i.e., the view that subscribes to the updates an `ObservableObject` sends), all three of these property wrappers behave exactly the same: the view (and its subviews) can subscribe to individual properties of the `ObservableObject` (by either using direct property access or bindings) and receive updates whenever any of the published properties of the object changes.

The only way `@StateObject`, `@ObservedObject`, and `@EnvironmentObject` differ from each other is how they manage data.

Before we look at how exactly they manage data, we need to understand how `ObservableObject` works.

ObservableObject

To turn a simple Swift class into an observable object, you need to conform it to the `ObservableObject` protocol. As this is a class protocol, you can only use it on classes, not on value types (such as structs or enums).

It's certainly no coincidence that SwiftUI doesn't define `ObservableObject` itself, but instead imports it from the Combine framework. SwiftUI makes use of Combine's publishers without requiring developers to have deep knowledge about the Combine framework and Functional Reactive Programming. It's definitely possible to build SwiftUI apps without knowing anything about Combine or using any of its advanced features. That being said, Combine provides many useful features such as debouncing, error handling, retrying, and other useful features. Once you are past the initial learning curve, integrating features like these in your applications will be much easier using Combine than implementing them manually.

Conforming a class to `ObservableObject` and marking some of its properties as `@Published` turns a class into a Combine Publisher that emits events whenever one of its published properties changes. Once you have declared a property on your view that is an `ObservableObject` and marked it as a `@StateObject`, `@ObservedObject`, or `@EnvironmentObject`, you can connect its properties to the view or its subviews.

SwiftUI will start observing the objects and rerender the view as needed to keep it in sync with the state of the model.

@StateObject

When using `@StateObject`, SwiftUI handles the life cycle of the underlying object, making sure it will only be created once, even if SwiftUI has to re-create the entire view in response to a model update.

This is important for views that can change in response to events outside of the view. Consider the following code snippet. It shows a screen that allows the user to pick a number using a Stepper. In addition, the user can change the foreground color of the screen by tapping on the ColorPicker view. The developer of this screen has decided to move the stepper and the object containing the data into a separate view, named StateStepper.

```
class Counter: ObservableObject {
  @Published var count = 0
}

struct StateStepper: View {
  @StateObject var stateCounter = Counter()
  var body: some View {
    Section(header: Text("@StateObject")) {
      Stepper("Counter: \(stateCounter.count)", value:
      $stateCounter.count)
    }
  }
}

struct ContentView: View {
  @State var color: Color = Color.accentColor

  var body: some View {
    VStack(alignment: .leading) {
      StateStepper()
      ColorPicker("Pick a color", selection: $color)
    }
    .foregroundColor(color)
  }
}
```

As soon as the color is changed, SwiftUI will re-render all elements that need to change their color. This will result in `StateStepper` to be re-created.

Since `stateCounter` is marked as `@StateObject`, the `Counter` object will only be created once, and SwiftUI will manage its life cycle. Consequently, the value of `stateCounter.count` will not be reset to zero when the user decides to change the color of the screen.

Had the developer chosen to use `@ObservedObject` instead, changing the color would result in the `stateCounter` being re-created, and the data inside being lost.

When to Use

Use `@StateObject`,

- when you need to listen to changes or updates in an `ObservableObject`

- and you create the instance you want to listen to in the view itself

That is, when the view you want to use the object in is the owner of the data.

@ObservedObject

Similar to `@StateObject`, an `@ObservedObject` wraps an `ObservableObject`, making it available in a view so that the view (and its subviews) can subscribe to published properties of the object.

Other than `@StateObject`, an object wrapped by `@ObservedObject` will be re-created every single time the view is re-created. Let's take the previous code snippet, but this time use a `@ObservedObject` instead of `@StateObject`:

```
class Counter: ObservableObject {
  @Published var count = 0
}

struct ObservedStepper: View {
  @ObservedObject var counter = Counter()
  var body: some View {
    Section(header: Text("@ObservedObject")) {
      Stepper("Counter: \(counter.count)", value:
      $counter.count)
    }
  }
}

struct ContentView: View {
  @State var color: Color = Color.accentColor

  var body: some View {
    VStack(alignment: .leading) {
      ObservedStepper()
      ColorPicker("Pick a color", selection: $color)
    }
    .foregroundColor(color)
  }
}
```

When running this code, `counter` will be re-created whenever the user picks a color, resulting in `count` being reset to zero. For the user, it appears as if the UI has amnesia.

In the first release of SwiftUI, `@ObservedObject` was the only way to create and observe an object inside a view. You can still do this (at least the compiler doesn't throw a warning, and presumably there are quite a few SwiftUI apps out there that still use this approach), but using `@ObservedObject` to *create* a model object is an antipattern that you should avoid.

So if you see code like this: `@ObservedObject var foo = Bar()`, you should refactor your code and use `@StateObject` instead.

When to Use

Use `@ObservedObject`,

- when you need to listen to changes and updates in an `ObservedObject`

- and the object you want to observe in a view is *not* created by the view, but outside of the view (e.g., in a parent view or the app struct)

@EnvironmentObject

Theoretically, `@StateObject` and `@ObservedObject` should give you enough flexibility to build any sort of app that requires access to shared state. In most cases, you can create an object somewhere in your app—for example, in the app object itself, or in one of its top-level views, such as the main navigation view. You can then pass on this object through the view hierarchy by injecting it into the constructor of any subview that requires access to it.

However, not all views might need access to all of the data. For example, your app might have a shared state that represents the logged-in user. You might want to display the user's avatar on the main screen, and you also might want to display their first and last name on a profile screen, but to get to the profile screen, the user might need to navigate through a couple of settings screens first. And those screens might not require access to the user object at all. Hauling the user object through the navigation hierarchy not only is unnecessary, but it would also create a tight coupling between the intermediary screens and the user object where it is not required.

For situations like these, you can use @EnvironmentObject. As the name implies, it fetches an ObservableObject from the environment and makes it available to the view. To inject an object into the environment, call .environmentObject(myObject) on any view. This will make myObject available to all sub views. To retrieve an object from the environment, declare a property on a view, and mark it as @EnvironmentObject.

```
class UserProfile: ObservableObject {
  @Published var name: String
}

struct EnvironmentObjectSampleScreen: View {
  @StateObject var profile = UserProfile(name: "Peter")
  @State var isSettingsShown = false
  var body: some View {
    VStack(alignment: .leading) {
      // ...
    }
    .sheet(isPresented: $isSettingsShown) {
      NavigationView {
        SettingsScreen()
      }
      .environmentObject(profile) // very important to put
      this here, NOT inside the NavigationView! See https://
      developer.apple.com/forums/thread/653367
    }
  }
}

struct SettingsScreen: View {
  var body: some View {
    VStack(alignment: .leading) {
      NavigationLink(destination: UserProfileScreen()) {
```

```swift
        Text("User Profile")
      }
    }
  }
}

struct UserProfileScreen: View {
  @EnvironmentObject var profile: UserProfile

  var body: some View {
    VStack(alignment: .leading) {
      Form {
        Section(header: Text("User profile")) {
          TextField("Name", text: $profile.name)
        }
      }
    }
  }
}
```

While it might be tempting to use @EnvironmentObject for all your state objects, it is worth noting that this approach has a serious drawback: the compiler has no way to check if you injected an ObservableObject into the environment before trying to fetch it using @EnvironmentObject. When trying to retrieve an object from the environment that doesn't exist, your app will crash with a runtime error.

The SwiftUI environment is a very powerful mechanism that we'll dive into much deeper detail in one of the following chapters.

When to Use

Use `@EnvironmentObject`,

- when you need to listen to changes and updates in an `ObservedObject`

- and you'd have to pass an `ObservedObject` through several views that don't need this object before it reaches the view where you need access to the object

Summary

In this chapter, you learned how SwiftUI handles state and makes sure that the user interface always stays in sync with application's state.

We briefly touched on SwiftUI's relation to the Combine framework and learned that an `ObservableObject` really is a Combine publisher that communicates all updates to its published properties to the SwiftUI views that are subscribed to it.

You learned about the three different property wrappers— `@StateObject`, `@ObservedObject`, and `@EnvironmentObject`—how they manage the life cycle of the observable objects they wrap, and when you should know which to connect your views to your application's state.

Congrats, you've mastered one of the key building blocks of SwiftUI apps!

CHAPTER 5

Displaying Data in Lists

List views are probably one of the most important UI structures in iOS apps, and you'll be hard-pressed to find an app that doesn't use some sort of list.

SwiftUI makes it particularly easy to build list views: it just takes three lines of code to create a simple list! At the same time, SwiftUI's List view is extremely powerful and versatile, so it pays off to get to know it in a little bit more detail.

In this chapter, you will learn everything you need to know about List views, from simple lists, styling lists and their items, displaying collections of data in list views, implementing actions on lists and individual list items, iOS, iPadOS, and macOS.

Getting Started with Lists in SwiftUI

When you create a new SwiftUI view, Xcode will use a template that looks like this:

```
struct ContentView: View {
  var body: some View {
    Text("Hello, world!")
  }
}
```

© Peter Friese 2023
P. Friese, *Asynchronous Programming with SwiftUI and Combine*,
https://doi.org/10.1007/978-1-4842-8572-5_5

The simplest way to build a list is to create a new SwiftUI view and wrap the *Hello World* text in a `List`:

```
struct StaticListView: View {
  var body: some View {
    List {
      Text("Hello, world!")
    }
  }
}
```

This will show a static text inside a list view.

Figure 5-1. *A simple list view with one static text item*

To add more items to the list, we can just add another line:

```
List {
  Text("Hello, world!")
  Text("Hello, SwiftUI!")
}
```

Using Other SwiftUI Views Inside List Rows

The cool thing about the List view is that you can use any type of SwiftUI view as a list row, not just Text. Labels, Sliders, Steppers, Toggles, TextFields, SecureFields for entering passwords, ProgressViews, and Pickers—you name it.

```
struct StaticListView2: View {
  @State var number: Int = 42
  @State var degrees: Double = 37.5
  @State var toggle = true
  @State var name = "Peter"
  @State var secret = "s3cr3t!"

  var fruits = ["Apples", "Bananas", "Mangoes"]
  @State var fruit = "Mangoes"

  var body: some View {
    List {
      Text("Hello, world!")
      Label("The answer", systemImage: "42.circle")
      Slider(value: $degrees, in: 0...50) {
        Text("\(degrees)")
      } minimumValueLabel: {
        Text("min")
      } maximumValueLabel: {
```

```
      Text("max")
    }

    Stepper(value: $number, in: 0...100) {
      Text("\(number)")
    }
    Toggle(isOn: $toggle) {
      Text("Checked")
    }
    TextField("Name", text: $name)
    SecureField("Secret", text: $secret)
    ProgressView(value: 0.3)
    Picker(selection: $fruit, label: Text("Pick your
    favourite fruit")) {
      ForEach(fruits, id: \.self) { fruit in
        Text(fruit)
      }
    }
  }
 }
}
```

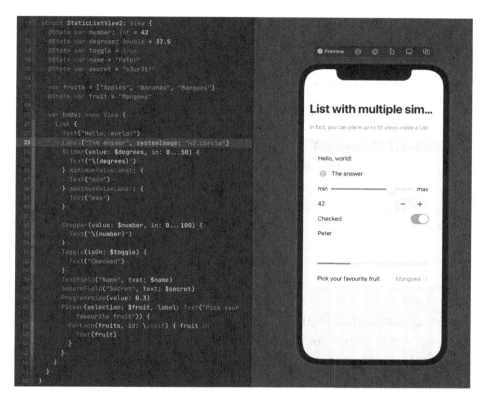

Figure 5-2. *List with advanced SwiftUI views*

Building Custom List Rows

And thanks to SwiftUI's stack-based layout system, you can easily create custom rows as well. In this example, we're using VStack to lay out two Text views on top of each other, replicating the typical title and details layout that is widely used in many iOS apps.

```
struct StaticListWithSimpleCustomRowView: View {
  var body: some View {
    List {
      VStack(alignment: .leading) {
```

```
        Text("Apples")
          .font(.headline)
        Text("Eat one a day")
          .font(.subheadline)
      }
      VStack(alignment: .leading) {
        Text("Bananas")
          .font(.headline)
        Text("High in potassium")
          .font(.subheadline)
      }
    }
  }
}
```

Adding custom rows like this is quick and easy, but the code will grow rapidly as we add more rows, and this will make it harder to understand and update it when we need to make changes. To prevent this from happening, we can extract the code for the list rows into a separate view, making it reusable:

```
struct StaticListWithSimpleCustomRowView: View {
  var body: some View {
    List {
      CustomRowView(title: "Apples", subtitle: "Eat one a day")
      CustomRowView(title: "Bananas", subtitle: "High in
      potassium")
    }
  }
}

private struct CustomRowView: View {
  var title: String
  var subtitle: String
```

```swift
    var body: some View {
      VStack(alignment: .leading) {
        Text(title)
          .font(.headline)
        Text(subtitle)
          .font(.subheadline)
      }
    }
  }
}
```

Figure 5-3. *Custom List Rows*

To learn more about refactoring SwiftUI code, check out this video[1], in which I show the process of refactoring SwiftUI views in more detail.

More Complex List Rows

SwiftUI's layout system is both flexible and easy to use and makes it easy to create even complex layouts using a combination of HStack, VStack, ZStack, and other SwiftUI views. Here is how you can create list rows with a title, a subtitle, a leading image, and a trailing number:

```
struct StaticListWithCustomRowView: View {
  var body: some View {
    List {
      CustomRowView("Apple", description: "Eat one a day",
        titleIcon: "🍎", count: 2)
      CustomRowView("Banana", description: "High in potassium",
        titleIcon: "🍌", count: 3)
      CustomRowView("Mango", description: "Soft and sweet",
        titleIcon: "🥭")
    }
  }
}


private struct CustomRowView: View {
  var title: String
  var description: String?
  var titleIcon: String
  var count: Int
```

---

[1]www.youtube.com/watch?v=UhDdtdeW63k

```swift
init(_ title: String, description: String? = nil, titleIcon:
String, count: Int = 1) {
  self.title = title
  self.description = description
  self.titleIcon = titleIcon
  self.count = count
}

var body: some View {
  HStack {
    Text(titleIcon)
      .font(.title)
      .padding(4)
      .background(Color(UIColor.tertiarySystemFill))
      .cornerRadius(10)
    VStack(alignment: .leading) {
      Text(title)
        .font(.headline)
      if let description = description {
        Text(description)
          .font(.subheadline)
      }
    }
    Spacer()
    Text("\(count)")
      .font(.title)
  }
}
}
```

115

Notice how we made use of a custom initializer for `CustomRowView`, allowing us to get rid of the parameter name for the `title` property and to define defaults for some of the properties. As a result, it is now more convenient to use the custom row view.

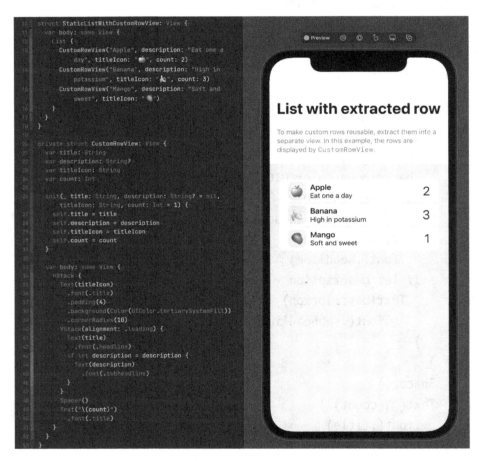

Figure 5-4. *Complex List Rows*

Dynamic Lists

So far, we looked at how to use List views to create *static* list views. Static list views are useful for creating menus or settings screens in iOS apps, but List views become a lot more useful when we connect them to a data source.

Let's now look at a couple of examples on how you can use List views to display a *dynamic* list of data, such as a list of books. We will also learn how to use some of the new features that Apple added to the latest version of SwiftUI in iOS 15, such as pull-to-refresh, a search UI, and an easy way to use async/await to fetch data from asynchronous APIs, such as remote services.

Displaying a List of Elements

There are a number of ways to create lists, and you can create both *flat* lists as well as *hierarchical, nested* lists. Since all list rows are computed on demand, List views perform well even for collections with many items.

The easiest way to create a List view based on a collection of elements is to use its constructor that takes a RandomAccessCollection and a view builder for the row content:

```
List(collection) { element in
  // use SwiftUI views to render an individual row to display
  `element`
}
```

Inside the view builder, we get access to the individual elements of the collection in a type-safe way. This means we can access the properties of the collection elements and use SwiftUI views like Text to render the individual rows, like in the following example:

```
struct Book: Identifiable {
  var id = UUID()
  var title: String
  var author: String
  var isbn: String
  var pages: Int
  var isRead: Bool = false
}

extension Book {
  static let samples = [
    Book(title: "Changer", author: "Matt Gemmell", isbn:
"9781916265202", pages: 476),
    Book(title: "SwiftUI for Absolute Beginners", author:
"Jayant Varma", isbn: "9781484255155", pages: 200),
    Book(title: "Why we sleep", author: "Matthew Walker", isbn:
"9780141983769", pages: 368),
    Book(title: "The Hitchhiker's Guide to the Galaxy", author:
"Douglas Adams", isbn: "9780671461492", pages: 216)
  ]
}

private class BooksViewModel: ObservableObject {
  @Published var books: [Book] = Book.samples
}

struct BooksListView: View {
  @StateObject fileprivate var viewModel = BooksViewModel()
  var body: some View {
    List(viewModel.books) { book in
      Text("\(book.title) by \(book.author)")
    }
  }
}
```

As this view acts as the owner of the data we want to display, we use a @StateObject to hold the view model. The view model exposes a published property which holds the list of books. In the interest of simplicity, this is a static list, but in a real-world application, you would fetch this data from a remote API or a local database.

Notice how we can access the properties of the Book elements inside the List by writing book.title or book.author. Here, we use a Text view to display the title and the author of a book using string interpolation.

Thanks to SwiftUI's declarative syntax, we can easily build more complex custom UIs to present data.

Let's replace the Text view in the preceding snippet with a more elaborate row that displays the book cover, title, author, and number of pages:

```
// ...
List(viewModel.books) { book in
  HStack(alignment: .top) {
    Image(book.mediumCoverImageName)
      .resizable()
      .aspectRatio(contentMode: .fit)
      .frame(height: 90)
    VStack(alignment: .leading) {
      Text(book.title)
        .font(.headline)
      Text("by \(book.author)")
        .font(.subheadline)
      Text("\(book.pages) pages")
        .font(.subheadline)
    }
    Spacer()
  }
}
// ...
```

Using Xcode's refactoring tools for SwiftUI, we can extract this code into a custom view, to make our code easier to read[2].

```
private struct BookRowView: View {
  var book: Book

  var body: some View {
    HStack(alignment: .top) {
      Image(book.mediumCoverImageName)
        .resizable()
        .aspectRatio(contentMode: .fit)
        .frame(height: 90)
      VStack(alignment: .leading) {
        Text(book.title)
          .font(.headline)
        Text("by \(book.author)")
          .font(.subheadline)
        Text("\(book.pages) pages")
          .font(.subheadline)
      }
      Spacer()
    }
  }
}
```

Since we're not planning to modify the data inside the list row (or inside a details view), we pass the list item to the row as a simple reference. If we wanted to modify the data inside the list row (e.g., by marking a book as a favorite, or passing it on to a child screen where the user can edit the book details), we'd have to use a list binding.

---

[2] Check out my video (Building SwiftUI Components—Getting Started http://www.youtube.com/watch?v=UhDdtdeW63k) on building SwiftUI views to see this (and other) refactoring in action.

Using List Bindings to Allow Modifying List Items

Normally, data inside a view is unmodifiable. To modify data, it needs to be managed as a `@State` property or a `@ObservedObject` view model. To allow users to modify data in a child view (e.g., a `TextField` or a details screen), we need to use a binding to connect the data in the child view to the state in the parent view.

Until SwiftUI 3, there wasn't a direct way to get a binding to the elements of the list, so people had to come up with their own solutions. I've written about this before in this blog post[3], in which I discuss incorrect and correct ways to do this.

With SwiftUI 3, Apple has introduced a straightforward way to access list items as bindings, using the following syntax:

```
List($collection) { $element in
  TextField("Name", text: $element.name)
}
```

To allow users of our sample app to edit the title of a book inline in the list view, all we have to do is to update the book list view as follows:

```
List($viewModel.books) { $book in
  TextField("Book title",
            text: $book.title,
            prompt: Text("Enter the book title"))
}
```

Of course, this also works for custom views—here is how to update the `BookRowView` to make the book title editable:

---

[3] https://peterfriese.dev/posts/swiftui-list-item-bindings-behind-the-scenes/

121

```swift
struct EditableBooksListView: View {
  // ...

  var body: some View {
    List($viewModel.books) { $book in
      EditableBookRowView(book: $book)
    }
  }
}

private struct EditableBookRowView: View {
  @Binding var book: Book

  var body: some View {
    HStack(alignment: .top) {
      Image(book.mediumCoverImageName)
        .resizable()
        .aspectRatio(contentMode: .fit)
        .frame(height: 90)
      VStack(alignment: .leading) {
        TextField("Book title", text: $book.title, prompt:
        Text("Enter the book title"))
          .font(.headline)
        Text("by \(book.author)")
          .font(.subheadline)
        Text("\(book.pages) pages")
          .font(.subheadline)
      }
      Spacer()
    }
  }
}
```

The key point here is to use @Binding in the child view. By doing so, the parent view retains ownership of the data that you pass in to the child view while letting the child view modify the data. The *source of truth* is the @Published property on the ObservableObject in the parent view.

To read more about list bindings, and how this feature works under the hood, check out my article SwiftUI List Bindings[4].

Asynchronously Fetching Data

The next sections of this chapter have one thing in common—they're all based on Apple's new APIs for handling asynchronous code.

At WWDC 21, Apple introduced Swift's new concurrency model as part of Swift 5.5.

In the previous examples, we used a static list of data. The advantage of this approach is that we didn't have to fetch (and wait for) this data, as it was already in memory. This was fine for the examples, as it allowed us to focus on what's relevant, but it doesn't reflect reality. In a real-world application, we usually display data from remote APIs, and this usually means performing asynchronous calls: while we're waiting for the results to come in from the remote API, the app needs to continue updating the UI. If it didn't do so, users might get the impression the app was hanging or even crashed.

So in the next examples, I'm going to demonstrate how to make use of Swift's new concurrency model to handle asynchronous code.

A good moment to fetch data is when the user navigates to a new screen and the screen just appears. In previous versions of SwiftUI, using the .onAppear view modifier was a good place to request data. Starting with iOS 15, SwiftUI includes a new view modifier that makes this even

---

[4]https://peterfriese.dev/posts/swiftui-list-item-bindings-behind-the-scenes/

easier: .task. It will start an asynchronous Task when the view appears and will cancel this task once the view disappears (if the task is still running). This is useful if your task is a long-running download that you automatically want to abort when the user leaves the screen.

Using .task is as easy as applying it to your List view:

```
struct AsyncFetchBooksListView: View {
  @StateObject fileprivate var viewModel =
  AsyncFetchBooksViewModel()

  var body: some View {
    List(viewModel.books) { book in
      AsyncFetchBookRowView(book: book)
    }
    .overlay {
      if viewModel.fetching {
        ProgressView("Fetching data, please wait...")
          .progressViewStyle(CircularProgressViewStyle(tint:
          .accentColor))
      }
    }
    .animation(.default, value: viewModel.books)
    .task {
      await viewModel.fetchData()
    }
  }
}
```

In the view model, you can then use asynchronous APIs to fetch data. In this example, I've mocked the backend to make the code a bit easier to read, and added an artificial delay:

```
private class AsyncFetchBooksViewModel: ObservableObject {
  @Published var books = [Book]()
  @Published var fetching = false

  func fetchData() async {
    fetching = true

    await Task.sleep(2_000_000_000)
    books = Book.samples

    fetching = false
  }
}
```

If you'd try and run the code like this, you would end up with a runtime warning, saying that *"Publishing changes from background threads is not allowed; make sure to publish values from the main thread (via operators like receive(on:)) on model updates."*

The reason for this runtime error is that the code inside `fetchData` is not executed on the main thread. However, UI updates *must* be executed on the main thread. In the past, we would've had to use `DispatchQueue.main.async { ... }` to make sure any UI updates are executed on the main thread. However, with Swift's new concurrency model, there is an easier way: all we have to do is to mark any methods (or classes) that perform UI updates using the `@MainActor` property wrapper. This instructs the compiler to switch to the main actor when executing this code and thus make sure any UI updates run on the main thread. Here's the updated code:

```
private class AsyncFetchBooksViewModel: ObservableObject {
  @Published var books = [Book]()
  @Published var fetching = false
```

```
@MainActor
func fetchData() async {
  fetching = true

  await Task.sleep(2_000_000_000)
  books = Book.samples

  fetching = false
  }
}
```

To learn more about Swift's new concurrency model, check out my video series[5], as well as the following articles on my blog:

— Getting Started with async/await in SwiftUI[6]

— Cooperative Task Cancellation - SwiftUI Concurrency Essentials[7]

Pull-to-Refresh

Unless you use an SDK like Cloud Firestore[8] that allows you to listen to updates in your backend in real time, you will want to add some UI affordances to your app that make it easy for your users to request the latest data. One of the most common ways to let users refresh data is *pull-to-refresh*, made popular in. 2008 by Loren Brichter in the Tweetie app[9] (later acquired by Twitter and relaunched as Twitter for iOS).

---

[5] https://bit.ly/swift-concurrency-video-series
[6] https://peterfriese.dev/swiftui-concurrency-essentials-part1/
[7] https://peterfriese.dev/swiftui-concurrency-essentials-part2/
[8] https://firebase.google.com/docs/firestore
[9] https://www.imore.com/hall-fame-loren-brichter-and-tweetie

SwiftUI makes it easy to add this functionality to your app with just a few lines of code, thanks to its declarative nature. And as mentioned earlier, this feature also makes use of Swift's new concurrency model to ensure that your app's UI remains responsive even while it needs to wait for any updates to arrive.

Adding the refreshable view modifier to your List view is all it takes to add *pull-to-refresh* to your app:

```
struct RefreshableBooksListView: View {
  @StateObject var viewModel = RefreshableBooksViewModel()
  var body: some View {
    List(viewModel.books) { book in
      RefreshableBookRowView(book: book)
    }
    .refreshable {
      await viewModel.refresh()
    }
  }
}
```

As indicated by the await keyword, refreshable opens an asynchronous execution context. This requires that the code you're calling from within refreshable can execute asynchronously (if the code you're calling can execute nonasynchronously, because it returns immediately, that's fine as well, but more often than not you'll want to communicate with a remote API that requires being called asynchronously).

To give you an idea of how this might look like, I've created a view model that simulates an asynchronous remote API by adding some artificial wait time:

```
class RefreshableBooksViewModel: ObservableObject {
  @Published var books: [Book] = Book.samples
```

```
private func generateNewBook() -> Book {
  let title = Lorem.sentence
  let author = Lorem.fullName
  let pageCount = Int.random(in: 42...999)
  return Book(title: title, author: author, isbn:
  "9781234567890", pages: pageCount)
}

func refresh() async {
  await Task.sleep(2_000_000_000)
  let book = generateNewBook()
  books.insert(book, at: 0)
}
}
```

Let's take a look at this code to understand what's going on.

1. As in the previous samples, books is a published property that the view subscribes to.

2. generateNewBook is a local function that produces a random new Book instance using the excellent LoremSwiftum[10] library.

3. Inside refresh, we call generateBook to produce a new book and then insert it into the published property books, but before we do so, we tell the app to sleep for 2 seconds, using the Task.sleep call. This is an asynchronous call, so we need to use await to call it.

---

[10] https://github.com/lukaskubanek/LoremSwiftum

Just the same as in the previous example, this code will produce a purple runtime warning: *"Publishing changes from background threads is not allowed; make sure to publish values from the main thread (via operators like receive(on:)) on model updates",* so we need to use @MainActor to ensure all updates happen on the main actor. This time, instead of marking just the refresh method, we're going to mark the entire view model as @MainActor:

```
@MainActor
class RefreshableBooksViewModel: ObservableObject {
  // ...

  func refresh() async {
    // ...
  }
}
```

One final adjustment before we can wrap up this section: you will notice that when adding new items to the list by pulling to refresh, the newly added items will appear instantly, without a smooth transition.

Thanks to SwiftUI's declarative syntax, adding animations to make this feel more natural is super easy: all we need to do is adding an animation view modifier to the List view:

```
// ...
List(viewModel.books) { book in
  RefreshableBookRowView(book: book)
}
.animation(.default, value: viewModel.books)
// ...
```

By providing the value parameter, we can make sure this animation is only run when the contents of the list view change, for example, when new items are inserted or removed.

To perfect the animations, we'll also add a short pause to the end of the refresh function on the view model—this makes sure that the new rows appear with a smooth transition before the progress spinner disappears:

```
func refresh() async {
  await Task.sleep(2_000_000_000)
  let book = generateNewBook()
  books.insert(book, at: 0)

  // the following line, in combination with the `.animation`
  modifier, makes sure we have a smooth animation
  await Task.sleep(500_000_000)
}
```

Searching

SwiftUI makes it easy to implement search in List views—all you need to do is apply the .searchable view modifier to the list view, and SwiftUI will handle all the UI aspects for you automatically: it will display a search field (and make sure it is offscreen when you first display the list view, just like you'd expect from a native app). It also has all the UI affordances to trigger the search and clear the search field).

The only thing that's left to do is to actually perform the search and provide the appropriate result set.

Generally speaking, a search screen can either act locally (i.e., filter the items being displayed in a list view) or remotely (i.e., perform a query against a remote API and only display the results of this call).

For this section, we're going to look at filtering the elements being displayed in the list view. To do so, we'll be using a combination of async/await and Combine.

To get started, we'll build a simple List view that displays a list of books from a view model. This should look very familiar to you, as we're in fact reusing much of the code we've used for the previous examples:

130

```swift
struct SearchableBooksListView: View {
  @StateObject var viewModel = SearchableBooksViewModel()
  var body: some View {
    List(viewModel.books) { book in
      SearchableBookRowView(book: book)
    }
  }
}

struct SearchableBookRowView: View {
  var book: Book

  var body: some View {
    HStack(alignment: .top) {
      Image(book.mediumCoverImageName)
        .resizable()
        .aspectRatio(contentMode: .fit)
        .frame(height: 90)
      VStack(alignment: .leading) {
        Text(book.title)
          .font(.headline)
        Text("by \(book.author)")
          .font(.subheadline)
        Text("\(book.pages) pages")
          .font(.subheadline)
      }
      Spacer()
    }
  }
}
```

The view model is very similar to the ones we used previously, with one important difference—the collection of books is empty initially:

```
class SearchableBooksViewModel: ObservableObject {
  @Published var books = [Book]()
}
```

To add a search UI to SearchableBooksListView, we apply the .searchable view modifier and bind its text parameter to a new searchTerm property on the view model:

```
class SearchableBooksViewModel: ObservableObject {
  @Published var books = [Book]()
  @Published var searchTerm: String = ""
}

struct SearchableBooksListView: View {
  @StateObject var viewModel = SearchableBooksViewModel()
  var body: some View {
    List(viewModel.books) { book in
      SearchableBookRowView(book: book)
    }
    .searchable(text: $viewModel.searchTerm)
  }
}
```

This will install the search UI in the List view, but if you run this code, nothing will happen. In fact, you won't even see any books in the list view.

To change this, we will add a new private property to the view model which holds the original unfiltered list of books. And finally, we will set up a Combine pipeline that filters this list based on the search term entered by the user:

```
class SearchableBooksViewModel: ObservableObject {
  @Published private var originalBooks = Book.samples
  @Published var books = [Book]()
  @Published var searchTerm: String = ""

  init() {
    Publishers.CombineLatest($originalBooks,
    $searchTerm) // (1)
      .map { books, searchTerm in // (2)
        books.filter { book in // (3)
          searchTerm.isEmpty
            ? true
            : (book.title.matches(searchTerm)
              || book.author.matches(searchTerm))
        }
      }
      .assign(to: &$books)
  }
}
```

How does this Combine pipeline work?

1. We use `Publishers.CombineLatest` to take the
   latest state of the two publishers, `$originalBooks`
   and `$searchTerm`. In a real-world application, we
   might receive updates to the collection of books in
   the background, and we'll want these to be included
   in the search result as well. The `CombineLatest`
   publisher will publish a new tuple containing the
   latest value of `originalBooks` and `searchTerm` every
   time one of those publishers sends a new event.

2.   We then use the .map operator to transform the (books, searchTerm) tuple into an array of books that we eventually assign to the published $books property, which is connected to the SearchableBooksListView.

3.   Inside the .map closure, we use filter to return only the books that contain the search term either in their title or in the author's name. This part of the process actually is not Combine-specific—filter is a method on Array.

If you run this code, you will notice that everything you type into the search field will be autocapitalized. To prevent this, we can apply the .autocapitalization view modifier—*after* the searchable view modifier:

```
struct SearchableBooksListView: View {
  @StateObject var viewModel = SearchableBooksViewModel()
  var body: some View {
    List(viewModel.books) { book in
      SearchableBookRowView(book: book)
    }
    .searchable(text: $viewModel.searchTerm)
    .autocapitalization(.none)
  }
}
```

Styling

Lists offer a wide range of styling options, and with SwiftUI 3, it is now possible to configure almost all aspects of list views:

- The overall appearance of the list itself (i.e., the list style)

- The look of the list cells

- The dividers (finally!)

- ...and much more

Let's look at what's possible.

List Styles

The overall look and feel of list views can be controlled with the `.listStyle` view modifier. SwiftUI supports six different looks:

1. `.automatic`

2. `.grouped`

3. `.inset`

4. `.insetGrouped`

5. `.plain`

6. `.sidebar`

```
List(items) { item in
  Text("\(item.label)")
}
.listStyle(.plain)
```

If you don't provide a style, SwiftUI will assume `.automatic`. On iOS, `.automatic` and `.insetGrouped` have the same look.

Instead of trying to describe in words how each of the styles looks like, here are the images that show each of the styles.

```
List Styles: 1
```

Figure 5-5. *List Styles*

```
List Styles: 2
```

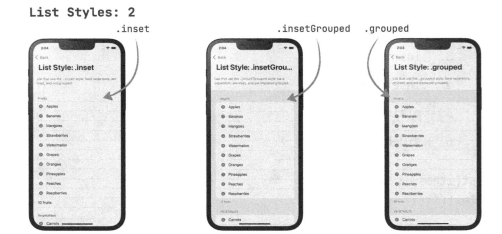

Figure 5-6. *More List Styles*

Headers and Footers

All of the List view styles support headers and footers. To specify a header and/or footer for a section, use one of the constructors that take a header or footer parameter.

It seems like my favorite way of creating headers and footers has been marked for deprecation:

```
@available(iOS 13.0, macOS 10.15, tvOS 13.0, watchOS 6.0, *)
extension Section where Parent : View, Content : View,
Footer : View {

    /// Creates a section with a header, footer, and the
    provided section content.
    /// - Parameters:
    ///    - header: A view to use as the section's header.
    ///    - footer: A view to use as the section's footer.
    ///    - content: The section's content.
    @available(iOS, deprecated: 100000.0, renamed: "Section
    (content:header:footer:)")
    @available(macOS, deprecated: 100000.0, renamed: "Section
    (content:header:footer:)")
    @available(tvOS, deprecated: 100000.0, renamed:
    "Section(content:header:footer:)")
    @available(watchOS, deprecated: 100000.0, renamed: "Section
    (content:header:footer:)")
    public init(header: Parent, footer: Footer, @ViewBuilder
    content: () -> Content)
}
```

Here is my preferred way of setting up header and footer for a section:

```
List {
  Section(header: Text("Fruits"), footer: Text("\(fruits.count)
  fruits")) {
    ForEach(fruits, id: \.self) { fruit in
      Label(fruit, systemImage: "\(fruits.firstIndex(of: fruit)
      ?? 0).circle.fill" )
    }
  }
}
```

And here is the new way of doing the same:

```
List {
  Section {
    ForEach(fruits, id: \.self) { fruit in
      Label(fruit, systemImage: "\(fruits.firstIndex(of: fruit)
      ?? 0).circle.fill" )
    }
  } header: {
    Text("Fruits")
  } footer: {
    Text("\(fruits.count) fruits")
  }
}
```

I leave it up to you to decide which one looks cleaner—when executed, they do exactly the same.

List Cells

Designing custom cells used to be a pretty complicated affair in the early days of UITableViewController, and thankfully, things have gotten a lot easier since then.

In SwiftUI, designing custom List rows is easy to get started (just use a plain Text view to represent the current item), but the possibilities are endless, as you can make use of SwiftUI's flexible stack-based layout system. For a general introduction to building custom List rows, check out the first part of this series, which covers some basic techniques.

In addition, SwiftUI supports a number of ways for styling common aspects of List rows, such as their background, their inset, accent color, tint, and badges.

Here is a code snippet that shows how you can configure a list row:

```
List(items, id: \.title) { item in
  Label(item.title, systemImage: item.iconName)
    .badge(item.badge)
    // listItemTint and foregroundColor are mutually exclusive
    // .listItemTint(listItemTintColor)
    .foregroundColor(foregroundColor)
    .listRowSeparator(showSeparators == true ? .visible :
    .hidden)
    .listRowSeparatorTint(separatorTintColor)
    .listRowBackground(rowBackgroundColor)
  }
}
```

Styling List Rows

Figure 5-7. *List Styles*

Separators

As any designer will be able to tell you, the space between items is as important as the items themselves. With SwiftUI 3, it is now possible to influence the style of row separators and section separators: both the tint color and the visibility can be controlled. SwiftUI's flexible DSL makes it easy to control this for an entire List view or for individual rows and sections.

To control the appearance of row separators, you can use .listRowSeparator() and .listRowSeparatorTint(). You can specify which edges (.top or .bottom) you want to configure. If you don't provide any value for the edges parameter, both top *and* bottom will be modified.

```
List {
  Text("Row 1")
  Text("Row 2 (separators hidden)")
    .listRowSeparator(.hidden)
  Text("Row 3")
```

```
    Text("Row 4 (separators tinted red)")
      .listRowSeparatorTint(.red)
    Text("Row 5")
    Text("Row 6 (bottom separator hidden)")
      .listRowSeparator(.hidden, edges: .bottom)
    Text("Row 7")
    Text("Row 8 (top separator tinted blue)")
      .listRowSeparatorTint(.blue, edges: .top)
    Text("Row 9")
    Text("Row 10")
}
```

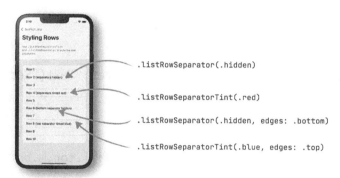

Figure 5-8. *Styling List Rows*

To control the appearance of section separators, use
`.listSectionSeparator()` and `.listSectionSeparatorTint()`. Just
like the view modifiers for list rows, both of these view modifiers support
specifying the edges you'd like to modify.

```
List {
  Section(header: Text("Section 1"), footer: Text("Section 1 -
  no styling")) {
    Text("Row 1")
  }
  Section(header: Text("Section 2"), footer: Text("Section 2 -
  section separators hidden")) {
    Text("Row 1")
  }
  .listSectionSeparator(.hidden)

  Section(header: Text("Section 3"), footer: Text("Section 3 -
  section separator tinted red")) {
    Text("Row 1")
  }
  .listSectionSeparatorTint(.red)

  Section(header: Text("Section 4"), footer: Text("Section 4 -
  section separators tinted green")) {
    Text("Row 1")
  }
  .listSectionSeparatorTint(.green, edges: [.top, .bottom])

  Section(header: Text("Section 5"), footer: Text("Section 5 -
  section separator (bottom) hidden")) {
    Text("Row 1")
  }
  .listSectionSeparator(.hidden, edges: .bottom)

  Section("Section 6") {
    Text("Row 1")
  }
}
```

Styling List Sections

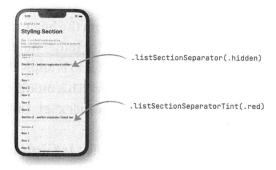

.listSectionSeparator(.hidden)

.listSectionSeparatorTint(.red)

Figure 5-9. *Styling List Sections*

Actions

Let's now look at Swipe Actions. Swipe Actions are used in many apps, most prominently in Apple's own Mail app. They provide a well-known and easy-to-use UI affordance to allow users to perform actions on list items.

UIKit has supported Swipe Actions since iOS 11, but SwiftUI didn't support Swipe Actions until WWDC 2021.

In this post, we will look at the following features:

- **Swipe-to-delete** using the onDelete modifier

- **Deleting and moving items** using EditButton and the .editMode environmental value

- Using **Swipe Actions** (this is the most flexible approach, which also gives us a wealth of styling options)

Swipe-to-Delete

This feature was available in SwiftUI right from the beginning. It is pretty straightforward to use, but also pretty basic (or rather inflexible). To add swipe-to-delete to a `List`view, all you need to do is apply the `onDelete` modifier to a `ForEach` loop inside a `List` view. This modifier expects a closure with one parameter that contains an `IndexSet`, indicating which rows to delete.

Here is a code snippet that shows a simple `List` with an `onDelete` modifier. When the user swipes to delete, the closure will be called, which will consequently remove the respective row from the array of items backing the `List` view:

```
struct SwipeToDeleteListView: View {
  @State fileprivate var items = [
    Item(title: "Puzzle", iconName: "puzzlepiece", badge:
    "Nice!"),
    Item(title: "Controller", iconName: "gamecontroller",
    badge: "Clicky!"),
    Item(title: "Shopping cart", iconName: "cart",
    badge: "$$$"),
    Item(title: "Gift", iconName: "giftcard", badge: ":-)"),
    Item(title: "Clock", iconName: "clock", badge:
    "Tick tock"),
    Item(title: "People", iconName: "person.2", badge: "2"),
    Item(title: "T-Shirt", iconName: "tshirt", badge: "M")
  ]

  var body: some View {
    List {
      ForEach(items) { item in
        Label(item.title, systemImage: item.iconName)
      }
```

```
  .onDelete { indexSet in
    items.remove(atOffsets: indexSet)
  }
    }
  }
}
```

It's actually quite convenient that `onDelete` passes an `IndexSet` to indicate which item(s) should be deleted, as `Array` provides a method `remove(atOffsets:)` that takes an `IndexSet`.

It is worth noting that you cannot apply `onDelete` to `List` directly—you need to use a `ForEach` loop instead and nest it inside a `List`[11].

Moving and Deleting Items Using EditMode

For some applications, it makes sense to let users rearrange items by dragging them across the list. SwiftUI makes implementing this super easy—all you need to do is apply the `onMove` view modifier to a `List` and then update the underlying data structure accordingly.

Here is a snippet that shows how to implement this for a simple array:

```
List {
  ForEach(items) { item in
    Label(item.title, systemImage: item.iconName)
  }
  .onDelete { indexSet in
    items.remove(atOffsets: indexSet)
  }
```

---

[11] I am not entirely sure why the SwiftUI team decided to implement it this way—if you have any clue (or work on the SwiftUI team), please get in touch with me!

```
.onMove { indexSet, index in
    items.move(fromOffsets: indexSet, toOffset: index)
  }
}
```

Again, this is made easy thanks to `Array.move`, which expects exactly the parameters that we receive in `onDelete`'s closure.

To turn on edit mode for a `List`, there are two options:

  - Using the `.editMode` environment value

  - Using the `EditButton` view

Under the hood, both approaches make use of SwiftUI's environment. The following snippet demonstrates how to use the `EditButton` to allow the user to turn on edit mode for the list:

```
List {
  ForEach(items) { item in
    Label(item.title, systemImage: item.iconName)
  }
  .onDelete { indexSet in
    items.remove(atOffsets: indexSet)
  }
  .onMove { indexSet, index in
    items.move(fromOffsets: indexSet, toOffset: index)
  }
}
.toolbar {
  EditButton()
}
```

Swipe Actions

For anything that goes beyond swipe-to-delete and `EditMode`, SwiftUI now supports Swipe Actions. This new API gives us a lot of control over how to display swipe actions:

- We can define different swipe actions per row.

- We can specify the text, icon, and tint color to use for each individual action.

- We can add actions to the leading and trailing edge of a row.

- We can enable or disable full swipe for the first action on either end of the row, allowing users to trigger the action by completely swiping the row to the respective edge.

Basic Swipe Actions

Let's look at a simple example on how to use this new API. To register a Swipe Action for a `List` row, we need to call the `swipeActions` view modifier. Inside the closure of the view modifier, we can set up one (or more) `Button`s to implement the action itself.

The following code snippet demonstrates how to add a simple swipe action to a `List` view:

```
List(viewModel.items) { item in
  Text(item.title)
    .fontWeight(item.isRead ? .regular : .bold)
    .swipeActions {
      Button (action: { viewModel.markItemRead(item) }) {
        if let isRead = item.isRead, isRead == true {
          Label("Read", systemImage: "envelope.badge.fill")
        }
```

```
    else {
      Label("Unread", systemImage: "envelope.open.fill")
    }
  }
  .tint(.blue)
}
}
```

It's worth noting that the `swipeActions` modifier is invoked on the view that represents the row. In this case, it is a simple `Text` view, but for more advanced lists, this might as well be a `HStack` or `VStack`. This is different from the `onDelete` modifier (which needs to be applied to a `ForEach` loop inside a `List` view), and it gives us the flexibility to apply a different set of actions depending on the row.

Also note that each swipe action is represented by a `Button`. If you use any other view, SwiftUI will not register it, and no action will be shown. Likewise, if you try to apply the `swipeActions` modifier to the `List` or a `ForEach` loop, the modifier will be ignored.

Specifying the Edge

By default, swipe actions will be added to the trailing edge of the row. This is why, in the previous example, the *mark as read/unread* action was added to the trailing edge. To add the action to the leading edge (just like in Apple's Mail app), all we have to do is specify the `edge` parameter, like so:

```
List(viewModel.items) { item in
  Text(item.title)
    .fontWeight(item.isRead ? .regular : .bold)
    .swipeActions(edge: .leading) {
      Button (action: { viewModel.markItemRead(item) }) {
```

```
      if let isRead = item.isRead, isRead == true {
        Label("Read", systemImage: "envelope.badge.fill")
      }
      else {
        Label("Unread", systemImage: "envelope.open.fill")
      }
    }
  .tint(.blue)
}
```

To add actions to either edge, we can call the swipeActions modifier multiple times, specifying the edge we want to add the actions to.

If you add swipe actions to both the leading and trailing edge, it is a good idea to be explicit about where you want to add the actions. In the following code snippet, we add one action to the leading edge and another one to the trailing edge:

```
List(viewModel.items) { item in
  Text(item.title)
    .fontWeight(item.isRead ? .regular : .bold)
    .swipeActions(edge: .leading) {
      Button (action: { viewModel.markItemRead(item) }) {
        if let isRead = item.isRead, isRead == true {
          Label("Read", systemImage: "envelope.badge.fill")
        }
        else {
          Label("Unread", systemImage: "envelope.open.fill")
        }
      }
      .tint(.blue)
  }
```

```
.swipeActions(edge: .trailing) {
  Button(role: .destructive, action: { viewModel.
  deleteItem(item) } ) {
    Label("Delete", systemImage: "trash")
  }
 }
}
```

You might notice that we used the role parameter on the Button to indicate it is .destructive—this instructs SwiftUI to use a red background color for this button. We still have to implement deleting the item ourselves, though. And since the action closure of the Button is inside the scope of the current row, it is now much easier to directly access the current list item—another advantage of this API design over the previous design for onDelete.

Swipe Actions and onDelete

After reading the previous code snippet, you might be wondering why we didn't use the onDelete view modifier instead of implementing a delete action ourselves. The answer is quite simple: as stated in the documentation, SwiftUI will stop synthesizing the delete functionality once you use the swipeActions modifier.

Adding More Swipe Actions

To add multiple swipe actions to either edge, we can call the swipeActions modifier multiple times:

```
List(viewModel.items) { item in
  Text(item.title)
    .fontWeight(item.isRead ? .regular : .bold)
    .swipeActions(edge: .leading) {
```

```
    Button (action: { viewModel.markItemRead(item) }) {
      if let isRead = item.isRead, isRead == true {
        Label("Read", systemImage: "envelope.badge.fill")
      }
      else {
        Label("Unread", systemImage: "envelope.open.fill")
      }
    }
    .tint(.blue)
  }
  .swipeActions(edge: .trailing) {
    Button(role: .destructive, action: { viewModel.
    deleteItem(item) } ) {
      Label("Delete", systemImage: "trash")
    }
  }
  .swipeActions(edge: .trailing) {
    Button (action: { selectedItem = item  } ) {
      Label("Tag", systemImage: "tag")
    }
    .tint(Color(UIColor.systemOrange))
  }
}
```

If this makes you feel uneasy, you can also add multiple buttons to the same swipeActions modifier. The following code snippet results in the same UI as the previous one:

```
List(viewModel.items) { item in
  Text(item.title)
    .fontWeight(item.isRead ? .regular : .bold)
    .badge(item.badge)
```

```
.swipeActions(edge: .leading) {
  Button (action: { viewModel.markItemRead(item) }) {
    if let isRead = item.isRead, isRead == true {
      Label("Read", systemImage: "envelope.badge.fill")
    }
    else {
      Label("Unread", systemImage: "envelope.open.fill")
    }
  }
  .tint(.blue)
}
.swipeActions(edge: .trailing) {
  Button(role: .destructive, action: { viewModel.
  deleteItem(item) } ) {
    Label("Delete", systemImage: "trash")
  }
  Button (action: { selectedItem = item  } ) {
    Label("Tag", systemImage: "tag")
  }
  .tint(Color(UIColor.systemOrange))
}
}
```

If you add multiple swipe actions to the same edge, they will be shown from the outside, that is, the first button will always appear closest to the respective edge.

> *Please note that, although there doesn't seem to be any limit as to how many swipe actions you can add to either edge of a row, the number of actions that a user can comfortably use depends on their device. For example, a list row on an iPhone 13 in portrait orientation can fit up to five swipe actions, but they completely fill up the entire row, which not only looks*

strange but also leads to some issues when trying to tap the right button. Smaller devices, like an iPhone 6 or even and iPhone 5, can fit even fewer swipe actions. Three or four swipe actions seem to be a sensible limit that should work on most devices.

Full Swipe

By default, the first action for any given swipe direction can be invoked by using a full swipe. You can deactivate this behavior by setting the allowsFullSwipe parameter to false:

```
.swipeActions(edge: .trailing, allowsFullSwipe: false) {
  Button(role: .destructive, action: { viewModel.
  deleteItem(item) } ) {
    Label("Delete", systemImage: "trash")
  }
}
```

Styling Your Swipe Actions

As mentioned before, setting the role of a swipe action's Button to .destructive will automatically tint the button red. If you don't specify a role, the Button will be tinted in light gray. You can specify any other color by using the tint modifier on a swipe action's Button—like so:

```
.swipeActions(edge: .trailing) {
  Button (action: { selectedItem = item  } ) {
    Label("Tag", systemImage: "tag")
  }
  .tint(Color(UIColor.systemOrange))
}
```

Inside the Button, you can display both text labels and/or icons, using Image, Text, or Label.

Managing Focus in Lists

Managing focus is an important aspect for almost any sort of UI—getting this right helps your users to navigate your app faster and more efficiently. In desktop UIs, we have come to expect being able to navigate through the input fields on a form by pressing the Tab key, and on mobile it's no less important. In Apple's Reminders app, for example, the cursor will automatically be placed in any new reminder you create and will advance to the next row when you tap the Enter key. This way, you can add new elements very efficiently.

Apple added support for focus management to SwiftUI in iOS 15—this includes both setting and observing focus.

Most examples both in Apple's own documentation and on other people's blogs and videos only discuss how to use this in simple forms, such as a login form. Advanced use cases, such as managing focus in an editable list, aren't covered.

In the following, I will show you how to manage focus state in an app that allows users to edit elements in a list. As an example, I am going to use Make It So, a to-do list app I am working on. Make It So is a replica of Apple's Reminders app, and the idea is to figure out how close we can get to the original using only SwiftUI and Firebase (for the backend services such as storage)[12].

How to Manage Focus in SwiftUI

At WWDC 2021, Apple introduced `@FocusState`, a property wrapper that can be used to track and modify focus within a scene.

---

[12] You can download the latest version of the app from its GitHub repository at `https://github.com/peterfriese/MakeItSo`

You can either use a `Bool` or an `enum` to track which element of your UI is focused.

The following example makes use of an `enum` with two cases to track focus for a simple user profile form. As you can see in the `Button`'s closure, we can programmatically set the focus, for example, if the user forgot to fill out a mandatory field.

```swift
enum FocusableField: Hashable {
  case firstName
  case lastName
}

struct FocusUsingEnumView: View {
  @FocusState private var focus: FocusableField?

  @State private var firstName = ""
  @State private var lastName = ""

  var body: some View {
    Form {
      TextField("First Name", text: $firstName)
        .focused($focus, equals: .firstName)
      TextField("Last Name", text: $lastName)
        .focused($focus, equals: .lastName)

      Button("Save") {
        if firstName.isEmpty {
          focus = .firstName
        }
        else if lastName.isEmpty {
          focus = .lastName
        }
```

```
      else {
        focus = nil
      }
    }
  }
}
}
```

This approach works fine for simple input forms that have all but a few input elements, but it's not feasible for List views or other dynamic views that display an unbounded number of elements.

How to Manage Focus in Lists

To manage focus in List views, we can make use of the fact that Swift enums support associated values. This allows us to define an enum that can hold the id of a list element we want to focus:

```
enum Focusable: Hashable {
  case none
  case row(id: String)
}
```

With this in place, we can define a local variable focusedReminder that is of this type and wrap it using @FocusState:

```
struct Reminder: Identifiable {
  var id: String = UUID().uuidString
  var title: String
}

struct FocusableListView: View {
  @State var reminders: [Reminder] = Reminder.samples
```

```swift
@FocusState var focusedReminder: Focusable?

var body: some View {
  List {
    ForEach($reminders) { $reminder in
      TextField("", text: $reminder.title)
        .focused($focusedReminder, equals: .row(id:
        reminder.id))
    }
  }
  .toolbar {
    ToolbarItemGroup(placement: .bottomBar) {
      Button(action: { createNewReminder() }) {
        Text("New Reminder")
      }
    }
  }
}
// ...
}
```

When the user taps the *New Reminder* toolbar button, we add a new Reminder to the reminders array. To set the focus into the row for this newly created reminder, all we need to do is create an instance of the Focusable enum using the new reminder's id as the associated value, and assign it to the focusedReminder property:

```swift
struct FocusableListView: View {

  // ...

  func createNewReminder() {
    let newReminder = Reminder(title: "")
```

```
    reminders.append(newReminder)
    focusedReminder = .row(id: newReminder.id)
  }

}
```

Handling the Enter Key

Let's now turn our focus to another feature of Apple's Reminder app that will improve the UX of our application: adding new elements (and focusing them) when the user hits the Enter key.

We can use the .onSubmit view modifier to run code when the user submits a value to a view. By default, this will be triggered when the user taps the Enter key:

```
...
TextField("", text: $reminder.title)
  .focused($focusedTask, equals: .row(id: reminder.id))
  .onSubmit {
    createNewTask()
  }
...
```

This works fine, but all new elements will be added to the end of the list. This is a bit unexpected in case the user was just editing a to-do at the beginning or in the middle of the list.

Let's update our code for inserting new items and make sure new items are inserted directly after the currently focused element:

```
...
func createNewTask() {
  let newReminder = Reminder(title: "")
```

```
// if any row is focused, insert the new task after the
focused row
if case .row(let id) = focusedTask {
  if let index = reminders.firstIndex(where: { $0.id ==
  id } ) {
    reminders.insert(newReminder, at: index + 1)
  }
}
// no row focused: append at the end of the list
else {
  reminders.append(newReminder)
}

// focus the new task
focusedTask = .row(id: newReminder.id)
}
...
```

This works great, but there is a small issue with this: if the user hits the *Enter* key several times in a row without entering any text, we will end up with a bunch of empty rows—not ideal. The Reminders app automatically removes empty rows, so let's see if we can implement this as well.

If you've followed along, you might notice another issue: the code for our view is getting more and more crowded, and we're mixing declarative UI code with a lot of imperative code.

What About MVVM?

Now those of you who have been following my blog and my videos know that I am a fan of using the MVVM approach in SwiftUI, so let's take a look at how we can introduce a view model to declutter the view code *and* implement a solution for removing empty rows at the same time.

Ideally, the view model should contain the array of Reminders, the focus state, and the code to create a new reminder:

```
class ReminderListViewModel: ObservableObject {
  @Published var reminders: [Reminder] = Reminder.samples

  @FocusState
  var focusedReminder: Focusable?

  func createNewReminder() {
    let newReminder = Reminder(title: "")

    // if any row is focused, insert the new reminder after the
    focused row
    if case .row(let id) = focusedReminder {
      if let index = reminders.firstIndex(where: { $0.id ==
      id } ) {
        reminders.insert(newReminder, at: index + 1)
      }
    }
    // no row focused: append at the end of the list
    else {
      reminders.append(newReminder)
    }

    // focus the new reminder
    focusedReminder = .row(id: newReminder.id)
  }
}
```

Notice how we're accessing the focusedReminder focus state inside of createNewReminder to find out where to insert the new reminder, and then set the focus on the newly added/inserted reminder.

Obviously, the FocusableListView view needs to be updated as well to reflect the fact that we're no longer using a local @State variable, but an @ObservableObject instead:

```
struct FocusableListView: View {
  @StateObject var viewModel = ReminderListViewModel().

  var body: some View {
    List {
      ForEach($viewModel.reminders) { $reminder in
        TextField("", text: $reminder.title)
          .focused(viewModel.$focusedReminder, equals:
          .row(id: reminder.id))
          .onSubmit {
            viewModel.createNewReminder()
          }
      }
    }
    .toolbar {
      ToolbarItem(placement: .bottomBar) {
        Button(action: { viewModel.createNewReminder() }) {
          Text("New Reminder")
        }
      }
    }
  }
}
```

This all looks great, but when running this code, you will notice the focus handling no longer works, and instead we receive a SwiftUI runtime warning that says *Accessing FocusState's value outside of the body of a View. This will result in a constant Binding of the initial value and will not update.*

Figure 5-10. *Runtime warning when accessing FocusState outside the body of a view*

This is because `@FocusState` conforms to `DynamicProperty`, which can only be used inside views.

So we need to find another way to synchronize the focus state between the view and the view model. One way to react to changes on properties of views is the `.onChange(of:)` view modifier.

To synchronize the focus state between the view model and the view, we can

1. Add the `@FocusState` back to the view

2. Mark `focusedReminder` as a `@Published` property on the view model

3. And sync them using `onChange(of:)`

Like this:

```
class ReminderListViewModel: ObservableObject {
  @Published var reminders: [Reminder] = Reminder.samples

  @Published var focusedReminder: Focusable?
  // ...
}
```

```swift
struct FocusableListView: View {
  @StateObject var viewModel = ReminderListViewModel()

  @FocusState var focusedReminder: Focusable?

  var body: some View {
    List {
      ForEach($viewModel.reminders) { $reminder in
        // ...
      }
    }
    .onChange(of: focusedReminder)  {
      viewModel.focusedReminder = $0
    }
    .onChange(of: viewModel.focusedReminder) {
      focusedReminder = $0
    }
    // ...
  }
}
```

Side note: this can be cleaned up even further by extracting the code for synching into an extension on View.

And with this, we've cleaned up our implementation—the view focuses on the display aspects, whereas the view model handles updating the data model and translating between the view and the model.

Eliminating Empty Elements

Using a view model gives us another nice benefit—since the focusedReminder property on the view model is a published property, we can attach a Combine pipeline to it and react to changes of the property.

This will allow us to detect when the previously focused element is an empty element and consequently remove it.

To do this, we will need an additional property on the view model to keep track of the previously focused Reminder and then install a Combine pipeline that removes empty Reminders once their row loses focus:

```
class ReminderListViewModel: ObservableObject {
  @Published var reminders: [Reminder] = Reminder.samples

  @Published var focusedReminder: Focusable?
  var previousFocusedReminder: Focusable?

  private var cancellables = Set<AnyCancellable>()

  init() {
    $focusedReminder
      .compactMap { focusedReminder -> Int? in
        defer { self.previousFocusedReminder =
        focusedReminder }

        guard focusedReminder != nil else { return nil }
        guard case .row(let previousId) = self.
        previousFocusedReminder else { return nil }
        guard let previousIndex = self.reminders.
        firstIndex(where: { $0.id == previousId } ) else { return nil }
        guard self.reminders[previousIndex].title.isEmpty else
        { return nil }

        return previousIndex
      }
      .delay(for: 0.01, scheduler: RunLoop.main)
      // <-- this helps reduce visual jank
      .sink { index in
        self.reminders.remove(at: index)
      }
```

```
        .store(in: &cancellables)
    }
    // ...
}
```

Summary

Congratulations, you made it until the end of one of the longest chapters in this book! Lists are not only one of the more frequently used UI patterns in SwiftUI; they also are very flexible and can be customized in many ways.

In this chapter, you learned a lot about Lists and their look and feel; we talked about static and dynamic lists (and how to connect them to your app's data model), how to style the lists themselves and their cells, and we talked about how to add interaction to lists by adding swipe actions.

Finally, we brought together what you learned so far and dived into how to manage focus in dynamic list views.

With this under your belt, you will be able to build even more sophisticated UIs.

In the next chapter, we will take a look at List view's cousin, Form, and you will learn how to build elegant input forms with surprisingly little effort.

CHAPTER 6

Building Input Forms

When you hear the term "forms," you probably don't think your app needs many forms, and you most definitely won't get excited (unless you're a person who likes filling out forms). However, you might be surprised to hear that forms are an important way to build UIs, especially on Apple's platforms.

Just think about it: your app most likely has a setting screen—and that's technically a form. Your app might also have a login screen—again, that's a form! And if you have any sort of data entry—guess what, that's a form too.

When Apple first released the iPhone iOS SDK (as it was called back then), they didn't provide a first-class way to build input forms. Developers quickly figured out that UITableView, originally built for tabular representations of data, could also be used to display input forms. However, as UITableView's APIs (UITableViewDataSource and UITableViewDelegate) weren't built with this use case in mind, it has always been a bit cumbersome to build forms based on these APIs—for example, you had to keep track of which row you're currently on to decide which subclass of UITableViewCell to vend to display the correct form cell.

SwiftUI gave Apple the opportunity to start from a clean slate and come up with concepts and APIs that better meet modern application's needs and finally address what developers had been telling them for years.

Being such an important part of many iOS apps, Apple added a dedicated API for building forms to SwiftUI.

© Peter Friese 2023
P. Friese, *Asynchronous Programming with SwiftUI and Combine*,
https://doi.org/10.1007/978-1-4842-8572-5_6

In this chapter, you will see that it is straightforward to build great-looking forms, and—who knows?—by the end of it maybe you'll be really excited about forms too!

Building Simple Forms

We'll first cover the basics and look at how to build a simple form for displaying static data. We will also learn how to bind a form's UI elements to your data model. From there, it's just a small step to learn how to use input elements like TextField or Toggle to edit form data. This will also give us the opportunity to discuss whether (or rather when) to use @State or @StateObject.

Getting started with forms is remarkably simple—the SwiftUI team has designed the forms API so that you can continue using the UI elements you already know (such as Text, Label, Button, Image, etc.), and SwiftUI will take care of rendering them so that they look like the stock forms UI we all know from the iOS settings app.

This is a recurring theme in SwiftUI—you as a developer/designer specify *what* you want to display, and SwiftUI will figure out *how* to best do this on the respective platform. In the end, it's a mixture of both—you'll end up tweaking your code quite a bit to make the UI look exactly as you'd like it to.

The simplest form you can build in SwiftUI is to wrap the *Hello World* text from the SwiftUI application template in a Form, like this:

```
struct ContentView: View {
  var body: some View {
    Form {
      Text("Hello, world!")
    }
  }
}
```

This turns the Text view into a simple tabular form.

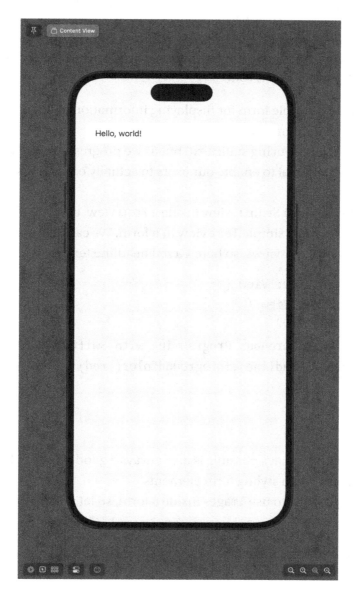

Figure 6-1. *Hello World in a form*

If you've done any UIKit development before, this will look remarkably like a UITableView to you, and Apple might actually be using a UITableView under the hood to achieve this look and feel—but we shouldn't make any assumptions, as Apple doesn't make any guarantees about how they render SwiftUI views on screen.

Let's build a simple form for displaying information about a book to get to know some additional form elements.

We'll start out by using static text, but as we progress, we will replace this with a data model to enable our users to actually edit the data on the form.

You can use most SwiftUI view inside a Form view, and you already learned how to use a simple Text view in a form. We can also use view modifiers to style our views, so here's a red headline text:

```
struct ContentView: View {
  var body: some View {
    Form {
      Text("Asynchronous Programming with SwiftUI and Combine")
        .font(.headline).foregroundColor(.red)
    }
  }
}
```

Not everything that's possible is also always a good idea, so please use good judgment when styling form elements.

It's also possible to use Images inside a form, so let's display the book cover, like this:

```
struct ContentView: View {
  var body: some View {
    Form {
      Text("Asynchronous Programming with SwiftUI and Combine")
```

170

```
            .font(.headline).foregroundColor(.red)
        Image("book-cover-combine")
      }
   }
}
```

Figure 6-2. *Displaying an image inside a form*

Now, we could display the book's author and the number of pages using a Text view, but wouldn't it be nice to display a little icon next to the text to make it easier for the user to quickly distinguish these fields at a glance? For this, we can use Label:

```
struct ContentView: View {
  var body: some View {
    Form {
      Text("Asynchronous Programming with SwiftUI and Combine")
        .font(.headline).foregroundColor(.red)
      Image("book-cover-combine")
      Label("Peter Friese",
            systemImage: "person.crop.rectangle")
      Label("451 pages", systemImage: "book")
    }
  }
}
```

Figure 6-3. *Using Label to display an icon alongside a text*

To track whether the user has already read the book, we might want to display a toggle, like this:

```
struct ContentView: View {
  var body: some View {
    Form {
      Text("Asynchronous Programming with SwiftUI and Combine")
        .font(.headline).foregroundColor(.red)
      Image("book-cover-combine")
      Label("Peter Friese",
            systemImage: "person.crop.rectangle")
      Label("451 pages", systemImage: "book")
      Toggle("Read", isOn: .constant(true))
    }
  }
}
```

As we're not yet binding any real data to the form, we're making use of the .constant() binding to bind the Toggle view to a true constant.

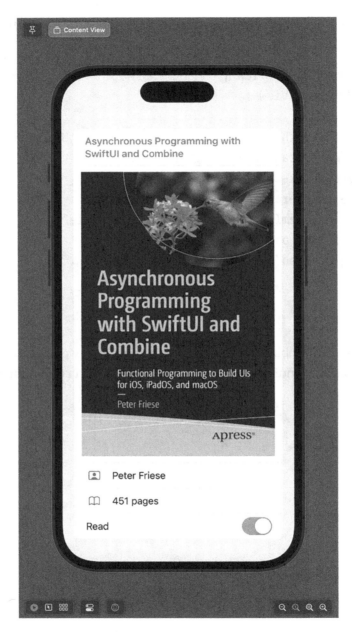

Figure 6-4. *Displaying a toggle inside a form*

Often, users need to take action on the form, and there is an easy way to add buttons to forms, too:

```
struct ContentView: View {
  var body: some View {
    Form {
      Text("Asynchronous Programming with SwiftUI and Combine")
        .font(.headline).foregroundColor(.red)
      Image("book-cover-combine")
      Label("Peter Friese",
            systemImage: "person.crop.rectangle")
      Label("451 pages", systemImage: "book")
      Toggle("Read", isOn: .constant(true))
      Button(action: {}) {
        Label("Share", systemImage: "square.and.arrow.up")
      }
    }
  }
}
```

In this example, I've used a Label to show an icon next to the button label, but you can use a regular Text just as well if you'd rather not show an icon.

Figure 6-5. *Displaying a button in a form*

Showing Data in a Form

Being able to display static data is useful for UIs that don't require any dynamic updates, such as your app's settings screen. However, most apps need to display data that is dynamically updating, so let's look at binding a forms UI to a data model and—in a second step—make it editable as well.

As the Forms API makes use of SwiftUI's regular UI views, all of their features continue to work as expected—the only thing that the Forms API influences is how the UI elements look inside a form.

Thanks to this, we can use all of SwiftUI's state management tools to bind the UI elements such as Text, Label, and Image and even more complex ones such as the pickers to our data model.

To continue with our example, let's assume we've got the following data model to represent books:

```
struct Book: Hashable, Identifiable {
  var id = UUID()
  var title: String
  var author: String
  var isbn: String
  var pages: Int
  var isRead: Bool = false
}

extension Book {
  var smallCoverImageName: String { return "\(isbn)-S" }
  var mediumCoverImageName: String { return "\(isbn)-M" }
  var largeCoverImageName: String { return "\(isbn)-L" }
}
```

To display data from a Book instance, we need to replace the static texts we used in the previous code snippets and access the model attributes instead. All of Swift's string interpolation capabilities work in SwiftUI

179

as well, so the following syntax: "\(book.pages) pages" will inject the current value of the pages property of the Book instance into the Text.

There is one notable exception—Toggle expects a binding, so it can update the underlying property whenever the user flips the switch. Since we want to display all information on BookDetailsView in read-only mode, we will use .constant() to turn the binding into a constant value. This effectively prevents the user from making any changes to the read status of the model.

Whenever the model (book) is updated, SwiftUI will rerender all UI elements that are bound to this model.

```swift
struct BookDetailsView: View {
  @State var book: Book

  var body: some View {
    Form {
      Text(book.title)
      Image(book.largeCoverImageName)
      Label(book.author, systemImage: "person.crop.rectangle")
      Label("\(book.pages) pages", systemImage: "book")
      Toggle("Read", isOn: .constant(book.isRead))
      Button(action: { /* add code to display the edit
      screen */ }) {
        Label("Edit", systemImage: "pencil")
      }
    }
    .navigationTitle(book.title)
  }
}
```

As expected, the result looks exactly like our static example.

Figure 6-6. *Displaying dynamic data*

Make It Editable

Displaying information is only part of the way to a fully data-driven app, and in the next step, we're going to create an editable version of this form.

Part of the iPhone's success is due to its slick and powerful UI, and most of its UI elements have been around since the unveiling of the original iPhone in 2007. Just like UIKit, SwiftUI contains a core set of input elements that allow developers to build easy-to-use, yet powerful and flexible UIs for entering data on (relatively) small screens.

We'll be using just a few of these input elements to build a form for editing a book, but we'll cover the remaining ones at the end of this chapter.

Probably the most versatile (and most often used) input element is TextField—it accepts alphanumeric input and can be customized to support a variety of data types such as email addresses, phone numbers, URLs, and many more.

To create a TextField in SwiftUI, you have to provide a title and a binding to a value to display and edit: TextField("title", $model. property).

Here is the basic version of a form to edit a book:

```
struct BookEditView: View {
  @State var book: Book

  var body: some View {
    Form {
      TextField("Book title", text: $book.title)
      Image(book.largeCoverImageName)
      TextField("Author", text: $book.author)
    }
  }
}
```

As you can see, we're using TextFields to edit the title and author properties of the current Book instance.

But what about the number of pages?

If you look at TextFields API, you will notice it supports editing arbitrary data types—all you have to do is provide a Formatter instance that translates between the data type and its textual representation that the user edits.

To edit an Int property like the number of pages, we can use a NumberFormatter, like so:

```
struct BookEditView: View {
  @State var book: Book

  var body: some View {
    Form {
      TextField("Book title", text: $book.title)
      Image(book.largeCoverImageName)
      TextField("Author", text: $book.author)
      TextField("Pages", value: $book.pages, formatter:
      NumberFormatter())
    }
  }
}
```

If you recall, the book also has a Boolean property, isRead, to track whether the user has read this book. Previously, we used a constant to display the state of this property, but now let's make it editable:

```
struct BookEditView: View {
  @State var book: Book

  var body: some View {
    Form {
      TextField("Book title", text: $book.title)
```

```
        Image(book.largeCoverImageName)
        TextField("Author", text: $book.author)
        TextField("Pages", value: $book.pages, formatter:
        NumberFormatter())
        Toggle("Read", isOn: $book.isRead)
      }
    }
}
```

To see this in action, we'll need to update the preview provider to inject one of the sample books into the view:

```
struct BookEditView_Previews: PreviewProvider {
  static var previews: some View {
    BookEditView(book: Book.samples[0])
  }
}
```

Drill-Down Navigation

Drill-down navigation is a popular UI pattern in iOS apps, probably best known from the built-in *Contacts* app: starting from the list of all their contacts, users can navigate into individual contacts to see their details and perform actions such as initiating a call or face-timing them. The contact details screen also features an *Edit* button, which will open the currently displayed contact in an editable form. Once the user has finished editing the contact, the updated contact details will be updated throughout the entire *Contacts* app.

In this section, we will take a quick look on how to implement this pattern for our Book management app based on the building blocks we've already got: the BookDetailsView and the BookEditView.

In addition to the Book struct, which serves as the model for an individual book, we need to establish a source of truth that contains a collection of all the books in our app. As we haven't implemented any data storage or backend connector yet, we're going to use a static list of books to initialize this source of truth.

As discussed in Chapter 4, the best way to hold a collection of elements and update any subscribers about changes to this list is to use an ObservableObject with a property that is marked as @Published:

```
class BooksViewModel: ObservableObject {
  @Published var books: [Book] = Book.samples
}
```

At a later stage, we might want to connect this view model to a database, but for now, we're assigning a static list of books, as defined here:

```
extension Book {
  static let sampleBooks = [
    Book(title: "Changer", author: "Matt Gemmell", isbn:
    "9781916265202", pages: 476),
    Book(title: "SwiftUI for Absolute Beginners", author:
    "Jayant Varma", isbn: "9781484255155", pages: 200),
    Book(title: "Asynchronous Programming with SwiftUI and
    Combine", author: "Peter Friese", isbn: "9781484285718",
    pages: 451),
    Book(title: "Modern Concurrency on Apple Platforms",
    author: "Andy Ibanez", isbn: "9781484286944", pages: 368)
  ]
}
```

This view model now needs to be instantiated and passed around to the individual views in our app. A good place to do this is in the main App struct—this makes sure our source of truth is shared among all windows of our application. This becomes important when your users run your application on a device that allows them to show multiple windows of your application at once (such as an iPad): any changes the user makes in one window of the app will be reflected in the other window immediately.

As mentioned in Chapter 4, we need to use @StateObject to tell SwiftUI that it needs to ensure to keep this instance of BooksViewModel alive across any screen redraws.

To pass the view model down the view hierarchy, we can either use the environment or inject the instance into a view's initializer.

Personally, I prefer using initializer injection, as it tends to be more explicit than using the environment.

```swift
import SwiftUI

@main
struct BookShelfApp: App {
  @StateObject var booksViewModel = BooksViewModel()

  var body: some Scene {
    WindowGroup {
      NavigationStack {
        BooksListView(booksViewModel: booksViewModel)
          .navigationTitle("Books")
      }
    }
  }
}
```

The root view of our navigation hierarchy is BooksListView, which displays a list of books. As our app's view model is owned by BookShelfApp, we can refer to it here using ObservableObject:

```swift
import SwiftUI

struct BooksListView: View {
  @ObservedObject var booksViewModel: BooksViewModel

  var body: some View {
    List {
      ForEach($booksViewModel.books) { $book in
        BookRowView(book: $book)
      }
      .onDelete { indexSet in
        booksViewModel.books.remove(atOffsets: indexSet)
      }
    }
    .navigationTitle("Books")
  }
}
```

You will notice we're using List bindings to ensure the individual items of the list are editable. See Chapter 5 if you need a refresher for how this works.

The binding to the current Book instance can now be passed down to the BookRowView, which displays the book details within the BookListView:

```swift
struct BookRowView: View {
  @Binding var book: Book

  var body: some View {
    NavigationLink(destination: BookDetailsView(book: $book)) {
      HStack(alignment: .top) {
        Image(book.mediumCoverImageName)
          .resizable()
          .aspectRatio(contentMode: .fit)
          .frame(height: 90)
```

```
            VStack(alignment: .leading) {
              Text(book.title)
                .font(.headline)
              Text("by \(book.author)")
                .font(.subheadline)
              Text("\(book.pages) pages")
                .font(.subheadline)
            }
            Spacer()
          }
        }
      }
}
```

You'll notice how we make use of NavigationLink to specify the destination view when the user taps on one of the books in the list. To pass on the binding, we make use of the $ syntax: NavigationLink(destination: BookDetailsView(book: $book)).

In the BookDetailsView, we need to change @State to @Binding to indicate that the parent view owns the data:

```
struct BookDetailsView: View {
  @Binding var book: Book
  @State var showEditBookView = false

  var body: some View {
    Form {
      Text(book.title)
      Image(book.largeCoverImageName)
        .resizable()
        .scaledToFit()
        .shadow(radius: 10)
        .padding()
      Label(book.author, systemImage: "person.crop.rectangle")
```

```
      Label("ISBN: \(book.isbn)", systemImage: "number")
      Label("\(book.pages) pages", systemImage: "book")
      Toggle("Read", isOn: .constant(book.isRead))
      Button(action: { showEditBookView.toggle() }) {
        Label("Edit", systemImage: "pencil")
      }
    }
    .sheet(isPresented: $showEditBookView) {
      BookEditView(book: $book)
    }
    .navigationTitle(book.title)
  }
}
```

When the user taps on the *Edit* button on the BookDetailsView, we
open a modal sheet to display BookEditView.

To pass a modifiable Book instance to the BookEditView, we make use
of the same pattern used previously: BookEditView(book: $book).

And finally, here is the code for BookEditView:

```
struct BookEditView: View {
  @Binding var book: Book

  var body: some View {
    Form {
      TextField("Book title", text: $book.title)
      Image(book.largeCoverImageName)
        .resizable()
        .scaledToFit()
        .shadow(radius: 10)
        .padding()
      TextField("Author", text: $book.author)
      TextField("Pages", value: $book.pages, formatter:
      NumberFormatter())
```

```
        Toggle("Read", isOn: .constant(true))
    }
    .navigationTitle(book.title)
  }
}
```

Any changes the user makes in this screen will be reflected immediately in the entire app. You can try this yourself by running the app on an iPad Simulator, opening two windows of the app side-by-side, and then updating a book title: as you type, the book title will be updated in the details view and the other window as well.

Figure 6-7. *Side-by-side editing a book, all updates are reflected in all instances of the app*

Input Validation

Quite often, in our input forms, we need some level of input validation. Some well-known examples for validating input are password fields on sign-up forms, where you want to make sure that the password the user enters meets certain criteria. Other apps don't enforce input validation—for example, you will find that the iOS *Contacts* app doesn't perform any input validation at all.

In our sample app, there is one field that would benefit from input validation: the ISBN field. ISBNs (short for *International Standard Book Number*) follow a specific scheme, with the last digit being the check number. Making sure the user enters a valid ISBN is important, as we use the ISBN to look up the cover for the book, so let's add a simple validation routine.

We're going to do this in multiple steps:

- First, we're going to add the validation directly to the `BookEditView`. This is the easiest and most straightforward way to implement this, but it is also the least maintainable and scalable, as we will see.

- Second, we're going to extract the validation logic into a view model. This might look like a lot of extra work, but you will see that this approach is a lot more scalable and makes it much easier to add validation for additional fields.

- And lastly, we're going to sprinkle some Combine over this second approach. This allows us to compose multiple validation steps into one, which is useful for forms that require several criteria to be met at once (sign-up forms are a well-known example: passwords need to meet certain criteria, and both the password and the password confirmation need to match).

191

Using .onChange(of:)

You can call .onChange(of:) on any SwiftUI view to trigger side effects whenever a property changes. This can be any Environment key or Binding on the view.

To observe changes to the ISBN attribute of the currently edited book, we can add .onChange(of: book.isbn) to any of the views in BookEditView. It's up to you whether you'd like to add it to the ISBN TextField or rather to the Form itself. Inside the closure, you will receive the *new* value:

```
struct BookEditView: View {
  @Binding var book: Book
  @State var isISBNValid = false

  var body: some View {
    Form {
      // ...
      VStack(alignment: .leading) {
        if !isISBNValid {
          Text("ISBN is invalid")
            .font(.caption)
            .foregroundColor(.red)
        }
        TextField("ISBN", text: $book.isbn)
      }
      // ...
    }
    .onChange(of: book.isbn) { value in
      self.isISBNValid = checkISBN(isbn: book.isbn)
    }
    .navigationTitle(book.title)
  }
}
```

We use checkISBN (which is a function in the Utils folder) to verify the ISBN and store the result of the check in the state attribute isISBNValid. This is bound to a conditional which will show or hide a Text with a warning message as appropriate.

While this approach does work, it doesn't scale well. Just imagine what happens if you try to implement validation logic for more than a handful of input fields—this will quickly become unmanageable.

Using a View Model to Handle Form Validation

So far, we've been using @State and @Binding to access the data we want to display or edit on a screen. This follows the guidelines discussed in Chapter 4:

> *If the data you want to display in a view is an enum, struct, or a simple type, you can either use @State or @Binding to wrap the variable, or bind to the variable directly.*

However, now that we want to add some business logic, we need to make a few changes. Adding validation logic to the data model might sound like a good idea, but we'd eventually pollute our data model with code that is only required in very specific locations in your app: it's appropriate to validate data in an input form, but you probably don't need to do that in your persistence of network layer.

Instead, let's use a *view model* to encapsulate the *view-specific* business logic. In addition to being able to perform data validation, this also gives us the opportunity to define additional properties for any warnings or error messages we might want to display.

To be able to bind the properties of the view model to the view, the view model needs to implement the ObservableObject protocol:

```
class BookEditViewModel: ObservableObject {
}
```

We can then move the Book variable into the view model, marking it as @Published. Classes don't have automatic memberwise initializers,[1] so we'll have to implement an initializer ourselves that takes a Book instance, like this:

```
class BookEditViewModel: ObservableObject {
  @Published var book: Book

  init(book: Book) {
    self.book = book
  }
}
```

And finally, we can move the isISBNValid check to the view model as well:

```
class BookEditViewModel: ObservableObject {
  @Published var book: Book

  var isISBNValid: Bool {
    checkISBN(isbn: book.isbn)
  }

  init(book: Book) {
    self.book = book
  }
}
```

---

[1] Structs do have memberwise initializers, but classes don't. The main reason is that classes support inheritance, and it would be pretty difficult to implement memberwise initializers in a way that doesn't break if you add new properties to one of the parent classes.

To use the view model inside the BookEditView, we need to first set it up using @ObservedObject and declare an initializer that BookEditView can call:

```
struct BookEditView: View {
  @ObservedObject var bookEditViewModel: BookEditViewModel

  init(book: Book) {
    self.bookEditViewModel = BookEditViewModel(book: book)
  }

  var body: some View {
    // ...
  }
}
```

Inside body, all views that were previously connected to book now need to be connected to $bookEditViewModel.book:

```
var body: some View {
  NavigationView {
    Form {
      TextField("Book title", text: $bookEditViewModel.
      book.title)
      Image(bookEditViewModel.book.largeCoverImageName)
      TextField("Author", text: $bookEditViewModel.
      book.author)
      VStack(alignment: .leading) {
        if !bookEditViewModel.isISBNValid {
          Text("ISBN is invalid")
            .font(.caption)
            .foregroundColor(.red)
        }
        TextField("ISBN", text: $bookEditViewModel.book.isbn)
```

```
    }
    TextField("Pages", value: $bookEditViewModel.book.
    pages, formatter: NumberFormatter())
    Toggle("Read", isOn: $bookEditViewModel.book.isRead)
  }
  .navigationTitle(bookEditViewModel.book.title)
}
}
```

Synchronizing a Local Source of Truth with the Global Source of Truth by Using @Binding and @ObservableObject

If you run this application now, you will notice something odd: the drill-down navigation works as expected, and you're able to edit a book using the BookEditView. But any changes aren't reflected in BookDetailsView or BooksListView.

This is because we create a new @ObservableObject every time the BookEditView is displayed, effectively installing a new source of truth.

To understand why this is the case, let's take a closer look at the flow of information:

- BookShelfApp holds a reference to BooksViewModel. By using the @StateObject property wrapper, we make sure this ObservableObject is only instantiated once, effectively turning it into the root source of truth for the application.

- BookShelfApp then passes a reference to this source of truth to BooksListView, which stores it in a local property as an @ObservedObject. Since this is a reference to the root source of truth, all changes we make to it inside BooksListView will not only be reflected in

BooksListView and its child views, but also on the app
and any child view that is connected to the
@StateObject in BookShelfApp.

— BooksListView uses list bindings to iterate over the
individual books contained in the array of books on
BooksViewModel, and instantiates a new BookRowView,
passing a Binding to the book.

— BookRowView displays some of the properties of the
book and passes the Binding to BookDetailsView.

— BookDetailsView passes this Binding to BookEditView.

So far, the flow of information is still connected both ways: any
changes to the source of truth in BookShelfApp will percolate down the
view hierarchy and will be reflected on the respective views. Likewise, any
changes to the book instance (which is a @Binding inside BookEditView)
will be reflected on the source of truth in BookShelfApp.

However, by instantiating a new @ObservedObject of
BookEditViewModel in BookEditView, we establish a new source of truth.
All UI elements in BookEditView are connected to this local source of
truth, so all changes the user makes in the UI will only be reflected on this
instance.

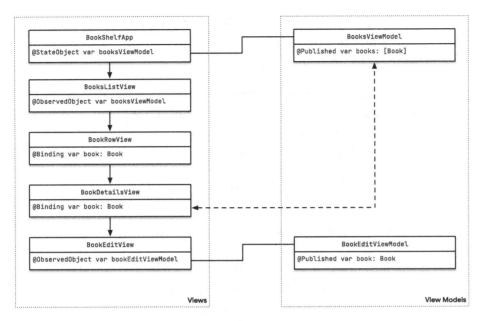

Figure 6-8. *Using @Binding to update the source of truth*

There are a couple of ways to work around this:

First, we could change the book property in BookEditViewModel to be a @Binding instead of an @Published property. However, this would prevent us from using this property as a Combine publisher (which we will get to in a minute).

The second option is to add a completion handler to BookEditViewModel, which we can call once the user finished editing the book. When the completion handler is called, we can update the edited book on the original source of truth. This option doesn't feel very SwiftUI-y, though. If you look at other SwiftUI components that are similar, such as ColorPicker, you will notice that they accept a Binding.

So let's look at another option: let's try passing in a Binding, copy its value into an @Published property on a view model that is local to the BookEditView only, and, once the user finishes editing, assign it back to the Binding.

To properly implement this functionality, let's first add a *Cancel* and *Save* button to the BookEditView and add handlers for their *tap* events:

```
struct BookEditView: View {
  @ObservedObject var bookEditViewModel: BookEditViewModel
  @Environment(\.dismiss) var dismiss

  // ...

  func cancel() {
    dismiss()
  }

  func save() {
    // (add code to update the binding)
    dismiss()
  }

  var body: some View {
    NavigationStack {
      Form {
        // ...
      }
      .navigationTitle(bookEditViewModel.book.title)
      .toolbar {
        ToolbarItem(placement: .navigationBarLeading) {
          Button(action: cancel) {
            Text("Cancel")
          }
        }
```

```
      ToolbarItem(placement: .navigationBarTrailing) {
        Button(action: save) {
          Text("Save")
        }
      }
    }
  }
}
```

By pulling in the dismiss action from the environment, we're able to programmatically dismiss the BookEditView when the user taps on either of the buttons.

Note: If you want to prevent the user from dismissing a dialog, you can use the interactiveDismissDisabled() view modifier.

With this in place, we can now implement handling the binding. To do this, we need to add the binding to the view and then use it to create the view model in the initializer:

```
struct BookEditView: View {
  @Binding var book: Book
  @ObservedObject var bookEditViewModel: BookEditViewModel
  @Environment(\.dismiss) var dismiss

  init(book: Binding<Book>) {
    self._book = book
    self.bookEditViewModel = BookEditViewModel(book: book.
    wrappedValue)
  }

  // ...
}
```

By using the underscore, we can assign the binding we receive in the initializer to the book property (which is a Binding<Book> itself).

Then, by creating the view model using the wrappedValue of the binding, we pass the underlying value object to the view model, where we use the @Published property wrapper to turn it into a publisher.

The missing piece to send any of the user's changes back to the caller (BookDetailsView in our case) is to update the save function:

```
func save() {
  self.book = bookEditViewModel.book
  dismiss()
}
```

This takes the updated Book from the view model and assigns it back to the binding. This will cause the *source of truth* to be updated, and the update will be reflected throughout the app.

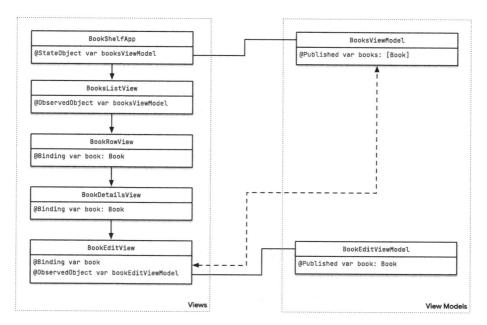

Figure 6-9. *Using @ObservedObject and @Binding to update local and global source of truth*

201

Using Combine to Perform Form Validation

In this final step, we're going to use Combine to improve the validation logic.

At the moment, the validation logic lives in a computed property in the view model:

```
class BookEditViewModel: ObservableObject {
  @Published var book: Book

  var isISBNValid: Bool {
    checkISBN(isbn: book.isbn)
  }

  init(book: Book) {
    self.book = book
  }
}
```

While this does work, it is less than ideal: SwiftUI will only cause your views to be updated if it receives an event from the published properties the views are subscribed to.

As isISBNValid is not an @Published property, it will not send any notifications when it is updated. So, why does the view update and reflect the correct state of this property anyway? Well, this is just by coincidence, actually: the view model will send an update event whenever the book (or any of its properties) is updated. It just so happens that the ISBN is a property of Book as well, so when you edit the ISBN of a book, the book will send an event which will cause SwiftUI to rerender. In the process of doing this, it will also rerender the VStack that conditionally shows an error message based on the state of the isISBNValid property.

To make this more solid and less coincidental, let's use Combine to compute the state of isISBNValid.

Let's first turn isISBNValid into a published property:

```
class BookEditViewModel: ObservableObject {
  @Published var book: Book
  @Published var isISBNValid: Bool = true

  // ...
}
```

Then, in the initializer, we can subscribe to any changes that are sent by the book publisher. These events will contain the current value of the book property. To determine whether the current ISBN of a book is valid, we will then map over the book value, verify its ISBN, and assign the resulting Bool value to the isISBNValid property:

```
init(book: Book) {
  self.book = book

  self.$book
    .map { book in
      return checkISBN(isbn: book.isbn)
    }
    .assign(to: &$isISBNValid)
}
```

We can condense the map closure even further thanks to implicit returns and implicit parameters:

```
self.$book
  .map { checkISBN(isbn: $0.isbn) }
  .assign(to: &$isISBNValid)
```

And with this, we've got a fully functional drill-down navigation for a data-driven application, including a simple Combine pipeline for validating form input.

Summary

In this chapter, you saw how easy it is to build form-based UIs in SwiftUI. By using the `Form` view, SwiftUI adapts regular views to match the look and feel we all know from the iOS settings screen. The SwiftUI DSL really comes into its own here, and you can see how the SwiftUI team harnesses the power of the DSL to allow developers to quickly build flexible and feature-rich UIs.

After looking at static forms, we jumped in at the deep end and took a closer look at how to use SwiftUI's state management tools to build drill-down navigation for a data-driven app—a UI pattern that you will find in many apps.

And finally, we implemented a simple business logic for validating form input. By using a view model, we were able to encapsulate this logic and avoid polluting the view. Using a view model added some challenges to our drill-down navigation, which we were able to overcome by using `@Binding` and `@ObservableObject` together to allow users to edit data while giving them the flexibility to change their mind and cancel any changes they made. Thanks to using Combine, we were able to implement this in a SwiftUI-compatible way.

This was quite a lot, but we're only getting started! In the next chapter, we will look at Functional Reactive Programming, why it's so cool, and how it relates to Combine!

Part 2

CHAPTER 7

Getting Started with Combine

Now, we have already used a bit of Combine in the previous chapters, and hopefully, they were easy enough to understand in the context of the SwiftUI UIs we used them with. But you might wonder how Combine really works and what goes on under the hood of SwiftUI's reactive state management system. In this chapter, we're going to dive into Combine, and you will learn about the underlying principles and why it works so well in combination with SwiftUI.

> *The source code for the code snippets in this chapter can be found in the GitHub repository for the book.*[1]

What Is Functional Reactive Programming?

Everything that happens in our computers can be thought of as an event—users tapping on a button, time passing, an API request returning some value, a network request failing. Most of these events happen asynchronously, which makes dealing with them challenging.

---

[1] https://github.com/peterfriese/SwiftUI-Combine-Book

© Peter Friese 2023
P. Friese, *Asynchronous Programming with SwiftUI and Combine*,
https://doi.org/10.1007/978-1-4842-8572-5_7

There are several ways to deal with asynchronous behavior. As iOS developers, we are well accustomed to using delegates and callbacks, but they have several drawbacks and result in code that is all over the place and hard to reason about.

Reactive programming is another way to deal with this situation. The basic idea in reactive programming is that everything is an event, and these happen asynchronously. Events are sent by an event source, and interested parties can register to receive certain events. More often than not, these streams of events need to be transformed to make them more useful for the respective subscriber.

There are numerous implementations of reactive programming. The most well known is probably Reactive Extensions (ReactiveX[2]), "an API for asynchronous programming with observable streams." The beauty of ReactiveX is that it is available for a wide range of platforms and languages: Java,[3] JavaScript,[4] C#,[5] Kotlin,[6] Swift,[7] and more.[8]

Apple introduced Combine as their take on reactive programming at WWDC 2019, and it is pretty similar to RxSwift. The main reason to use Combine over RxSwift is that it is more deeply integrated into Apple's platforms. It works especially well with SwiftUI, so if you're targeting iOS 13 or higher (which is the minimum target platform for both Combine and SwiftUI), you should take a closer look.

Combine is a unified, declarative API for processing values over time.

---

[2] http://reactivex.io/

[3] https://github.com/ReactiveX/RxJava

[4] https://github.com/ReactiveX/rxjs

[5] https://github.com/Reactive-Extensions/Rx.NET

[6] https://github.com/ReactiveX/RxKotlin

[7] https://github.com/kzaher/RxSwift

[8] http://reactivex.io/languages.html

Combine defines three main concepts to implement the idea of reactive programming:

1. Publishers

2. Subscribers

3. Operators

Publishers deliver values over time, and **subscribers** act on these values as they receive them. **Operators** sit in the middle between publishers and subscribers and can be used to manipulate the stream of values.

Let's take a closer look.

Publishers

As the name suggests, publishers emit values over time. To signal error conditions, publishers may also publish errors. Each publisher defines which kinds of values and errors (if any) it publishes.

The most basic publisher is Just—it emits just one value and never fails:

```
Just(42)
```

Figure 7-1. *A publisher that emits a single value*

Sending a single value is certainly useful in many situations, but most of the time, we'll want to send several values. Combine makes it easy to turn almost anything into a publisher. For example, here is how you would turn an array of the ten most popular[9] pizza toppings[10] into a publisher:

---

[9] Sausage—really? I mean, Salami, yes—but Sausage?

[10] www.huffpost.com/entry/popular-pizza-toppings_n_4261085

```
["Pepperoni", "Mushrooms", "Onions", "Sausage", "Bacon", "Extra
cheese", "Black olives", "Green peppers"].publisher
```

Figure 7-2. *A publisher that emits a number of pizza toppings and then terminates*

Using simple values or sequences as publishers might seem a bit boring, but it is definitely something that comes in handy later when we need to compose pipelines from multiple Combine publishers.

Time to spice it up a bit!

Let's imagine we're building a pizza ordering app. Here is some code that creates an order and sets up a publisher. This particular publisher will emit events whenever NotificationCenter sends a notification named .didUpdateOrderStatus to the pizzaOrder object.

```
// create the order
let pizzaOrder = Order()

let pizzaOrderPublisher = NotificationCenter
  .default
  .publisher(for: .didUpdateOrderStatus,
            object: pizzaOrder)
```

When the user wants to place the order, a different part of the app will use NotificationCenter to send this notification. This might be called when the user taps on the *Place order* button.

```
// once the user is ready to place the order
NotificationCenter
  .default
  .post(name: .didUpdateOrderStatus,
      object: pizzaOrderPublisher,
      userInfo: ["status": OrderStatus.processing])
```

If you run this code, nothing will happen—this is because publishers will only start to emit events once a subscriber has been registered with the publisher. So let's now take a look at subscribers.

Subscribers

Subscribers receive values from the upstream publisher they are subscribed to. Each subscriber defines which types of values and errors it is willing to receive.

The Combine framework comes with two main subscribers that are extremely versatile—sink and assign.

- sink is the most generic one; you can use it to receive values from a Combine publisher and then execute whatever code you like inside its closure.

- assign lets you assign any received values to a property or to another Publisher.

In the earlier examples, the publishers didn't really do anything. Let's use sink to subscribe to the list of most popular pizza toppings and print the emitted values to the console.

```
["Pepperoni", "Mushrooms", "Onions", "Salami", "Bacon", "Extra
cheese", "Black olives", "Green peppers"]
  .publisher
  .sink { topping in
      print("\(topping) is a popular topping for pizza")
  }
```

You will notice I've taken the liberty to replace *Sausage* with *Salami*...

Coming back to our pizza ordering example, here is how you can subscribe to the pizzaOrderPublisher and print any order status updates:

```
// create the order
let pizzaOrder = Order()

let pizzaOrderPublisher = NotificationCenter
  .default
  .publisher(for: .didUpdateOrderStatus, object: pizzaOrder)

pizzaOrderPublisher.sink { notification in
  print(notification)
}

// once the user is ready to place the order
NotificationCenter
  .default
  .post(name: .didUpdateOrderStatus,
        object: pizzaOrder,
        userInfo: ["status": OrderStatus.processing])
```

Printing values to the console is all nice and dandy, but let's take it one step further and assign the order status to the order. To do so, we will use the `assign` subscriber.[11]

A first attempt at assigning the order status to the status field on our pizza order might look like this:

```
pizzaOrderPublisher
  .assign(to: \.status, on: pizzaOrder)
```

However, this code doesn't compile. Instead, the compiler issues an error: `Key path value type 'OrderStatus' cannot be converted to contextual type 'NotificationCenter.Publisher.Output' (aka 'Notification')`

---

[11] You will find yourself using `assign` a lot when working with @Published properties on view models, as we will see later.

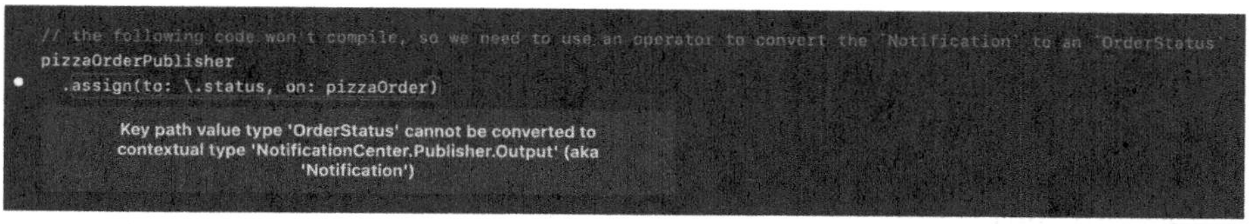

Figure 7-3. *pizzaOrderPublisher emits Notification, but OrderStatus was expected*

This is because `pizzaOrderPublisher` emits `Notification` values, but the property status is of type `OrderStatus`. We somehow need to extract the `OrderStatus` from the `UserInfo` dictionary on the `Notification`.

To convert values from upstream publishers, Combine provides a concept named *Operators*.

Operators

Often, you will need to modify the values before they can be used by the subscriber. These can be simple transformations, such as extracting a specific property from a more complex value, or filtering elements, so the subscriber only receives elements that meet a certain condition. Combine has a wide range of operators that can be combined (excuse the pun) to form powerful pipelines.

The names of many of the operators will sound familiar to you, as the Combine team decided to name them after existing operations in other parts of the Swift Standard Library.

One such operator is `map`—you might have already used its namesake sibling[12] to transform elements of an array or some other sequence. Similarly, in Combine, `map` is used to transform elements[13] from upstream publishers.

---

[12] https://developer.apple.com/documentation/swift/array/3017522-map
[13] https://bit.ly/3uXNzcO

213

In our example, we can use map to transform the Notifications we receive to the OrderStatus values we want to assign to the status property:

```
pizzaOrderPublisher
  .map { notification in
      notification.userInfo?["status"] as?
      OrderStatus ?? OrderStatus.placing
  }
  .assign(to: \.status, on: pizzaOrder)
```

Inside the map closure, we extract the OrderStatus enum from the UserInfo dictionary of the notification. Since this is optional and might be nil, we need to perform this rather clumsy-looking check and return a default value in case there is no status.

Fortunately, Combine has an operator that allows us to handle situations like these much more elegantly and safer: .compactMap. CompactMap *calls a closure with each received element and publishes any returned optional that has a value* (Apple docs[14]). This means two things:

1. All nil values will be removed from the result.

2. The result will no longer be optional.

```
pizzaOrderPublisher
  .compactMap { notification in
      notification.userInfo?["status"] as? OrderStatus
  }
  .assign(to: \.status, on: pizzaOrder)
```

The resulting code is much more concise and ... compact[15].

---

[14] https://bit.ly/3i8PRUO

[15] alright—no more puns, I promise ;-)

Composing Operators

Let's take a closer look at operators to better understand how they work. Operators are so special because they can subscribe to a publisher and act as a publisher at the same time. For example, here is the simplified declaration of CompactMap, and the extension to the Publisher protocol that enables us to compose Combine pipelines using a fluent syntax:[16]

```
extension Publishers {
  public struct CompactMap<Upstream, Output> : Publisher
      where Upstream : Publisher {
    public typealias Failure = Upstream.Failure
    public let upstream: Upstream

    public let transform: (Upstream.Output) ->
      Output?
  }
}

extension Publisher {
  public func compactMap<T>(_ transform: @escaping
    (Self.Output) -> T?) -> Publishers.CompactMap<Self, T>
}
```

And since all operators follow this pattern, this means we can chain several operators to create more powerful pipelines.

To show this in action, let's create a new publisher for our pizza delivery service. This time, we want to implement adding new toppings to an existing order.

---

[16]https://en.wikipedia.org/wiki/Fluent_interface#Swift

Let's start with a plain Margherita:

```
let margheritaOrder = Order(toppings: [
  Topping("tomatoes", isVegan: true),
  Topping("vegan mozarella", isVegan: true),
  Topping("basil", isVegan: true)
])
```

Now, let's create a publisher on NotificationCenter that publishes all Notifications that contain a message named .addTopping:

```
let extraToppingPublisher = NotificationCenter
  .default
  .publisher(for: .addTopping,
             object: margheritaOrder)

extraToppingPublisher
  .compactMap { notification in
    notification.userInfo?["extra"] as? Topping
  }
  .sink { value in
    if margheritaOrder.toppings != nil {
      margheritaOrder.toppings!.append(value)
      print("Adding \(value.name)")
      print("Your order now contains \(margheritaOrder.
        toppings!.count) toppings")
    }
  }

// send some notifications to add extra toppings
NotificationCenter
  .default
  .post(name: .addTopping,
        object: margheritaOrder,
        userInfo: ["extra": Topping("salami", isVegan: false)])
```

216

```
NotificationCenter
  .default
  .post(name: .addTopping,
        object: margheritaOrder,
        userInfo: ["extra": Topping("olives", isVegan: true)])
NotificationCenter
  .default
  .post(name: .addTopping,
        object: margheritaOrder,
        userInfo: ["extra": Topping("pepperoni", isVegan: true)])
NotificationCenter
  .default
  .post(name: .addTopping,
        object: margheritaOrder,
        userInfo: ["extra": Topping("capers", isVegan: true)])
```

Just like in our previous example, we use `.compactMap` to extract the Topping. Eventually, we use a `sink` subscriber to receive the topping and add it to the order.

So far, this is pretty similar to what we've done before. But recently, the owners of the delivery service decided to go vegan. So let's update our pipeline to make sure we only accept vegan toppings. We can do so by inserting the `filter` operator into our pipeline:

```
let extraToppingPublisher = NotificationCenter
  .default
  .publisher(for: .addTopping,
             object: margheritaOrder)

extraToppingPublisher
  .compactMap { notification in
    notification.userInfo?["extra"] as? Topping
  }
```

```
.filter{ topping in
  return topping.isVegan
}
.sink { value in
  if margheritaOrder.toppings != nil {
    margheritaOrder.toppings!.append(value)
    print("Adding \(value.name)")
    print("Your order now contains \(margheritaOrder.
      toppings!.count) toppings")
  }
}
```

```
// send some notifications to add extra toppings
NotificationCenter
  .default
  .post(name: .addTopping,
       object: margheritaOrder,
       userInfo: ["extra": Topping("salami", isVegan: false)])
NotificationCenter
  .default
  .post(name: .addTopping,
       object: margheritaOrder,
       userInfo: ["extra": Topping("extra cheese",
       isVegan: true)])
```

And thanks to implicit parameters and implicit returns, we can simplify this even further:

```
extraToppingPublisher
  .compactMap { notification in
    // ...
  }
```

```
.filter { $0.isVegan }
.sink { value in
  // ...
}
```

How about making sure people can only add three *extra* toppings? That's easy enough by using the `.prefix` operator—this operator only publishes up to a certain number of values:

```
extraToppingPublisher
  .compactMap { notification in
    // ...
  }
  .filter { $0.isVegan }
  .prefix(3)
  .sink { value in
    // ...
  }
```

And of course, it'd be a good idea to make sure to only accept changes to the list of toppings as long as the pizza isn't in the oven (or out for delivery) yet:

```
extraToppingPublisher
  .compactMap { notification in
    // ...
  }
  .filter { $0.isVegan }
  .prefix(3)
  .prefix(while: { topping in
    margheritaOrder.status == .placing
  })
  .sink { value in
    // ...
  }
```

Combining Publishers

When building applications, we find ourselves quite often in need of observing multiple events. In the pizza delivery service, we want to make sure to not keep our delivery couriers waiting. So, we will only ask them to get ready once the order has actually been placed and the address has been validated.

Updating the order status and validating the address are two different processes, so we have two separate publishers for them:

```
let orderStatusPublisher = NotificationCenter
  .default
  .publisher(for: .didUpdateOrderStatus, object: margheritaOrder)
  .compactMap { notification in
    notification.userInfo?["status"] as? OrderStatus
  }
  .eraseToAnyPublisher()

let shippingAddressValidPublisher = NotificationCenter
  .default
  .publisher(for: .didValidateAddress,
             object: margheritaOrder)
  .compactMap { notification in
    notification.userInfo?["addressStatus"] as? AddressStatus
  }
  .eraseToAnyPublisher()
```

By calling the .eraseToAnyPublisher() operator at the end of a pipeline, the type of the pipeline gets erased to AnyPublisher<Output, Never>. The unerased type of this publisher is Publishers.CompactMap <NotificationCenter.Publisher, OrderStatus>, which is a lot harder to read. It is a good idea to type-erase the result type of any pipelines you want to pass on to a different part of your code, for example, as a return type of a function or a property.

To determine whether we can ship the order, we need to evaluate the results of both of these pipelines. We only want to allocate a delivery courier if the order has been placed and the address is valid.

To achieve this, we need to create a new publisher that subscribes to orderStatusPublisher and shippingAddressValidPublisher and returns true once the order is .placed and the address is .valid. Combining several pipelines into one is a task that is rather common in Combine, and there are several publishers that we can choose from:

- Zip

- Merge

- CombineLatest

- ...and more

The one that's most suitable for our use case is CombineLatest—it takes the latest value from each of the upstream publishers.

```
let readyToProducePublisher = Publishers
  .CombineLatest(orderStatusPublisher,
                 shippingAddressValidPublisher)

readyToProducePublisher
  .print()
  .map { (orderStatus, addressStatus) in
    orderStatus == .placed && addressStatus == .valid
  }
  .sink {
    print("- Ready to ship order: \($0)")
  }
```

To make it easier to see the flow of events, I've added the .print()
operator to the pipeline. Let's send a couple of events to simulate a pizza
ordering process:

```
NotificationCenter
  .default
  .post(name: .didValidateAddress,
        object: margheritaOrder,
        userInfo: ["addressStatus": AddressStatus.invalid])
NotificationCenter
  .default
  .post(name: .didUpdateOrderStatus,
        object: margheritaOrder,
        userInfo: ["status": OrderStatus.placed])
NotificationCenter
  .default
  .post(name: .didValidateAddress,
        object: margheritaOrder,
        userInfo: ["addressStatus": AddressStatus.valid])
```

In the beginning, the address isn't valid yet, and the order is placed
before we can verify the address (we might be using a third-party service
that takes a moment to perform the check).

Here is the output:

```
receive subscription: (CombineLatest)
request unlimited
receive value: ((Combine_Playground_Sources.OrderStatus.placed,
Combine_Playground_Sources.AddressStatus.invalid))
- Ready to ship order: false
receive value: ((Combine_Playground_Sources.OrderStatus.placed,
Combine_Playground_Sources.AddressStatus.valid))
- Ready to ship order: true
receive cancel
```

The lines not starting with a dash are the debug output of the `.print()` operator. You can see how the order is deemed ready for shipment only once we receive an `OrderStatus` of `.placed` and an `AddressStatus` of `.valid`.

Summary

In this chapter, you learned the basics of Combine:

- Publishers emit values (such as the text a user enters into a text input field) over time.

- Subscribers can receive values, and can either assign them to variables (using the `.assign` subscriber), or process them further (using the `.sink` subscriber).

- Often, you need to transform values to make them useful for subscribers, and this is where Operators come into play.

You learned how to use Combine's operators to transform events they receive from upstream publishers and how this makes consuming events easier for subscribers. Apps often need to observe multiple event streams (e.g., the state of the fields on a shipping form), and you learned how to use Combine's operators to combine multiple event streams into one.

Combine almost feels like a DSL (domain-specific language) for describing the processing of the events that occur in our apps. This declarative approach makes it very similar to SwiftUI, and that's one of the reasons why they go together well.

In the next chapter, we will dive deeper into how you can combine SwiftUI and Combine and how using Combine in your SwiftUI apps will make it easier to implement your user-facing application logic.

CHAPTER 8

Driving UI State with Combine

Modern UIs have to respond to a multitude of input signals at the same time: users can communicate with an app using keyboard input, multitouch, physical gestures, and even voice commands. On top of this, applications might receive data from remote servers and local APIs.

Juggling all these input sources and the plethora of events they're sending is a challenging task for us developers, as we often find ourselves in situations that require us to combine several input sources, and making sure the app and its user interface always stay in sync.

In this and the following chapters, we're going to look at how Combine helps us build UIs that handle several event sources at the same time, such as the user's input and results from local and remote validation logic, making sure the UI reflects the state of the app at all times.

At the end of Chapter 6, you already saw how to use Combine to implement input validation for a single input field on an input form. Back then, we implemented validation logic for an ISBN field, both using onChange(of:) and Combine. To demonstrate the power of Combine, we are going to implement a more complex example with multiple event sources.

© Peter Friese 2023
P. Friese, *Asynchronous Programming with SwiftUI and Combine*,
https://doi.org/10.1007/978-1-4842-8572-5_8

Input Validation Using Combine

Let's assume that we've decided to add some social features to our book tracking app. To do so, we will ask users to sign up and create a user account. When signing up, users will need to choose a username and a password:

Figure 8-1. *A simple sign-up form*

To keep our users' data safe and secure, there are a couple of preconditions that need to be met:

- The username should consist of at least three characters. This is something we can check locally while the user types in their desired username.

- Usernames need to be unique, and we need to ensure the chosen username isn't already taken by any other user. This is a check we need to perform on our backend—there needs to be some API endpoint we can query to see if the name is still available.

- The user's password needs to meet certain complexity criteria (i.e., it needs to be strong enough).

- And to make sure the user can recall their password, we will ask them to repeat the password in a second password input field.

Only if all of these conditions are met, we can create a new user account. The button for creating a new user account should remain disabled until all conditions are met.

As you can see, we have a number of events that we need to route:

- The *Sign up* button must only be enabled if the form is valid.

- The *Username* input field needs to display a warning if the username is too short, or if it is no longer available.

- The *Password* fields need to display a warning if the password isn't strong enough, or if they don't match.

The Sign-Up Form View

In this chapter, we will use a Form to handle all user input. To display any error messages or warnings, we will use the header/footers of the respective form Section. In Chapter 14, we will take it one step further and build a reusable and configurable text input field with a floating label that can display error messages inline.

227

Note *You will find the code for the sample app in the Git-Hub repository*[1] *for this book, in the folder* Chapter 8—Driving UI State with Combine. *The individual steps can be found in the* steps *folder, and the final version in the* final *folder.*

```
struct SignUpForm: View {
  @StateObject var viewModel = SignUpFormViewModel()

  var body: some View {
    Form {
      // Username
      Section {
        TextField("Username", text: $viewModel.username)
          .autocapitalization(.none)
          .disableAutocorrection(true)
      } footer: {
        Text(viewModel.usernameMessage)
          .foregroundColor(.red)
      }

      // Password
      Section {
        SecureField("Password",
                    text: $viewModel.password)
        SecureField("Repeat password",
                    text: $viewModel.passwordConfirmation)
      } footer: {
        Text(viewModel.passwordMessage)
          .foregroundColor(.red)
      }
```

---

[1]https://github.com/peterfriese/Asynchronous-Programming-with-SwiftUI-and-Combine

```
// Submit button
Section {
  Button("Sign up") {
    print("Signing up as \(viewModel.username)")
  }
  .disabled(!viewModel.isValid)
  }
 }
 }
}
```

Handling all the input fields and making sure all form elements display the correct information (or warnings) for all the different states of the form usually require writing a lot of code, and it is easy to get things wrong and miss an important condition—especially when having to deal with asynchronous event sources like a remote API.

By using Combine and functional reactive programming, it will be much easier to implement this sign-up form.

In this chapter, we will focus on validating the username length requirement and the password strength requirements. In the next chapter, we will look at how to use Combine for networking and how we can use it to connect to a server and find out the username the user chose is still available.

The View Model

To perform input validation, our code needs to react to any changes the user makes to the sign-up form. In particular, we are interested in observing changes to the `username, password`, and `passwordConfirmation` text input fields. As we have already seen in the previous chapters, it is not possible to manipulate SwiftUI views directly or ready their state by accessing their properties. Instead, SwiftUI manages UI state outside of the view elements, in what is called the *source of truth*.

To make this possible, SwiftUI provides a number of property wrappers we can use to connect the source of truth to the views of an application. In Chapter 4, we discussed how those property wrappers work and which ones to use in which situation.

You might recall that we can use @State to handle local state in a view, so you might be tempted to use a local @State property to hold the username, password, and password confirmation for the sign-up form. However, @State is not a publisher, so we cannot use it to drive any Combine pipelines.

Instead, we will create a view model with username, password, and passwordConfirmation published properties that we can bind to the respective UI views.

```
class SignUpFormViewModel: ObservableObject {
  // Input
  @Published var username: String = ""
  @Published var password: String = ""
  @Published var passwordConfirmation: String = ""

  // Output
  @Published var usernameMessage: String = ""
  @Published var passwordMessage: String = ""
  @Published var isValid: Bool = false
}
```

Marking a property as @Published turns it into a Combine publisher. Not only does this allow us to bind the property to a UI element—we can also attach a Combine pipeline to it and run our validation logic inside the pipeline. We can then assign the result of the pipeline to another published property, which allows us to drive the UI with the result. For example, we can disable the *Submit* button as long as the form input is invalid.

By conforming the view model to ObservableObject, we make it observable. Whenever one of the published properties changes, the view model will emit the changes values, telling SwiftUI to update all affected views.

Using Combine in this way helps us to define the behavior of our application in a functional way, making sure that the UI and the application state are always in sync.

On a high level, the flow of information looks like this:

- The user types their preferred username into the username text input field.

- Every time the user types a character, the `TextField` view assigns the text entered so far to the username published property of the `SignUpFormViewModel`.

- Since `username` is a publisher, it sends events for any change to all of its subscribers.

- One of those subscribers is a Combine pipeline that checks if the length of the `username` is greater than three characters.

- The result of this pipeline is then used together with the result of other pipelines to determine the overall valida-tion result of the input form.

The basic version of our view model is already connected to the views of the sign-up form, so let's now look at how to implement the validation logic using Combine.

Validating the Username

Let's start with a simple verification and check the username length. We can access the publisher of a published property using the $propertyName syntax[2]. This will allow us to subscribe to any events the publisher sends (e.g., when the underlying property is changed because the user starts typing their username).

The input to our pipeline is a String, but we want to return a Bool indicating whether the length of the username is valid. For transformations like these, we can use Combine's map operator. Inside its closure, we can operate on the elements it receives from the upstream publisher and transform them into the required result.

So to verify if the username has at least three characters, we can check whether the count property of the input string is three or more. This check will either return true or false:

```
$username
  .map { username in
    return username.count >= 3
  }
```

And since this check is the only statement[3] we execute inside the closure, we can use an implicit return to simplify the code:

```
$username
  .map { username in
    username.count >= 3
  }
```

---

[2] The $ indicates we would like to access the property's so-called *projected value*. This is a concept introduced by Swift's property wrappers.

[3] This was introduced in SW-0255, "Implicit returns from single-expression functions": https://bit.ly/3ZgWDrd

Or, by using positional arguments:

```
$username
  .map { $0.count >= 3 }
```

Ultimately, the result of this pipeline (and others) needs to be assigned to the isValid property of the view model. As this currently is our only pipeline, we can do this in the view model's initializer:

```
class SignUpFormViewModel: ObservableObject {
  // Input
  @Published var username: String = ""
  @Published var password: String = ""
  @Published var passwordConfirmation: String = ""

  // Output
  @Published var usernameMessage: String = ""
  @Published var passwordMessage: String = ""
  @Published var isValid: Bool = false

  init() {
    $username
      .map { $0.count >= 3 }
      .assign(to: &$isValid)
  }
}
```

At the end of the pipeline, we use the assign(to:) operator to assign the result of the pipeline to the isValid property.

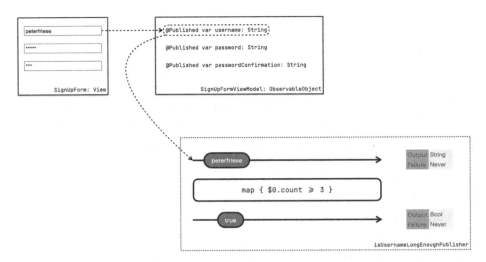

Figure 8-2. *The Combine pipeline for validating the username length*

If you run the app now, you will be able to see that the *Submit* button is disabled until you enter a username that has at least three characters.[4] However, there is no feedback for the user, and they might be wondering why the button is disabled, or what's the minimum username length.

Displaying Validation Messages

So, before we move on to implementing the password validation, let's make sure to provide some guidance for the user and display a suitable validation message. The view model already has a property usernameMessage that is bound to the footer of the form section that contains the username input field. All that's left to do for us is to implement the Combine pipeline that computes the validation message based on the length of the username.

---

[4] The code for the current state of the app can be found in the steps/step 1 subfolder of Chapter 8.

A naive implementation might look like this:

```
class SignUpFormViewModel: ObservableObject {

  // ...

  init() {
    $username
      .map { $0.count >= 3 }
      .assign(to: &$isValid)

    $username
      .map {
        $0.count >= 3
          ? ""
          : "Username must be at least three characters!"
      }
      .assign(to: &$usernameMessage)

  }
}
```

While this solution works fine, it has a number of drawbacks:

1. It contains duplicate logic for checking the username length. This might not be an issue now, but it might end up becoming a maintenance burden once we add more pipelines that contain a hard-coded version of the requirement that usernames must have at least three characters.

2. It is not scalable. At the moment, there is just one rule, but what happens if we add another rule, such as that usernames have to be unique, which will require us to communicate with a backend system. Combining several rules will be very complicated or even impossible with this approach.

To address these issues, we will make our Combine pipelines reusable by encapsulating them in computed properties.

Encapsulating Combine Pipelines in Computed Properties

An easy way to make Combine publishers reusable is to encapsulate them in private computed properties.

As you have learned in Chapter 7, a `Publisher` is a generic type that has two associated types for specifying the result and error cases. In our case, the result is of type `Bool`, and the pipeline will never fail, so the failure type is `Never`.

When putting together pipelines, the type of the pipeline will be a nested generic type representing the return types of all the publishers and operators we assembled along the way. In our case, this would be `Publishers.Map<Published<String>.Publisher, Bool>`. To avoid having to deal with such a complicated type, we can use type erasure. Combine provides an operator `eraseToAnyPublisher` that erases the type of a pipeline to `AnyPublisher`, which allows us to wrap our pipeline in a computed property like this:

```
private var isUsernameLengthValidPublisher:
  AnyPublisher<Bool, Never>
{
  $username
    .map { $0.count >= 3 }
    .eraseToAnyPublisher()
}
```

Having moved the pipeline into a computed property, we can now update the call site in the view model's initializer:

```
init() {
  isUsernameLengthValidPublisher
    .assign(to: &$isValid)
}
```

The next step is to reuse the publisher to drive the pipeline for computing the validation message:

```
init() {
  isUsernameLengthValidPublisher
    .assign(to: &$isValid)

  isUsernameLengthValidPublisher
    .map {
      $0 ? ""
        : "Username too short. Needs to be at least 3 characters."
    }
    .assign(to: &$usernameMessage)
}
```

By refactoring our code like this, we have moved the business logic ("usernames must have at least three characters") to one single location, where it is easier to update. This also enables us to reuse the publisher for composing more complex rules, as we will see shortly.

But before we do so, I'd like to call your attention to a small, but potentially serious aspect: the code we moved into the isUsernameLengthValidPublisher property will create a new pipeline every time it gets called. When using this publisher in more than one context—like we just did—we would end up not with one, but multiple instances of the same pipeline. Not only would this waste memory, but it'd also become a more serious issue once we build a pipeline that makes network calls or accesses a database. Creating and using multiple instances of a pipeline that performs a network access each time it processes an event would result in duplicate network requests for each extra instance of the pipeline—definitely not what we want.

To prevent this from happening, we need to convert the computed property into a lazy property. Lazy properties are computed once, and only the first time you access them. Converting a computed property into a lazy property requires only a few changes:

```
private lazy var isUsernameLengthValidPublisher:
 AnyPublisher<Bool, Never> =
{
  $username
    .map { $0.count >= 3 }
    .eraseToAnyPublisher()
}()
```

The great thing is that we can use lazy properties just like any other property—no need to change the call site. With this change in place, we've made sure that we only create the pipeline once, when the view model is initialized.

Validating the Password

A valid username is just one requirement for being able to create a new user account in our app—providing a password is another one. In this section, we will build on what you've learned in the previous section to implement a Combine pipeline that allows us to implement a flexible and easily enhanceable mechanism for validating passwords.

The first step is to make sure the password is not empty. We can implement this verification using a simple publisher, similar to how we implemented the username length check:

```
private lazy var isPasswordEmptyPublisher:
  AnyPublisher<Bool, Never> =
{
  $password
    .map { $0.isEmpty }
    .eraseToAnyPublisher()
}()
```

Just like before, we're using a lazy computed property to make sure we only create one instance of the pipeline.

As a small optimization, we can access the isEmpty property of the password string using a key path. Combine includes an extension on Publisher with overloaded versions of the map function that allow us to address up to three key paths in the map operator.

```
private lazy var isPasswordEmptyPublisher:
  AnyPublisher<Bool, Never> =
{
  $password
    .map(\.isEmpty)
    .eraseToAnyPublisher()
}()
```

In the next step, we will compare the password and the password confirmation field to make sure the user enters the same password twice. Both password and passwordConfirmation are published properties, so we can subscribe to them to receive events whenever the user types in their password.

But how can we consume the latest password and the latest password confirmation?

Combine provides a number of operators that allow us to combine several publishers in the same pipeline. Publishers.CombineLatest allows us to use the latest events sent by two upstream publishers. The following code snippet subscribes to $password and $passwordConfirmation and compares their latest output (which is the text the user entered into the password fields) using the equality operator ==:

```
private lazy var isPasswordMatching:
  AnyPublisher<Bool, Never> =
{
  Publishers.CombineLatest($password, $passwordConfirmation)
    .map(==)
    .eraseToAnyPublisher()
}()
```

You will notice I used the key path version of the map operator—the closure version would look like this: map { $0 == $1 }. Which one you use is largely a matter of style and personal preference.

Now that we can determine if the password is not empty and that both password and its confirmation match, we need to determine the overall password validity: the password is valid if it is not empty and if it matches the password confirmation.

You might have guessed it: we will use Publishers.CombineLatest to combine the latest state of the isPasswordEmptyPublisher and the isPasswordMatching publishers into yet another publisher that we're going to name isPasswordValidPublisher:

```
private lazy var isPasswordValidPublisher:
  AnyPublisher<Bool, Never> =
{
  Publishers.CombineLatest(
    isPasswordEmptyPublisher,
    isPasswordMatchingPublisher
  )
```

```
  .map { !$0 && $1 }
  .eraseToAnyPublisher()
}()
```

By now, this code should look familiar to you. To display a meaningful validation message, add the following code to the initializer of your view model:

```
Publishers.CombineLatest(
  isPasswordEmptyPublisher,
  isPasswordMatchingPublisher
)
.map { isPasswordEmpty, isPasswordMatching in
  if isPasswordEmpty {
    return "Password must not be empty"
  }
  else if !isPasswordMatching {
    return "Passwords do not match"
  }
  return ""
}
.assign(to: &$passwordMessage)
```

Putting It All Together

As a final step, we need to combine the username validation and password validation and assign the result to the isValid property of the view model. This will enable the submit button if the form is valid.

Similar to how we computed the overall validation state of the password, we will use Publishers.CombineLatest to determine the overall state of the form based on the isUsernameLengthValidPublisher and the isPasswordValidPublisher:

```
private lazy var isFormValidPublisher:
  AnyPublisher<Bool, Never> =
{
  Publishers.CombineLatest(
    isUsernameLengthValidPublisher,
    isPasswordValidPublisher
  )
  .map { $0 && $1 }
  .eraseToAnyPublisher()
}()
```

In the initializer of the view model, replace the first line (which uses just the isUsernameLengthValidPublisher) and use isFormValidPublisher to drive the submit button state:

```
init() {
  isFormValidPublisher
    .assign(to: &$isValid)

  isUsernameLengthValidPublisher
    .map {
      $0 ? ""
        : "Username too short. Needs to be at least 3
          characters."
    }
    .assign(to: &$usernameMessage)

  Publishers.CombineLatest(
    isPasswordEmptyPublisher,
    isPasswordMatchingPublisher
  )
```

```
.map { isPasswordEmpty, isPasswordMatching in
  if isPasswordEmpty {
    return "Password must not be empty"
  }
  else if !isPasswordMatching {
    return "Passwords do not match"
  }
  return ""
}
.assign(to: &$passwordMessage)
}
```

Exercises[5]

Choosing a strong password is not easy, and many sign-up forms provide a visual clue to help users pick a strong password. Our sign-up form is pretty lenient in this regard and allows users to pick anything as a password, which isn't very secure. Use what you've learned so far to encourage users to pick a strong password:

1. Implement a password length requirement: make sure the user's password has at least eight characters. If it has less than eight characters, display a warning in the footer of the password section of the form.

---

[5] The solutions for the exercises can be found in the `exercises` sub-folder of this chapter.

2. Verify the password strength and reject any passwords that aren't strong enough. An easy way to do this is to use a library like *Navajo-Swift*,[6] which computes the strength on a scale of `very weak`, `weak`, `reasonable`, `strong`, `very strong`. Make sure the sign-up form only becomes valid if the user picks password with at least `reasonable` strength.

3. Add a progress bar to the footer of the password section and display the password strength, coloring the progress bar in red, yellow, and green to indicate the password strength.

Summary

In this chapter, you learned how to use Combine publishers to drive the state of a UI with complex business logic, and how breaking down the logic of your app into smaller Combine pipelines can help to keep your code manageable.

We looked at separating the business logic from your UI by moving it into a view model. This helped us keep our view lean and easy to read.

You then learned about several techniques for creating Combine pipelines and how to manage them in your view model. For simple pipelines, it is OK to create them in your view model's initializer. Once you need to reuse pipelines, it's a good idea to move them into private properties. Keep in mind that you should use lazy computed properties to make sure you don't create multiple instances of the same pipeline, resulting in memory waste and potentially extra network calls.

---

[6]See `https://github.com/jasonnam/Navajo-Swift`

Combine offers a wide range of operators to transform the output you receive from upstream publishers. In this chapter, we used the following:

- map allows us to transform input from one publisher into a different format. You saw how you can either use map with a closure to perform more complex transformation logic, or use its key path overload to create concise, yet powerful transformations that directly access attributes of the input.

- Publishers.CombineLatest is another operator you will use frequently—it combines the latest events from several upstream publishers and makes them available to its closure. You can think of it as a sort of *Y*-shaped junction that allows you to join several streams of events, converting them into a single unified output stream.

This chapter provided a first glimpse into what's possible with Combine and SwiftUI and how using Combine will make it easier to write SwiftUI apps.

In the next chapter, we will switch gears and look at how we can use Combine to access the network and combine the results of remote API calls with local events in your app's UI.

CHAPTER 9

Networking with Combine

We live in a networked world, and most modern applications need to access the network to retrieve information stored on a server running on the Internet (or on the user's local network).

Even on a superfast connection, a request usually takes several milliseconds. Using blocking I/O and waiting for a response on the foreground thread of the application is not an option, as it would freeze the app and result in a pretty terrible user experience. Users would probably assume your app has died, and kill it. To prevent this behavior, we need to offload asynchronous work to a background thread, so the foreground thread is free to perform UI updates and respond to user interactions. This is why modern networking APIs need to be called asynchronously.

The most popular way to implement asynchronous APIs in Swift is to use *callbacks*. Usually, these are implemented as closures, and thanks to Swift's trailing closure syntax, they look rather elegant and are easy to use once you understand how they work.

Other ways to call asynchronous APIs are *async/await* and *Combine*. In this chapter, we will dive into how to use Combine to implement a networking layer for your app. We will first look at the traditional, callback-driven way to fetch data from the network using `URLSession`. Then, we will refactor this code to make use of Combine's `DataTaskPublisher`. You will learn how Combine makes mapping data and handling errors easier that

© Peter Friese 2023
P. Friese, *Asynchronous Programming with SwiftUI and Combine*,
https://doi.org/10.1007/978-1-4842-8572-5_9

will result in more readable and more bug-free code. In Chapters 14 and 15, you will learn how to use `async/await` to perform asynchronous calls, and we will look at the differences between Combine and async/await.

Keeping your application's user interface in sync with the application's state has always been difficult, and the development community has come up with a plethora of approaches to address this challenge.

Reactive programming is one such approach, and SwiftUI's reactive state management makes this a lot easier by introducing the notion of a *source of truth* that can be shared across your app using SwiftUI's property wrappers such as `@EnvironmentObject`, `@StateObject`, and `@ObservedObject`.

This *source of truth* is usually your in-memory data model, and combining your local source of truth to the network might sound complicated. In this chapter, you will learn how you can use Combine to make combining your local source of truth with data from a remote service a lot easier than you maybe think.

You will first learn how to connect a network-driven Combine pipeline to a SwiftUI user interface. We will then optimize the implementation to ensure your app doesn't overwhelm your backend server. Combine provides a couple of operators that will help us significantly reduce the number of requests your app sends to the server. This will also improve the user experience of your application, leaving you to wonder how you ever got by without using Combine.

Let's kick things off by looking into how to use Combine to fetch data from a server and map the result to a Swift `struct`.

Fetching Data Using URLSession

We will continue working on the sign-up form we started building in the previous chapter. Let's assume one of the requirements is to check if the user's preferred username is still available.

This requires us to communicate with our authorization server to check if the desired username already is taken by someone else. Here is a request that shows how we might try to find out if the username *sjobs* is still available:

```
GET localhost:8080/isUserNameAvailable?userName=sjobs HTTP/1.1
```

The server will reply with a short JSON document stating whether the username is still available or not:

```
HTTP/1.1 200 OK
content-type: application/json; charset=utf-8
content-length: 39
connection: close
date: Thu, 06 Jan 2022 16:09:08 GMT

{"isAvailable":false, "userName":"sjobs"}
```

To perform this request in Swift, we can use URLSession. The traditional way to fetch data from the network using URLSession looks like this:

```
func checkUserNameAvailableOldSchool(userName: String,
completion: @escaping (Result<Bool, NetworkError>) -> Void) {
  guard let url = URL(string: "http://localhost:8080/
  isUserNameAvailable?userName=\(userName)") else { // (2)
    completion(.failure(.invalidRequestError("URL invalid")))
    return
  }

  let task = URLSession.shared.dataTask(with: url) { data,
  response, error in
    if let error = error { // (3)
      completion(.failure(.transportError(error)))
      return
    }
```

```
if let response = response as? HTTPURLResponse,
!(200...299).contains(response.statusCode) { // (4)
  completion(.failure(.serverError(
    statusCode: response.statusCode
  )))
  return
}

guard let data = data else { // (5)
  completion(.failure(.noData))
  return
}

do {
  let decoder = JSONDecoder()
  let userAvailableMessage =
    try decoder.decode(UserNameAvailableMessage.self,
                       from: data)
  completion(.success(
    userAvailableMessage.isAvailable)) // (1)
}
catch {
  completion(.failure(.decodingError(error)))
}
}

task.resume() // (6)
}
```

And while this code works fine and nothing is inherently wrong with it, it does have several issues:

1.   It's not immediately clear what the happy path is—the only location that returns a successful result is pretty hidden (1).

2. Developers who are new to using completion handlers might be confused by the fact that the happy path doesn't even use a `return` statement to deliver the result of the network call to the caller.

3. Error handling is scattered all over the place (2, 3, 4, 5).

4. There are several exit points, and it's easy to forget one of the `return` statements in the `if let` conditions.

5. Overall, it is hard to read and maintain, even if you're an experienced Swift developer.

6. It's easy to forget you have to call `resume()` to actually perform the request (6). I am pretty sure most of us have been frantically looking for bugs when using `URLSession`, only to find out we forgot to actually kick off the request using `resume`. And yes, I think `resume` is not a great name for an API that is supposed to *send* the request.

RUNNING THE CODE SAMPLES

You will find all the code samples in the accompanying GitHub repository,[1] *in the* `Networking` *folder. To be able to benefit the most, I've also provided a demo server (built with Vapor) in the* `server` *subfolder. To run it on your machine, do the following:*

```
$ cd server
$ swift run
```

---

[1] https://github.com/peterfriese/SwiftUI-Combine-Book

Using Combine to Fetch Data

When they introduced Combine, Apple added publishers for many of their own asynchronous APIs. Developers can now use these publishers to replace their existing, callback-driven code.

The resulting code has fewer exit points, follows a straight line, and thus is easier to read and maintain. It's also less prone to subtle bugs.

To get a better understanding of what this means, let's look at how the previous (callback-based) code snippet looks like after refactoring it to make use of Combine:

```
func checkUserNameAvailableNaive(userName: String) ->
  AnyPublisher<Bool, Never>
{
  guard let url = URL(string: "http://127.0.0.1:8080/
isUserNameAvailable?userName=\(userName)") else {
    return Just(false).eraseToAnyPublisher()
  }

  return URLSession.shared.dataTaskPublisher(for: url) // (1)
    .map { data, response in // (2)
      do {
        let decoder = JSONDecoder()
        let userAvailableMessage =
          try decoder.decode(UserNameAvailableMessage.self,
                             from: data)
        return userAvailableMessage.isAvailable
      }
      catch {
        return false // (4)
      }
    }
```

```
    .replaceError(with: false) // (5)
    .eraseToAnyPublisher()
}
```

Let's walk through the code step by step:

1. We use dataTaskPublisher to perform the request.
   This publisher is a one-shot publisher and will emit
   an event once the requested data has arrived. It's
   worth keeping in mind that Combine publishers
   don't perform any work if there is no subscriber.
   This means that this publisher will not perform
   any call to the given URL until you add at least one
   subscriber. I will later show you how to connect this
   pipeline to the UI and make sure it gets called every
   time the user enters text into the username field.

2. Once the request returns, the publisher emits a
   value that contains both the data and the response.
   In this line, we use the map operator to transform
   this result. As you can see, we can reuse most of the
   data mapping code from the previous version of the
   code, except for a couple of minor changes.

3. Instead of calling the completion closure, we can
   return a Boolean value to indicate whether the
   username is still available or not. This value will be
   passed down the pipeline.

4. In case the data mapping fails, we catch the error
   and return false, which seems to be a good
   compromise.

5. We do the same for any errors that might occur
   when accessing the network. This is a simplification
   that we might need to revisit in the future.

Also note that (except for the `guard` statement that makes sure we've got a valid URL) there is just *one* exit point.

This looks a lot better and easier to read than the initial version. We could leave it there and use this code in our app.

But we can do better. In the following three sections, we will look at a few changes that will make the code more linear and easier to reason about.

Destructuring Tuples Using Key Paths

We often find ourselves in a situation where we need to extract a specific attribute from a variable. In the preceding code, `dataTaskPublisher` returns a result containing the `data` and the `response` for the URL request we sent. The type of the result is a tuple, as we can see from `DataTaskPublisher`'s declaration:

```
public struct DataTaskPublisher : Publisher {

  /// The kind of values published by this publisher.
  public typealias Output = (data: Data, response: URLResponse)
  ...
}
```

Extracting the individual elements from the tuple is called *destructuring*. Combine provides an overloaded version of the `map` operator that allows us to destructure the tuple and access just the attribute we care for:

```
return URLSession.shared.dataTaskPublisher(for: url)
  .map(\.data)
```

Mapping Data

Since mapping data is such a common task, Combine comes with a dedicated operator to make this easier: `decode(type:decoder:)`.

```
return URLSession.shared.dataTaskPublisher(for: url)
  .map(\.data)
  .decode(type: UserNameAvailableMessage.self,
          decoder: JSONDecoder())
```

This will extract the data value from the upstream publisher and decode it into a UserNameAvailableMessage instance.

And finally, we can use the map operator again to destructure the UserNameAvailableMessage and access its isAvailable attribute:

```
return URLSession.shared.dataTaskPublisher(for: url)
  .map(\.data)
  .decode(type: UserNameAvailableMessage.self,
          decoder: JSONDecoder())
  .map(\.isAvailable)
```

Fetching Data Using Combine, Simplified

With all these changes in place, we now have a version of the pipeline that is easy to read and has a linear flow:

```
class AuthenticationService {
  func checkUserNameAvailable(userName: String) ->
    AnyPublisher<Bool, Never>
  {
    guard let url = URL(string: "http://127.0.0.1:8080/
isUserNameAvailable?userName=\(userName)") else {
        return Just(false).eraseToAnyPublisher()
    }

      return URLSession.shared.dataTaskPublisher(for: url)
        .map(\.data)
        .decode(type: UserNameAvailableMessage.self,
                decoder: JSONDecoder())
```

```
        .map(\.isAvailable)
        .replaceError(with: false)
        .eraseToAnyPublisher()
    }
}
```

It's a good idea to keep this code in a separate type, together with any other further code that communicates directly with the authentication server. Modularizing our code like this helps us to keep our code base neatly organized.

Connecting to the UI

Let's now look at how to integrate this new Combine pipeline in the sign-up form we started in the previous chapter.

Here is a condensed version of the sign-up form. I've removed some of the code to avoid distracting you from what we want to focus on in this chapter. For the discussion in this chapter, we just care about the username field, the Text label to display a message, and a sign-up button. I've commented out the code for the password fields we discussed in the previous chapter.

```
struct SignUpForm: View {
  @StateObject private var viewModel = SignUpFormViewModel()

  var body: some View {
    Form {
      // Username
      Section {
        TextField("Username", text: $viewModel.username)
          .autocapitalization(.none)
          .disableAutocorrection(true)
```

```
  } footer: {
    Text(viewModel.usernameMessage)
      .foregroundColor(.red)
  }

  // (code for password fields removed for brevity)

  // Submit button
  Section {
    Button("Sign up") {
      print("Signing up as \(viewModel.username)")
    }
    .disabled(!viewModel.isValid)
  }
    }
  }
}
```

Here are the parts of the view model that are relevant for our discussion—again, some of the code from the previous chapter is stripped out for simplicity.

```
class SignUpScreenViewModel: ObservableObject {
  private var authenticationService = AuthenticationService()

  // MARK: Input
  @Published var username: String = ""

  // MARK: Output
  @Published var usernameMessage: String = ""
  @Published var isValid: Bool = false
  ...
}
```

Since @Published properties are Combine publishers, we can subscribe to them to receive updates whenever their value changes.

This will allow us to take the user's most recent input and pass it to the checkUserNameAvailable publisher to see if this username is still available.

To pass events from one publisher to another one, we can use the flatMap operator:

```
$username
  .flatMap { username -> AnyPublisher<Bool, Never> in
    self.authenticationService.checkUserNameAvailable(userName:
      username)
  }
```

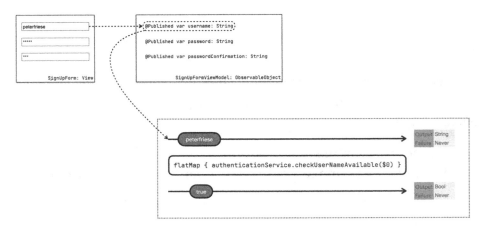

Figure 9-1. *Combine pipeline for calling the authentication service to check if the username is available*

This pipeline takes input events from the username publisher (i.e., what the user types into the *username* text input field) and sends them to the checkUserNameAvailable publisher. This publisher will return a Bool for each input event, indicating whether the respective username is still available. This means that subscribers will receive a stream of Bools.

We want to use the result of this pipeline to drive the state of the sign-up form: as long as the pipeline returns true to indicate that the chosen username is available, we want to enable the *Submit* button. At the same time, we want to display an error message as soon as the result of the pipeline is false.

This means we need to add two different subscribers to the pipeline: the enabled state of the *Submit* button and the text of the error message label.

To preserve memory and avoid wasting CPU cycles, let's make the pipeline reusable. One way to do this to wrap it inside a lazy computed property. Lazy computed properties are computed only once, and only if they are accessed.

As a reminder, the general form of a lazy computed property is as follows:

```
lazy var propertyName: Type = {
  // compute the property's value inside the closure
}() // <- don't forget the parentheses
```

Using a lazy computed property ensures that the pipeline will only be instantiated once, making sure we're using the same instance for every subscriber.

```
private lazy var isUsernameAvailablePublisher:
    Publishers.FlatMap<AnyPublisher<Bool, Never>,
Published<String>.Publisher> = {
  $username
    .flatMap { username in
      self.authenticationService
        .checkUserNameAvailable(userName: username)
    }
}()
```

At this point, the result type of the pipeline is `Publishers.`
`FlatMap<AnyPublisher<Bool, Never>, Published<String>.Publisher>`.
Not only is this hard to read, but it's also difficult to use in the calling
code. To prevent having to use a complicated signature like this, Combine
provides the `eraseToAnyPublisher` operator that allows us to erase
the type of a pipeline to `AnyPublisher<Type, Error>`. By appending
this operator to the end of our pipeline, we erase the pipeline's type
to `AnyPublisher<Bool, Never>`—much easier to use.

```
private lazy var isUsernameAvailablePublisher:
  AnyPublisher<Bool, Never> =
{
  $username
    .flatMap { username in
      self.authenticationService
        .checkUserNameAvailable(userName: username)
    }
    .eraseToAnyPublisher()
}()
```

In the next step, we will connect the result of the
`isUsernameAvailablePublisher` to the UI. Take a look at the view model:
we've got two properties in the output section of the view model—one
for any message related to the username and another one that holds the
overall validation state of the form.

Combine publishers can be connected to more than one subscriber,
so we can connect both `isValid` and `usernameMessage` to the
`isUsernameAvailablePublisher`:

```
class SignUpScreenViewModel: ObservableObject {
  ...
  init() {
    isUsernameAvailablePublisher
```

```
        .assign(to: &$isValid)

    isUsernameAvailablePublisher
      .map {
        $0 ? ""
            : "Username not available. Try a different one."
      }
      .assign(to: &$usernameMessage)
  }
}
```

Using this approach allows us to reuse the isUsernameAvailablePublisher and use it to drive both the overall isValid state of the form (which will enable/disable the *Submit* button) and the usernameMessage label, which informs the user whether their chosen username is still available or not.

Ensure the demo server is running, launch the app, and try typing in a few different usernames. The demo server has a hard-coded list of usernames that it regards as unavailable, so try these to see how the Combine pipeline we developed so far drives the UI: peterfriese, johnnyappleseed, page, johndoe.

Observe the server's console output while typing, and you will notice a few things:

1. The API endpoint gets called several times for each character you type.

2. Xcode tells you that you shouldn't update the UI from a background thread.

Let's look at these and try to understand how we can fix them.

261

Handling Multithreading

When building Combine pipelines that access the network, you might end up seeing error messages like the following in Xcode's console output:

[SwiftUI] Publishing changes from background threads is not allowed; make sure to publish values from the main thread (via operators like receive(on:)) on model updates.

Sometimes,[2] Xcode will display a purple warning in the code editor, making it easier to find the offending piece of code.

The reason for this error message is that URLSession will execute the network request on a background thread. When the request is fulfilled, dataTaskPublisher will send an event with the result of the request onto the pipeline. Our code retrieves this result, maps it to the data type we need for our UI, and assigns it to one of the published properties of the view model. This, in turn, will prompt SwiftUI to update the UI with the new value of the property.

All of this happens on the same thread—a background thread. However, accessing the UI from a background thread is discouraged, and this is why SwiftUI raises a warning.

To prevent this from happening, we need to instruct Combine to switch to the foreground thread once it has received the result of the network request. To tell Combine to receive an event on a specific thread, we can use the receive(on:) operator:

```
private lazy var isUsernameAvailablePublisher:
  AnyPublisher<Bool, Never> =
{
```

---

[2] Technically, this should work for all versions of Xcodes starting with version 12. However, I found that in some combinations of Xcode and iOS, this sometimes doesn't work. As the error messages show up in the console, I am inclined to think this is an IPC issue that hopefully should be resolved in future Xcode versions.

```
$username
  .flatMap { username -> AnyPublisher<Bool, Never> in
    self.authenticationService
      .checkUserNameAvailable(userName: username)
  }
  .receive(on: DispatchQueue.main)
  .eraseToAnyPublisher()
}()
```

We will dive deeper into the topic of threading in the chapter about Combine schedulers, but for now, this line will fix our threading issues.

Optimizing Network Access

With high-speed, low-latency Internet available in most places, it is easy to forget that not all of our users might be on a fast, low-latency uplink when using our apps. Even in cities like Hamburg or London, you will find areas with patchy or no connectivity at all.

When building apps that access the Internet, we should be mindful of this and make sure we don't waste bandwidth.

When running the app and inspecting the logs of our test server, you saw that the isUserNameAvailable endpoint got called multiple times for each character typed. This is clearly not ideal: not only does it waste CPU cycles on our server (which might become an issue if you're hosting your server with a cloud provider that charges you by the number of calls or CPU uptime), but it also means we're adding extra network overhead to our application.

You might barely notice this when running the test server locally, but you will definitely notice it when you're on an Edge connection, talking to a remote instance of your server.

The problem gets worse if your API endpoints aren't *idempotent*: imagine calling an API endpoint for reserving a seat or buying a concert ticket. By sending two (or more) requests instead of one, you would end up reserving more seats than you require, or buying more concert tickets than you wanted.

Finding the Root Cause

First of all, we need to find out what's causing all those extra requests.

An easy way to figure out what's going on with a Combine pipeline is to add some debugging code. Let's add the print() operator to the pipeline:

```
private lazy var isUsernameAvailablePublisher:
  AnyPublisher<Bool, Never> =
{
  $username
    .print("username")
    .flatMap { username -> AnyPublisher<Bool, Never> in
      self.authenticationService
        .checkUserNameAvailable(userName: username)
    }
    .receive(on: DispatchQueue.main)
    .eraseToAnyPublisher()
}()
```

This operator logs a couple of useful things to the console:

1. Any life-cycle events of the pipeline (e.g., subscriptions being added)

2. Any values being sent/received

We can specify a prefix ("username") to make the log statements stand out on the console.

Rerunning the app, we immediately see the following output—even without typing anything into the text field:

```
username: receive subscription: (PublishedSubject)
username: request unlimited
username: receive value: ()
username: receive subscription: (PublishedSubject)
username: request unlimited
username: receive value: ()
```

This indicates we've got *two* subscribers for our pipeline!

Looking at our code, we can spot those subscribers in the initializer of the view model:

```
init() {
  isUsernameAvailablePublisher
    .assign(to: &$isValid)

  isUsernameAvailablePublisher
    .map {
      $0 ? ""
        : "Username not available. Try a different one."
    }
    .assign(to: &$usernameMessage)
}
```

The first subscriber is the pipeline that feeds the isValid property, which we ultimately use to enable/disable the submit button on the sign-up form.

The second subscriber is the pipeline that produces an error message in case the chosen username is not available. The result of this pipeline will be displayed on the sign-up form as well.

Every time the user types a character, the isUsernameAvailablePublisher pipeline needs to process the current value of the username field, so the result can ultimately be assigned to the subscribers.

No big deal for a pipeline that runs locally (although we should try to not waste CPU cycles), but this becomes a much bigger issue for pipelines that access the network, like ours does.

Now that we've identified what's causing multiple subscriptions to our publisher, let's see what we can do to fix the problem.

Using the `share` Operator to Share a Publisher

Having multiple subscribers for a single publisher is a common pattern, especially in UIs, where a single UI element might have an impact on multiple other views.

If you need to share the results of a publisher with multiple subscribers, you can use the `share()` operator. According to Apple's documentation:

The publisher returned by this operator supports multiple subscribers, all of whom receive unchanged elements and completion states from the upstream publisher.

This is exactly what we need. By applying the `share` operator to the end of the pipeline in `isUsernameAvailablePublisher`, we share the result of the pipeline for each event (i.e., each character the user enters in the username input field) with all subscribers of the publisher:

```
private lazy var isUsernameAvailablePublisher:
  AnyPublisher<Bool, Never> =
{
  $username
    .print("username")
    .flatMap { username -> AnyPublisher<Bool, Never> in
      self.authenticationService
        .checkUserNameAvailable(userName: username)
    }
```

```
.receive(on: DispatchQueue.main)
.share()
.eraseToAnyPublisher()
}()
```

When running the updated code, we can see that the $username publisher no longer has two subscribers, but instead just one:

```
username: receive subscription: (PublishedSubject)
username: request unlimited
username: receive value: ()
```

Now, you might be wondering why it's only one subscriber, since we clearly still have two published properties (isValid and usernameMessage) subscribed to the pipeline.

Well, the answer is simple: the share operator ultimately is this one subscriber, and it in turn is being subscribed to by isValid and isUsernameAvailablePublisher. To prove this, let's add another print() operator to the pipeline:

```
private lazy var isUsernameAvailablePublisher:
  AnyPublisher<Bool, Never> =
{
  $username
    .print("username")
    .flatMap { username -> AnyPublisher<Bool, Never> in
      self.authenticationService
        .checkUserNameAvailable(userName: username)
    }
    .receive(on: DispatchQueue.main)
    .share()
    .print("share")
    .eraseToAnyPublisher()
}()
```

In the resulting output, we can see that share receives two subscriptions (1, 2) and username just one (3):

```
share: receive subscription: (Multicast)            // (1)
share: request unlimited
username: receive subscription: (PublishedSubject) // (3)
username: request unlimited
username: receive value: ()
share: receive subscription: (Multicast)            // (2)
share: request unlimited
share: receive value: (true)
share: receive value: (true)
```

You can think of share() as a fork that receives events from its upstream publisher and multicasts them to all of its subscribers.

IS IT A BUG OR A FEATURE?

Go ahead and type a few characters into the username field, and you will find that for every character you type, you will still see two requests being made to the server.

This might be an issue in iOS 15—I debugged into this a bit, and it seems like TextField emits every keystroke twice. In prior versions of iOS, this wasn't the case, and I am inclined to think this is a bug in iOS 15, so I created a sample project to reproduce this issue (see AppleFeedback/ FB9826727 at main · peterfriese/AppleFeedback (https://github.com/ peterfriese/AppleFeedback/tree/main/FB9826727)), and filed a Feedback (FB9826727) with Apple.

If you agree with me that this is a regression, consider filing a feedback as well—the more duplicates a bug receives, the more likely it will be addressed.

Using debounce to Further Optimize the UX

When building UIs that communicate with a remote system, we need to keep in mind that the user usually types a lot faster than the system can deliver feedback.

For example, when picking a username, I usually type my favorite username without stopping to type in the middle of the word. I don't care if the first few letters of this username are available—I am interested in the full name. Sending the incomplete username over to the server after every single keystroke doesn't make a lot of sense and seems like a lot of waste.

To avoid this, we can use Combine's debounce operator: it will drop all events until there is a pause. It will then pass on the most recent event to the downstream publisher:

```
private lazy var isUsernameAvailablePublisher:
  AnyPublisher<Bool, Never> =
{
  $username
    .debounce(for: 0.8, scheduler: DispatchQueue.main)
    .print("username")
    .flatMap { username -> AnyPublisher<Bool, Never> in
      self.authenticationService
        .checkUserNameAvailable(userName: username)
    }
    .receive(on: DispatchQueue.main)
    .share()
    .print("share")
    .eraseToAnyPublisher()
}()
```

By doing so, we tell Combine to disregard all updates to username until there is a pause of 0.8 seconds and then send the most recent username on to the next operator on the pipeline (in this case, the print operator, which will then pass the event on to the flatMap operator).

This suits a normal user input behavior much more and will result in the app sending fewer requests to the server.

Using `removeDuplicates` to Avoid Sending the Same Request Twice

Have you ever spoken to a person and asked them the same question twice? It's a bit of an awkward situation, and the other person probably wonders if you've been paying attention to them at all.

Now, even though AI is making advances, I am sure that computers don't have emotions, so they won't hold a grudge if you send the same API request twice. But to give our users the best experience possible, we should try to eliminate sending duplicate requests if we can.

Combine has an operator for this: `removeDuplicates`—it will remove any duplicate events from the stream of events if they follow each other *subsequently*.

This works really well in conjunction with the debounce operator, and we can use those two operators combined (sorry, I guess you'll have to live with the puns) for a little further optimization of our username availability check:

```
private lazy var isUsernameAvailablePublisher:
  AnyPublisher<Bool, Never> =
{
  $username
    .debounce(for: 0.8, scheduler: DispatchQueue.main)
    .removeDuplicates()
    .print("username")
    .flatMap { username -> AnyPublisher<Bool, Never> in
      self.authenticationService
        .checkUserNameAvailable(userName: username)
    }
```

```
.receive(on: DispatchQueue.main)
.share()
.print("share")
.eraseToAnyPublisher()
}()
```

Together, they will further reduce the number of requests we send to our server in case the user mistypes and then corrects their spelling.

Let's look at an example:

```
jonyive [pause] s [backspace]
```

This will send the following requests:

1. jonyive

2. No request for jonyives (as the s got deleted before the debounce timed out)

3. No second request for jonyive, as this got filtered by removeDuplicates

It's just a tiny change, and the impact might not be huge—but every little helps.

Bringing It All Together

In the last chapter, we implemented a check to ensure usernames have at least three characters. To verify that the username has at least characters and is still available, we need to combine the isUsernameLengthPublisher and isUsernameAvailablePublisher. Just like we did before, we can use Publishers.CombineLatest() for this.

Let's create a new publisher, isUsernameValidPublisher, that combines the events that isUsernameLengthValidPublisher and isUsernameAvailablePublisher send:

```
enum UserNameValid {
  case valid
  case tooShort
  case notAvailable
}

private lazy var isUsernameValidPublisher:
  AnyPublisher<UserNameValid, Never> =
{
  Publishers.CombineLatest(
    isUsernameLengthValidPublisher, isUsernameAvailablePublisher
  )
  .map { longEnough, available in
    if !longEnough {
      return .tooShort
    }
    if !available {
      return .notAvailable
    }
    return .valid
  }
  .share()
  .eraseToAnyPublisher()
}()
```

Introducing the UserNameValid enum helps us to return a semantically meaningful result to the subscribers of the pipeline.

To use this new publisher, we need to update isFormValidPublisher accordingly:

```
private lazy var isFormValidPublisher:
  AnyPublisher<Bool, Never> =
{
```

```
Publishers.CombineLatest(
  isUsernameValidPublisher,
  isPasswordValidPublisher
)
.map { ($0 == .valid) && $1 }
.eraseToAnyPublisher()
}()
```

Exercises

1. `isUsernameValidPublisher` is a bit inefficient: it will ping the server even if the username is too short. Try improving this by gating the pipeline on the length of the username.

2. Improve error handling. Instead of mapping a server error to the username not being available, return a Result from `checkUsernameAvailable`. In case of a success, the result should contain the `UserAvailableMessage`, otherwise the server error. Update the pipelines to inform the user that, because the server is not available, we cannot determine whether the username is available, and we'll just assume it is available for now, and we will perform a final availability check once the user actually hits the submit button.

Summary

In this chapter, I showed you how to access the network using Combine and how this enables you to write straight-line code that should be easier to read and maintain than the respective callback-driven counterpart.

We also looked at how to connect a Combine pipeline that makes network requests to SwiftUI by using a view model and attaching the pipeline to an @Published property.

We also discussed how Combine can make communicating with a remote server (or any asynchronous API, in fact) more efficient.

By using the share operator, we can attach multiple subscribers to a publisher/pipeline and avoid running expensive/time-consuming processing for each of those subscribers. This is particularly useful when accessing APIs with a higher latency than an in-process module, such as a remote server or anything involving I/O.

The debounce operator allows us to deal more efficiently with any events that occur in short bursts, like user input. Instead of processing every single event coming down the pipeline, we wait for a pause and only operate on the most recent event.

We can use the removeDuplicates operator to avoid processing duplicate events. As the name suggests, it removes any directly subsequent duplicate events, such as the user adding and then removing a character when we also use the debounce operator.

Together, these operators can help us build clients that access remote servers and other asynchronous APIs more efficiently.

One thing we need to spend more time on is how to properly deal with errors and other unexpected situations. In this chapter, we used replaceError(with:) to replace any errors with a nil value. This helped us to get unblocked, but in a real-world application, we need a more flexible way to handle errors. In the next chapter, we're going to discuss a couple of options for doing this.

CHAPTER 10

Error Handling in Combine

As developers, we tend to be a rather optimistic bunch of people. At least that's the impression you get when looking at the code we write—we mostly focus on the happy path and tend to spend a lot less time and effort on error handling.

Even in the previous chapter, we've been neglecting error handling. In fact, we've mostly ignored it: we replaced any errors with a default value, which was OK for prototyping our app, but this probably isn't a solid strategy for any app that goes into production.

In this chapter, let's take a closer look at how we can handle errors appropriately!

We will continue working on the sign-up form we started working on in the previous chapters. As a reminder, we use Combine to validate the user's input, and as part of this validation, the app also calls an endpoint on the app's authentication server to check if the username the user chose is still available. The endpoint will return `true` or `false` depending on whether the name is still available. In addition, the server will return the appropriate HTTP status codes and an error payload in case anything goes wrong when validating the username.

© Peter Friese 2023
P. Friese, *Asynchronous Programming with SwiftUI and Combine*,
https://doi.org/10.1007/978-1-4842-8572-5_10

Error Handling Strategies

Before we dive deeper into how to handle errors, let's talk about a couple of error-handling strategies and whether they are appropriate in our scenario.

Ignoring the Error

This might sound like a terrible idea at first, but it's actually a viable option when dealing with certain types of errors under specific circumstances. Here are some examples:

- The user's device is *temporarily* offline or there is another reason why the app cannot reach the server.

- The server is down at the moment, but will be back up *soon.*

In many cases, the user can continue working offline, and the app can sync with the server once the device comes back online. Of course, this requires some sort of offline capable sync solution (like Cloud Firestore)[1].

It is good practice to provide some user feedback to make sure users understand their data hasn't been synchronized yet. Many apps show an icon (e.g., a cloud with an upward pointing arrow) to indicate the sync process is still in progress, or a warning sign to alert the user they need to manually trigger the sync once they're back online.

Retrying (with Exponential Backoff)

In other cases, ignoring the error is not an option. Imagine the booking system for a popular event: the server might be overwhelmed by the amount of requests. In this case, we want to make sure that the system

---

[1] A NoSQL cloud database with realtime sync capabilities that is part of Firebase, see https://firebase.google.com/products/firestore

will not be thrashed by the users hitting "refresh" every couple of seconds. Instead, we want to spread out the time between retries. Using an exponential backoff strategy is both in the user's and the system's operator's best interest: the operator can be sure their server will not be overwhelmed even more by users trying to get through by constantly refreshing, and the users should eventually get their booking through thanks to the app automatically retrying.

Showing an Error Message

Some errors require the user's action—for example, if saving a document failed. In this case, it is appropriate to show a model dialog to get the user's attention and ask them how to proceed. For less severe errors, it might be sufficient to show a toast (an overlay that shows for a brief moment and then disappears).

Replacing the Entire View with an Error View

Under some circumstances, it might even be appropriate to replace the entire UI with an error UI. A well-known example for this is Chrome—if the device is offline, it will display the Chrome Dino to let users know their device is offline, and to help them spend the time until their connection restores with a fun jump-and-run game.

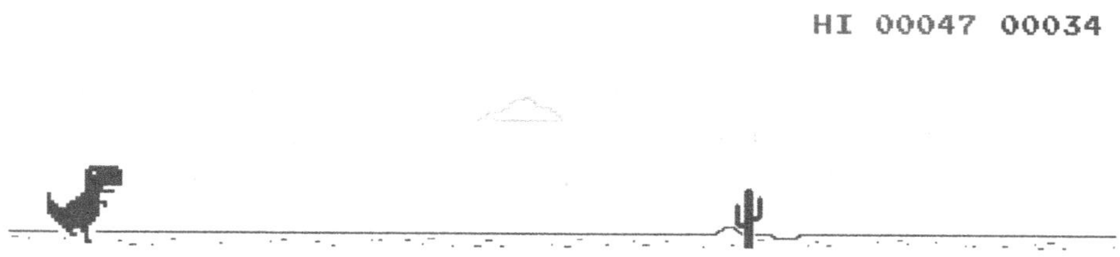

Figure 10-1. *The Chrome Dino game*

Showing an Inline Error Message

This is a good option in case the data the user has provided isn't valid. Not all input errors can be detected by a local form validation. For example, an online store might have a business rule that mandates shipments worth more than a certain amount must be shipped using a specific transport provider. It's not always feasible to implement all of these business rules in the client app (a configurable rules engine definitely might help here), so we need to be prepared to handle these kinds of semantic errors.

Ideally, we should show those kind of errors next to the respective input field to help the user provide the correct input.

Typical Error Conditions and How to Handle Them

To give you a better understanding of how to apply this in a real-world scenario, let's add some error handling to the sign-up form we created earlier in this series. In particular, we'll deal with the following error conditions:

- Device/network offline

- Semantic validation errors

- Response parsing errors/invalid URL

- Internal server errors

If you want to follow along, you will find the code for this chapter in the GitHub repository[2] for the book, in the folder for this chapter. The server *subfolder contains a local server that helps us simulate all the error conditions we will cover.*

---

[2] https://github.com/peterfriese/SwiftUI-Combine-Book

Implementing a Fallible Network API

In the previous chapter, we implemented an AuthenticationService that interfaces with an authentication server. This helps us to keep everything neatly organized and separated by concerns:

- The view (SignUpScreen) displays the state and takes the user's input.

- The view model (SignUpScreenViewModel) holds the state the view displays. In turn, it uses other APIs to react to the user's actions. In this particular app, the view model uses the AuthenticationService to interact with the authentication server.

- The service (AuthenticationService) interacts with the authentication server. Its main responsibilities are to bring the server's responses into a format that the client can work with. For example, it converts JSON into Swift structs, and (most relevant for this post) it handles any network-layer errors and converts them into UI-level errors that the client can better work with.

The following diagram provides an overview of how the individual types work together.

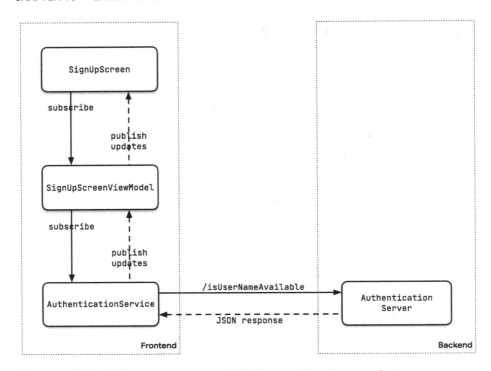

Figure 10-2. *The components making up the sign-up form*

If you take a look at the code we wrote in the previous chapter, you will notice that the checkUserNamerAvailablePublisher has a failure type of Never—that means it claims there is never going to be an error.

```
func checkUserNameAvailablePublisher(userName: String) ->
AnyPublisher<Bool, Never> { ... }
```

That's a pretty bold statement, especially given network errors are really common! We were only able to guarantee this because we replaced any errors with a return value of false:

```
func checkUserNameAvailablePublisher(userName: String)
    -> AnyPublisher<Bool, Never> {
```

```
guard let url = URL(string: "http://127.0.0.1:8080/
isUserNameAvailable?userName=\(userName)") else {
  return Just(false).eraseToAnyPublisher()
}

return URLSession.shared.dataTaskPublisher(for: url)
  .map(\.data)
  .decode(type: UserNameAvailableMessage.self,
          decoder: JSONDecoder())
  .map(\.isAvailable)
  .replaceError(with: false)
  .eraseToAnyPublisher()
}
```

To turn this rather lenient implementation into something that returns meaningful error messages to the caller, we first need to change the failure type of the publisher, and stop glossing over any errors by returning false:

```
enum APIError: LocalizedError {
  /// Invalid request, e.g., invalid URL
  case invalidRequestError(String)
}

struct AuthenticationService {

  func checkUserNameAvailablePublisher(userName: String)
      -> AnyPublisher<Bool, Error> {
    guard let url =
        URL(string: "http://127.0.0.1:8080/
        isUserNameAvailable?userName=\(userName)") else {
      return Fail(error: APIError.invalidRequestError("URL
      invalid"))
        .eraseToAnyPublisher()
    }
```

```
    return URLSession.shared.dataTaskPublisher(for: url)
      .map(\.data)
      .decode(type: UserNameAvailableMessage.self,
              decoder: JSONDecoder())
      .map(\.isAvailable)
//      .replaceError(with: false)
      .eraseToAnyPublisher()
  }

}
```

We also introduced a custom error type, APIError. This will allow us
to convert any errors that might occur inside our API (be it network errors
or data mapping errors) into a semantically rich error that we can handle
more easily in our view model.

Calling the API and Handling Errors

Now that the API has a failure type, we need to update the caller as well.
Once a publisher emits a failure, the pipeline will terminate—unless
you capture the error. A typical approach to handling errors when using
flatMap is to combine it with a catch operator:

```
somePublisher
  .flatMap { value in
    callSomePotentiallyFailingPublisher()
    .catch { error in
      return Just(someDefaultValue)
    }
  }
  .eraseToAnyPublisher()
```

Applying this strategy to the code in our view model results in the following code:

```
private lazy var isUsernameAvailablePublisher:
  AnyPublisher<Bool, Never> =
{
  $username
    .debounce(for: 0.8, scheduler: DispatchQueue.main)
    .removeDuplicates()
    .flatMap { username -> AnyPublisher<Bool, Never> in
      self.authenticationService
        .checkUserNameAvailablePublisher(userName: username)
        .catch { error in // (1)
          return Just(false) // (2)
        }
        .eraseToAnyPublisher()
    }
    .receive(on: DispatchQueue.main)
    .share()
    .eraseToAnyPublisher()
}()
```

And just like that, we end up where we started! If the API emits a failure (e.g., the username was too short), we catch the error (1) and replace it with false (2)—this is exactly the behavior we had before. Except, we wrote a lot more code...

Seems like we're getting nowhere with this approach, so let's take a step back and look at the requirements for our solution:

- We want to use the emitted values of the pipeline to drive the state of the submit button and to display a warning message if the chosen username is not available.

- If the pipeline emits a failure, we want to disable the submit button and display the error message in the error label below the username input field.

- How exactly we handle the errors will depend on the type of failure, as we will discuss later in this chapter.

This means

- We need to make sure we can receive both failures and successes

- We need to make sure the pipeline doesn't terminate if we receive a failure

To achieve all of this, we will map the result of the checkUserNameAvailablePublisher to a Result type. Result is an enum that can capture both success and failure states. Mapping the outcome of checkUserNameAvailablePublisherto Result also means the pipeline will no longer terminate in case it emits a failure.

Let's first define a typealias for the Result type to make our life a little easier:

```
typealias Available = Result<Bool, Error>
```

To turn the result of a publisher into a Result type, we can use the following operator that John Sundell implemented in his article "The power of extensions in Swift"[3]:

```
extension Publisher {
  func asResult() ->
    AnyPublisher<Result<Output, Failure>, Never>
  {
    self
```

---

[3] https://bit.ly/3GH1WZT

```
    .map(Result.success)
    .catch { error in
      Just(.failure(error))
    }
    .eraseToAnyPublisher()
  }
}
```

This allows us to update the isUsernameAvailablePublisher in our view model like this:

```
private lazy var isUsernameAvailablePublisher:
  AnyPublisher<Available, Never> =
{
  $username
    .debounce(for: 0.8, scheduler: DispatchQueue.main)
    .removeDuplicates()
    .flatMap { username -> AnyPublisher<Available, Never> in
      self.authenticationService
        .checkUserNameAvailablePublisher(userName: username)
        .asResult()
    }
    .receive(on: DispatchQueue.main)
    .share()
    .eraseToAnyPublisher()
}()
```

With this basic plumbing in place, let's look at how to handle the different error scenarios I outlined earlier.

Handling Device/Network Offline Errors

On mobile devices, it is pretty common to have spotty connectivity: especially when you're on the move, you might be in an area with bad or no coverage.

Whether or not you should show an error message depends on the situation:

For our use case, we can assume that the user at least has intermittent connectivity. Telling the user that we cannot reach the server would be rather distracting while they're filling out the form. Instead, we should ignore any connectivity errors for the form validation (and instead run our local form validation logic).

Once the user has entered all their details and submits the form, we should show an error message if the device is still offline.

Catching this type of error requires us to make changes at two different places. First, in checkUserNameAvailablePublisher, we use mapError to catch any upstream errors and turn them into an APIError:

```
enum APIError: LocalizedError {
  /// Invalid request, e.g. invalid URL
  case invalidRequestError(String)

  /// Indicates an error on the transport layer,
  /// e.g. not being able to connect to the server
  case transportError(Error)
}

struct AuthenticationService {

  func checkUserNameAvailablePublisher(userName: String)
    -> AnyPublisher<Bool, Error>
  {
    guard let url = URL(string: "http://127.0.0.1:8080/
    isUserNameAvailable?userName=\(userName)") else {
```

```
      return Fail(error: APIError.invalidRequestError("URL
      invalid"))
        .eraseToAnyPublisher()
    }

    return URLSession.shared.dataTaskPublisher(for: url)
      .mapError { error -> Error in
        return APIError.transportError(error)
      }
      .map(\.data)
      .decode(type: UserNameAvailableMessage.self,
              decoder: JSONDecoder())
      .map(\.isAvailable)
      .eraseToAnyPublisher()
  }
}
```

Then, in our view model, we map the result to detect if it was a failure (1, 2). If so, we extract the error and check if it is a network transport error. If that's the case, we return an empty string (3) to suppress the error message:

```
class SignUpScreenViewModel: ObservableObject {

  // ...

  init() {
    isUsernameAvailablePublisher
      .map { result in
        switch result {
        case .failure(let error): // (1)
          if case APIError.transportError(_) = error {
            return "" // (3)
```

```
        }
        else {
          return error.localizedDescription
        }
      case .success(let isAvailable):
        return isAvailable ? ""
                          : "This username is not available"
      }
    }
    .assign(to: &$usernameMessage) // (4)

  isUsernameAvailablePublisher
    .map { result in
      if case .failure(let error) = result { // (2)
        if case APIError.transportError(_) = error {
          return true
        }
        return false
      }
      if case .success(let isAvailable) = result {
        return isAvailable
      }
      return true
    }
    .assign(to: &$isValid) // (5)
  }
}
```

In case isUsernameAvailablePublisher returned a success, we
extract the Bool telling us whether or not the desired username is available
and map this to an appropriate message.

And finally, we assign the result of the pipeline to the `usernameMessage` (4) and `isValid` (5) published properties which drive the UI on our view.

Keep in mind that ignoring the network error is a viable option for this kind of UI—it might be an entirely different story for your use case, so use your own judgment when applying this technique.

So far, we haven't exposed any errors to the user, so let's move on to a category of errors that we actually want to make the user aware of.

Handling Validation Errors

Most validation errors should be handled locally on the client, but sometimes we cannot avoid running some additional validation steps on the server. Ideally, the server should return a HTTP status code in the 4xx range, and optionally a payload that provides more details.

In our example app, the server requires a minimum username length of four characters, and we have a list of usernames that are forbidden (such as "admin" or "superuser").

For these cases, we want to display a warning message and disable the submit button.

Our backend implementation is based on Vapor and will respond with a HTTP status of 400 and an error payload for any validation errors. If you're curious about the implementation, check out the code in `routes.swift` in the implementation of the server.

Handling this error scenario requires us to make changes in two places: the service implementation and the view model. Let's take a look at the service implementation first.

Since we should handle any errors before even trying to extract the payload from the response, the code for handling server errors needs to run after checking for `URLErrors` and before mapping data:

```
struct APIErrorMessage: Decodable {
  var error: Bool
```

```
  var reason: String
}

// ...

struct AuthenticationService {

  func checkUserNameAvailablePublisher(userName: String) ->
  AnyPublisher<Bool, Error> {
    guard let url = URL(string: "http://127.0.0.1:8080/
    isUserNameAvailable?userName=\(userName)") else {
      return Fail(error: APIError.invalidRequestError("URL
      invalid"))
        .eraseToAnyPublisher()
    }

    return URLSession.shared.dataTaskPublisher(for: url)
      // handle URL errors (most likely not able to connect to
      the server)
      .mapError { error -> Error in
        return APIError.transportError(error)
      }

      // handle all other errors
      .tryMap { (data, response) -> (data: Data, response:
      URLResponse) in
        print("Received response from server, now checking
        status code")

        guard let urlResponse = response as?
        HTTPURLResponse else {
          throw APIError.invalidResponse // (1)
        }
```

```
      if (200..<300) ~= urlResponse.statusCode { // (2)
      }
      else {
        let decoder = JSONDecoder()
        let apiError = try decoder.decode(APIErrorMessage.self,
                from: data) // (3)

        if urlResponse.statusCode == 400 { // (4)
          throw APIError.validationError(apiError.reason)
        }
      }
      return (data, response)
    }

    .map(\.data)
    .decode(type: UserNameAvailableMessage.self,
            decoder: JSONDecoder())
    .map(\.isAvailable)
//      .replaceError(with: false)
    .eraseToAnyPublisher()
  }

}
```

Let's take a closer look at what the code in this snippet does:

1. If the response isn't a `HTTPURLResonse`, we return `APIError.invalidResponse`.

2. We use Swift's pattern matching to detect if the request was executed successfully, that is, with a HTTP status code in the range of 200 to 299.

3. Otherwise, some error occurred on the server. Since we use Vapor, the server will return details about the error in a JSON payload (https://docs.vapor.codes/4.0/errors/), so we can now map this information to an APIErrorMessage struct and use it to create more meaningful error message in the following code.

4. If the server returns a HTTP status of 400, we know that this is a validation error (see the server implementation for details), and return an APIError.validationError including the detailed error message we received from the server.

In the view model, we can now use this information to tell the user that their chosen username doesn't meet the requirements:

```
init() {
  isUsernameAvailablePublisher
    .map { result in
      switch result {
      case .failure(let error):
        if case APIError.transportError(_) = error {
          return ""
        }
        else if case APIError.validationError(let reason)
        = error {
          return reason
        }
        else {
          return error.localizedDescription
        }
      case .success(let isAvailable):
```

```
        return isAvailable ? "" : "This username is not
        available"
    }
}
.assign(to: &$usernameMessage)
```

That's right—just three lines of code. We've already done all the hard work, so it's time to reap the benefits. 🎉

Handling Response Parsing Errors

There are many situations in which the data sent by the server doesn't match what the client expected:

- The response includes additional data, or some fields were renamed.

- The client is connecting via a captive portal (e.g., in a hotel).

In these cases, the client receives data, but it's in the wrong format. To help the user resolve the situation, we'll need to analyze the response and then provide suitable guidance, for example:

- Download the latest version of the app.

- Sign in to the captive portal via the system browser.

The current implementation uses the decode operator to decode the response payload and throw an error in case the payload couldn't be mapped. This works well, and any decoding error will be caught and show on the UI. However, an error message like *The data couldn't be read because it is missing* isn't really user friendly. Instead, let's try to show a message that is a little bit more meaningful for users and also suggest to upgrade to the latest version of the app (assuming the server is returning additional data that the new app will be able to leverage).

To be able to provide more fine-grained information about decoding errors, we need to part ways with the decode operator and fall back to manually mapping the data (don't worry, thanks to JSONDecoder and Swift's Codable protocol, this is pretty straightforward):

```
// ...
.map(\.data)
// .decode(type: UserNameAvailableMessage.self,
//         decoder: JSONDecoder())
.tryMap { data -> UserNameAvailableMessage in
  let decoder = JSONDecoder()
  do {
    return try decoder.decode(UserNameAvailableMessage.self,
                              from: data)
  }
  catch {
    throw APIError.decodingError(error)
  }
}
.map(\.isAvailable)
// ...
```

By conforming APIError to LocalizedError and implementing the errorDescription property, we can provide a more user-friendly error message (I included custom messages for the other error conditions as well):

```
enum APIError: LocalizedError {
  /// Invalid request, e.g. invalid URL
  case invalidRequestError(String)

  /// Indicates an error on the transport layer, e.g. not being
  able to connect to the server
  case transportError(Error)
```

```
/// Received an invalid response, e.g. non-HTTP result
case invalidResponse

/// Server-side validation error
case validationError(String)

/// The server sent data in an unexpected format
case decodingError(Error)

var errorDescription: String? {
  switch self {
  case .invalidRequestError(let message):
    return "Invalid request: \(message)"
  case .transportError(let error):
    return "Transport error: \(error)"
  case .invalidResponse:
    return "Invalid response"
  case .validationError(let reason):
    return "Validation Error: \(reason)"
  case .decodingError:
    return "The server returned data in an unexpected format.
      Try updating the app."
  }
 }
}
```

Now, to make it abundantly clear to the user that they should update the app, we will also display an alert. Here is the code for the alert:

```
struct SignUpScreen: View {
  @StateObject private var viewModel = SignUpScreenViewModel()

  var body: some View {
    Form {
```

```
    // ...
  }

  // show update dialog
  .alert("Please update", isPresented: $viewModel.
  showUpdateDialog, actions: {
    Button("Upgrade") {
      // open App Store listing page for the app
    }
    Button("Not now", role: .cancel) { }
  }, message: {
    Text("It looks like you're using an older version of this
    app. Please update your app.")
  })

  }
}
```

You'll notice that the presentation state of this alert is driven by a published property on the view model, showUpdateDialog. Let's update the view model accordingly (1) and also add the Combine pipeline that maps the results of isUsernameAvailablePublisher to this new property:

```
class SignUpScreenViewModel: ObservableObject {
  // ...

  @Published var showUpdateDialog: Bool = false // (1)

  // ...

  private lazy var isUsernameAvailablePublisher:
    AnyPublisher<Available, Never> =
    $username
      .debounce(for: 0.8, scheduler: DispatchQueue.main)
      .removeDuplicates()
```

```
    .flatMap { username -> AnyPublisher<Available, Never> in
      self.authenticationService
        .checkUserNameAvailablePublisher(userName: username)
        .asResult()
    }
    .receive(on: DispatchQueue.main)
    .share() // (3)
    .eraseToAnyPublisher()
  }()

  init() {
    // ...

    // decoding error: display an error message
    // suggesting to download a newer version
    isUsernameAvailablePublisher
      .map { result in
        if case .failure(let error) = result {
          if case APIError.decodingError = error // (2) {
            return true
          }
        }
        return false
      }
      .assign(to: &$showUpdateDialog)
  }
}
```

As you can see, nothing too fancy—we essentially just take any events coming in from the isUsernameAvailablePublisher and convert them into a Bool that only becomes true if we receive a .decodingError (2).

We're now using `isUsernameAvailablePublisher` to drive three different Combine pipelines, and I would like to explicitly call out that—since `isUsernameAvailablePublisher` eventually will cause a network request to be fired—it is important to make sure we're only sending *at most* one network request per keystroke. The previous chapter explains how to do this in depth using the `share()` operator (3).

Handling Internal Server Errors

In some rare cases, the backend of our app might be having some issues—maybe part of the system is offline for maintenance, some process died, or the server is overwhelmed. Usually, servers will return a HTTP status code in the 5xx range to indicate this.

SIMULATING ERROR CONDITIONS

The sample server includes code that simulates some of the error conditions discussed in this article. You can trigger the error conditions by sending specific `username` values:

- *Any username with less than four characters will result in a `tooshort` validation error, signaled via a HTTP 400 status code and a JSON payload containing a detailed error message.*

- *An empty username will result in an `emptyName` error message, indicating the username mustn't be empty.*

- *Some usernames are forbidden: "admin" or "superuser" will result in an `illegalName` validation error.*

- *Other usernames such as "peterfriese", "johnnyappleseed", "page", and "johndoe" are already taken, so the server will tell the client these aren't available any more.*

- *Sending "illegalresponse" as the username will return a JSON response that has too few fields, resulting in a decoding error on the client.*

- *Sending "servererror" will simulate a database problem (databaseCorrupted) and will be signaled as a HTTP 500 with no retry hint (as we assume that this is not a temporary situation, and retrying would be futile).*

- *Sending "maintenance" as the username will return a maintenance error, along with a retry-after header that indicates the client can retry this call after a period of time (the idea here is that the server is undergoing scheduled maintenance and will be back up after rebooting).*

Let's add the code required to deal with server-side errors. As we did for previous error scenarios, we need to add some code to map the HTTP status code to our `APIError` enum:

```
if (200..<300) ~= urlResponse.statusCode {
}
else {
  let decoder = JSONDecoder()
  let apiError = try decoder.decode(APIErrorMessage.self,
                                    from: data)

  if urlResponse.statusCode == 400 {
    throw APIError.validationError(apiError.reason)
  }
```

```
  if (500..<600) ~= urlResponse.statusCode {
    let retryAfter = urlResponse.value(
                        forHTTPHeaderField: "Retry-After")
    throw APIError.serverError(
      statusCode: urlResponse.statusCode,
      reason: apiError.reason,
      retryAfter: retryAfter)
  }

}
```

To display a user-friendly error message in our UI, all we need to do is add a few lines of code to the view model:

```
isUsernameAvailablePublisher
  .map { result in
    switch result {
    case .failure(let error):
      if case APIError.transportError(_) = error {
        return ""
      }
      else if case APIError.validationError(let reason)
      = error {
        return reason
      }
      else if case APIError.serverError(statusCode: _, reason:
      let reason, retryAfter: _) = error {
        return reason ?? "Server error"
      }
      else {
        return error.localizedDescription
      }
    case .success(let isAvailable):
```

```
   return isAvailable ? "" : "This username is not
   available"
 }
}
.assign(to: &$usernameMessage)
```

So far, so good.

For some of the server-side error scenarios, it might be worthwhile to retry the request after a short while. For example, if the server underwent maintenance, it might be back up again after a few seconds.

Combine includes a `retry` operator that we can use to automatically retry any failing operation. Adding it to our code is a simple one-liner:

```
return URLSession.shared.dataTaskPublisher(for: url)
  .mapError { ... }
  .tryMap { ... }
  .retry(3)
  .map(\.data)
  .tryMap { ... }
  .map(\.isAvailable)
  .eraseToAnyPublisher()
```

However, as you will notice when you run the app, this will result in *any* failed request to be retried three times. This is not what we want—for example, we want any verification errors to bubble up to the view model. Instead, they will be captured by the retry operator as well.

What's more, there is no pause between retries. If our goal was to reduce the pressure on a server that is already overwhelmed, we've made it even worse by sending not one, but four requests (the original request, plus three retries).

So how can we make sure that

1. We only retry certain types of failures?

2. There is a pause before we retry a failed request?

Our implementation needs to be able to catch any upstream errors and propagate them down the pipeline to the next operator. When we catch a serverError, however, we want to pause for a moment and them start the entire pipeline again so it can retry the URL request.

Let's first make sure we can (1) catch all errors, (2) filter out the serverError, and (3) propagate all other errors along the pipeline. The tryCatch operator "handles errors from an upstream publisher by either replacing it with another publisher or throwing a new error." This is exactly what we need:

```
return URLSession.shared.dataTaskPublisher(for: url)
  .mapError { ... }
  .tryMap { ... }
  .tryCatch { error -> AnyPublisher<(data: Data, response:
  URLResponse), Error> in // (1)
    if case APIError.serverError(_, _, let retryAfter) = error
    { // (2)
      // ...
    }
    throw error // (3)
  }
  .map(\.data)
  .tryMap { ... }
  .map(\.isAvailable)
  .eraseToAnyPublisher()
```

When we catch a serverError, we want to wait for a short amount of time and then restart the pipeline.

We can do this by firing off a new event (using the Just publisher), delaying it for a few seconds, and then using flatMap to kick off a new dataTaskPublisher. Instead of pasting the entire code for the pipeline inside the if statement, we assign the dataTaskPublisher to a local variable:

```
let dataTaskPublisher = URLSession.shared.
dataTaskPublisher(for: url)
  .mapError { ... }
  .tryMap { ... }

return dataTaskPublisher
  .tryCatch { error -> AnyPublisher<(data: Data, response:
  URLResponse), Error> in
    if case APIError.serverError = error {
      return Just(()) // (1)
        .delay(for: 3, scheduler: DispatchQueue.global())
        .flatMap { _ in
          return dataTaskPublisher
        }
        .retry(10) // (2)
        .eraseToAnyPublisher()
    }
    throw error
  }
  .map(\.data)
  .tryMap { ... }
  .map(\.isAvailable)
  .eraseToAnyPublisher()
```

A couple of notes about this code:

1. The Just publisher expects *some* value it can
    publish. Since it really doesn't matter which value
    we use, we can send anything we want. I decided
    to send an empty tuple, which is often used in
    situations when you mean "nothing".

2. We retry sending the request 10 times, meaning it will be sent up to 11 times in total (the original call plus the 10 retries).

The only reason why this number is so high is to make it easier to see that the pipeline comes to an end as soon as the server returns a successful result. The demo server can simulate recovering from scheduled maintenance when you send *maintenance* as the username: it will throw `InternalServerError.maintenance` (which is mapped to HTTP 500) for every first and second request. Every third request, it will return a `success` (i.e., HTTP 200). The best way to see this in action is to run the server from inside Xcode (run open the `server` project and press the *Run* button). Then, create a *Sound* breakpoint for the line that contains `throw InternalServerError.maintenance`.

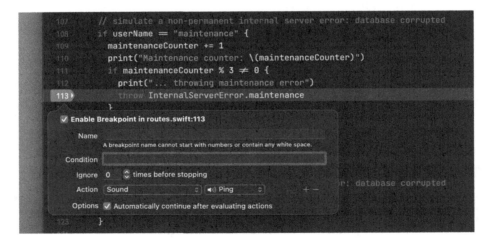

Figure 10-3. *Setting up a sound breakpoint*

Every time the server receives a request for `username=maintenance`, you will hear a sound. Now, run the sample app and enter *maintenance* as the username. You will hear the server responding with an error two times, before it will return a success.

Summary

After using a rather lenient approach to handle errors in the recent chapter, we took things a lot more serious this time around.

In this chapter, we used a couple of strategies to handle errors and expose them to the UI. Error handling is an important aspect of developer quality software, and there is a lot of material out there. However, the aspect of how to expose errors to the user isn't often discussed, and I hope this article provided you with a better understanding of how you can achieve this.

In comparison to the original code, the code became a bit more complicated, and this is something we're going to address in the next chapter when we will look at implementing your own Combine operators. To demonstrate how this works, we will implement an operator that makes handling incremental backoff as easy as adding one line to your Combine pipeline!

CHAPTER 11

Implementing Custom Combine Operators

In the previous chapters, you learned how to use Combine to access the network, handle errors, and expose any errors that might occur in a way that's meaningful for the users of your app.

Not surprisingly, we ended up with code that looked a bit more complicated than what we had in the beginning. After all, properly handling errors will take up more lines of code than not handling errors at all (or just ignoring them).

In this chapter, we are going to improve this situation by making use of one of Combine's most powerful tools: operators. You've already used operators in the previous chapters, and in this chapter, we're going to take a closer look at what they are, how they work, and—most importantly—how refactoring our code into a custom Combine operator will make it easier to reason about and more reusable at the same time.

What Is a Combine Operator?

Combine defines three main concepts to implement the idea of reactive programming:

1.   Publishers

© Peter Friese 2023
P. Friese, *Asynchronous Programming with SwiftUI and Combine*,
https://doi.org/10.1007/978-1-4842-8572-5_11

2. Subscribers

3. Operators

Publishers deliver values over time, and **subscribers** act on these values as they receive them. **Operators** sit in the middle between publishers and subscribers and can be used to manipulate the stream of values.

There are a few reasons why we need operators:

- Publishers don't always produce events in the format that is required by the subscriber. For example, a publisher might emit the result of a HTTP network request, but our subscriber needs a custom data structure. In this situation, we can use an operator like map or decode to turn the output of the publisher into the data structure the subscriber expects.

- Publishers might produce more events than the subscriber is interested in. For example, when typing a search term, we might not be interested in every single keystroke but only the final search term. In this situation, we can use operators like debounce or throttle to reduce the number of events our subscriber has to handle.

Operators help us to take the output produced by a publisher and turn it into something that the subscriber can consume. We've already used a number of built-in operators in previous chapters, for example:

- map (and its exceptional friend, tryMap) to transform elements

- debounce to publish elements only after a pause between two events

- removeDuplicates to remove duplicate events

- flatMap to transform elements into a new publisher

Implementing Custom Operators

Usually, when creating Combine pipelines, we will start with a publisher and then connect a bunch of Combine's built-in operators to process the events emitted by the publisher. At the end of any Combine pipeline is a subscriber that receives the events. As you saw in Chapter 10, pipelines can become complicated quite quickly.

Technically, operators are just functions that create other publishers and subscribers which handle the events they receive from an upstream publisher.

This means we can create our own custom operators by extending `Publisher` with a function that returns a publisher (or subscriber) that operates on the events it receives from the publisher we use it on.

Let's see what this means in practice by implementing a simple operator that allows us to inspect events coming down a Combine pipeline using Swift's `dump()` function. This function prints the contents of a variable to the console, showing the structure of the variable as a nested tree—similar to the debug inspector in Xcode.

You might be aware of Combine's `print()` operator, which works very similarly. However, it doesn't provide as much detail and—more importantly—doesn't show the result as a nested structure.

To add an operator, we first need to add an extension to the `Publisher` type. As we don't want to manipulate the events this operator receives, we can use the upstream publisher's types as the result types as well and return `AnypPublisher<Self.Output, Self.Failure>` as the result type:

```
extension Publisher {
  func dump() -> AnyPublisher<Self.Output, Self.Failure> {
  }
}
```

Inside the function, we can then use the handleEvents operator to examine any events this pipeline processes. handleEvents has a bunch of optional closures that get called when the publisher receives new subscriptions, new output values, a cancellation event, when it is finished, or when the subscriber requests more elements. As we are only interested in new Output values, we can ignore most of the closures and just implement the receiveOutput closure.

Whenever we receive a value, we will use Swift's dump() function to print the contents of the value to the console:

```
extension Publisher {
  func dump() -> AnyPublisher<Self.Output, Self.Failure> {
    handleEvents(receiveOutput:  { value in
      Swift.dump(value)
    })
    .eraseToAnyPublisher()
  }
}
```

We can use this operator like any of Combine's built-in operators. In the following example, we attach our new operator to a simple publisher that emits the current date:

```
Just(Date())
  .dump()

// prints:

∇ 2022-03-02 09:38:49 +0000
  - timeIntervalSinceReferenceDate: 667906729.659255
```

Implementing a Retry Operator with a Delay

Now that we've got a basic understanding of how to implement a simple operator, let's see if we can refactor the code from the previous episode. Here is the relevant part:

```
return dataTaskPublisher
  .tryCatch { error -> AnyPublisher<(data: Data, response:
  URLResponse), Error> in
    if case APIError.serverError = error {
      return Just(Void())
        .delay(for: 3, scheduler: DispatchQueue.global())
        .flatMap { _ in
          return dataTaskPublisher
        }
        .print("before retry")
        .retry(10)
        .eraseToAnyPublisher()
  }
    throw error
  }
  .map(\.data)
```

Let's begin by constructing an overloaded extension for the retry operator on Publisher:

```
extension Publisher {
  func retry<T, E>(_ retries: Int, withDelay delay: Int)
    -> Publishers.TryCatch<Self, AnyPublisher<T, E>>
      where T == Self.Output, E == Self.Failure
  {
  }
}
```

This defines two input parameters, `retries` and `withDelay`, which we can use to specify how many times the upstream publisher should be retried and how much time (in seconds) should be left between each retry.

Since we are going to use the `tryCatch` operator inside our new operator, we need to use its publisher type, `Publishers.TryCatch`, as the return type.

With this in place, we can now implement the body of the operator by pasting the existing implementation:

```
extension Publisher {
  func retry<T, E>(_ retries: Int, withDelay delay: Int)
    -> Publishers.TryCatch<Self, AnyPublisher<T, E>>
      where T == Self.Output, E == Self.Failure
  {
    return self.tryCatch { error -> AnyPublisher<T, E> in
      return Just(Void())
        .delay(for: .init(integerLiteral: delay),
               scheduler: DispatchQueue.global())
        .flatMap { _ in
          return self
        }
        .retry(retries)
        .eraseToAnyPublisher()
    }
  }
}
```

You might have noticed that we removed the error check. This is because `APIError` is an error type that is specific to our application. As we are interested in making this an implementation that can be used in other apps as well, let's see how we can make this more flexible.

Conditionally Retrying

To make this code reusable in other contexts, let's add a parameter for a trailing closure that the caller can use to control whether the operator should retry or not.

```
func retry<T, E>(_ retries: Int, withDelay delay: Int,
condition: ((E) -> Bool)? = nil) -> Publishers.TryCatch<Self,
AnyPublisher<T, E>> where T == Self.Output, E == Self.Failure {
  return self.tryCatch { error -> AnyPublisher<T, E> in
    if condition?(error) == true {
      return Just(Void())
        .delay(for: .init(integerLiteral: delay),
               scheduler: DispatchQueue.global())
        .flatMap { _ in
          return self
        }
        .retry(retries)
        .eraseToAnyPublisher()
    }
    else {
      throw error
    }
  }
}
```

If the caller doesn't provide the closure, the operator will retry using the parameters retries and delay.

With this in place, we can simplify the original call:

```
// ...
return dataTaskPublisher
  .retry(10, withDelay: 3) { error in
```

```
    if case APIError.serverError = error {
      return true
    }
      return false
    }
  .map(\.data)
  // ...
```

Implementing a Retry Operator for Exponential Backoff

Now, let's take this one step further and implement a version of the `retry` operator with exponential backoff.

> *Exponential backoff is commonly utilised as part of rate limiting[1] mechanisms in computer systems such as web services[2], to help enforce fair distribution of access to resources and prevent network congestion[3]. (Wikipedia[4])*

To increment the delay between two requests, we introduce a local variable that holds the current interval and double it after each request. To make this possible, we need to wrap the inner pipeline that kicks off the original pipeline in a pipeline that increments the backoff variable:

```
func retry<T, E>(_ retries: Int,
             withBackoff initialBackoff: Int,
             condition: ((E) -> Bool)? = nil)
    -> Publishers.TryCatch<Self, AnyPublisher<T, E>>
    where T == Self.Output, E == Self.Failure
{
```

---

[1]https://en.wikipedia.org/wiki/Ratelimiting
[2]https://en.wikipedia.org/wiki/Web_service
[3]https://en.wikipedia.org/wiki/Networkcongestion
[4]https://en.wikipedia.org/wiki/Exponential_backoff

```
return self.tryCatch { error -> AnyPublisher<T, E> in
  if condition?(error) ?? true {
    var backOff = initialBackoff
    return Just(Void())
      .flatMap { _ -> AnyPublisher<T, E> in
        let result = Just(Void())
          .delay(for: .init(integerLiteral: backOff),
                 scheduler: DispatchQueue.global())
          .flatMap { _ in
            return self
          }
        backOff = backOff * 2
        return result.eraseToAnyPublisher()
      }
      .retry(retries - 1)
      .eraseToAnyPublisher()
  }
  else {
    throw error
  }
}
}
```

To use exponential backoff only for certain kinds of errors, we can implement the closure to inspect the error, just like before. Here is a code snippet that shows how to use incremental backoff with an initial interval of 3 seconds for any APIError.serverError:

```
return dataTaskPublisher
  .retry(2, withBackoff: 3) { error in
    if case APIError.serverError(_, _, _) = error {
      return true
    }
```

```
  else {
    return false
  }
}
// ...
```

To use exponential backoff regardless of the error, this becomes even more compact:

```
return dataTaskPublisher
  .retry(2, withIncrementalBackoff: 3)
  // ...
```

Summary

Combine is a very powerful framework that allows us to put together very efficient data and event processing pipelines for our apps.

In this chapter, you learned how to refactor your existing Combine pipelines into reusable Combine operators, making your code more readable.

CHAPTER 12

Wrapping Existing APIs in Combine

Apple provides Combine publishers for many of their APIs, making it easy for us to integrate those APIs in our Combine pipelines. However, there are many APIs that don't support Combine even though they produce events over time. Thankfully, Apple gives us the tools we need to wrap APIs in Combine publishers and make them accessible to Combine pipelines.

In this chapter, I'm going to walk you through the process of wrapping existing APIs using Combine.

A Case Study

We're going to use a Firebase API as a case study. Firebase is a backend as a service (BaaS) that provides a whole range of services that make developing apps easier. For example, it provides an authentication service (Firebase Authentication), a document-based NoSQL database (Cloud Firestore), a service for storing large files in the cloud (Cloud Storage), a crash reporting service (Crashlytics), and much more.[1]

---

[1] https://firebase.google.com/

© Peter Friese 2023
P. Friese, *Asynchronous Programming with SwiftUI and Combine*,
https://doi.org/10.1007/978-1-4842-8572-5_12

Most of Firebase's APIs are asynchronous, meaning that whenever you make a call, it will get sent to one of the Firebase backend services, where it will be processed. Once the result is ready, it will be returned to the client SDK, and your code will be called back. There are multiple ways to asynchronously call Firebase services: completion handlers, Combine, and async/await. I've written about this before in *Calling asynchronous Firebase APIs from Swift - Callbacks, Combine, and async/await*[2]—and also published a video about this topic[3] as well.

For this chapter, we will take two methods from Cloud Firestore and turn them into Combine publishers. Cloud Firestore is a horizontally scaling document-based NoSQL database in the cloud. Similar to CloudKit,[4] but as a truly cross-platform solution: you can access Cloud Firestore from iOS, Android, the Web, and via a REST API.[5] Data stored in Firestore is organized in documents—a document is like a Swift struct: it can have any number of fields of different data types. Documents are organized in collections, and documents can contain subcollections, allowing you to build nested data structures.

The Firestore SDK provides methods to access data in single documents and collections. For example, here is a code snippet that shows how to fetch data from a collection of Firestore documents and map them to an array of Swift structs using Swift's Codable API:

```
db.collection("books").getDocuments { querySnapshot, error in
  guard let documents = querySnapshot?.documents else {
    return
  }
```

---

[2] https://peterfriese.dev/posts/firebase-async-calls-swift/
[3] https://youtu.be/j5htIyxmmzA
[4] https://developer.apple.com/icloud/cloudkit/
[5] https://firebase.google.com/docs/firestore/use-rest-api

```
let books = documents.compactMap { [weak self]
queryDocumentSnapshot in
  let result = Result {
    try queryDocumentSnapshot.data(as: Book.self)
  }
  switch result {
    case .success(let book):
      return book
    case .failure(let error):
      return nil
  }
}
print(books.count)
}
```

In addition to being able to fetch data on demand, Firestore also supports real-time live sync. This means your app will receive updates for any document or collection of document it subscribes to in real time. This is a great feature for any app that allows users to share data with other users (e.g., a chat app), or with the user's other devices (e.g., a to-do list app that you can use on your iPhone, iPad, an Mac and in a web application).

To receive updates, you register a snapshot listener for a specific document or collection of documents. Whenever the document or one of the documents in the collection is updated or deleted, or a document is inserted into the collection, Firestore will trigger the snapshot listener, and you will receive the update in the closure of the listener. The following code snippet shows how to receive updates for any changes on a collection of books:

```
db.collection("books")
  .addSnapshotListener { [weak self] (querySnapshot, error) in
    guard let documents = querySnapshot?.documents else {
      return
    }
```

```
self?.books = documents.compactMap {
queryDocumentSnapshot in
  let result = Result {
    try queryDocumentSnapshot.data(as: Book.self)
  }
  switch result {
    case .success(let book):
      return book
    case .failure(let error):
      return nil
  }
}
}
```

The sample code for this chapter is an application that demonstrates how to use both the closure-based APIs and the Combine-based version that we build in this chapter. Note that the Firebase SDK for Apple platforms includes experimental support for Combine—you can use this in your own apps by importing the respective modules. This chapter is intended to explain how the Firebase team implemented this Combine support.

In order to run the sample application, follow these steps:

1. Create a new Firebase projects via the Firebase console.[6]

2. Add your Xcode project to the Firebase project.

3. Download the GoogleService-Info.plist file and add it to your project.

4. Install the local Firebase Emulator Suite.[7]

5. Run the Firebase Emulator Suite by executing start.sh in the root of the sample project.

---

[6]https://console.firebase.google.com
[7]https://firebase.google.com/docs/emulator-suite/install_and_configure

6.   Launch the iOS app on a Simulator (so it can attach to the Emulator).

The `start.sh` script will make sure to populate the Firebase Emulator with some seed data so you can fetch data from Firestore.

Once the application has started, go into one of the menu items that use a snapshot listener for live syncing. Then, open the Emulator console at `http://localhost:4000/firestore` and make changes to the Firestore documents. Once you commit a change in the Emulator UI, observe how the data immediately updates in the app's UI.

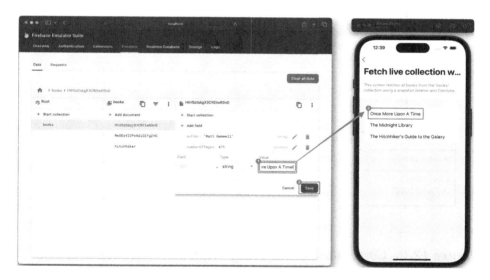

Figure 12-1. *Making changes in the Firebase Emulator UI will reflect in the app's UI as soon as you you click on Save*

Using Combine to Access Firestore

Let's now look at how we can make the data we receive from Firestore accessible from Combine. A common reason for doing this is to transform the data and combine it with events we receive from other Combine publishers, for example, the filter criteria on a search/filter dialog.

Using View Models and Published Properties

An easy and rather common way to feed data into a Combine pipeline is to create a published property in a view model. You might have seen this in many of the code samples on my blog[8] or in the Firebase Quick Starts.[9]

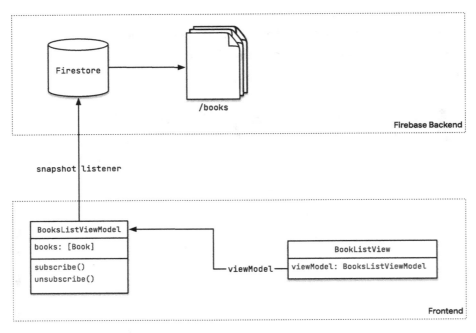

Figure 12-2. *Conceptual overview of the app's architecture*

In code, this looks as follows:

```
private class BookListViewModel: ObservableObject {
  @Published var books = [Book]()
  @Published var errorMessage: String?
```

---

[8] https://peterfriese.dev/
[9] https://github.com/firebase/quickstart-ios/tree/master/firestore

```swift
private var db = Firestore.firestore()
private var listenerRegistration: ListenerRegistration?

public func unsubscribe() {
  if listenerRegistration != nil {
    listenerRegistration?.remove()
    listenerRegistration = nil
  }
}

func subscribe() {
  if listenerRegistration == nil {
    listenerRegistration = db.collection("books")
      .addSnapshotListener { [weak self] (querySnapshot,
      error) in
        guard let documents = querySnapshot?.documents else {
          self?.errorMessage =
            "No documents in 'books' collection"
          return
        }

        self?.books = documents.compactMap {
        queryDocumentSnapshot in
          let result = Result {
            try queryDocumentSnapshot.data(as: Book.self)
          }
          switch result {
          case .success(let book):
            // Value successfully initialized from
            // DocumentSnapshot
            self?.errorMessage = nil
            return book
```

```
          case .failure(let error):
            // Value could not be initialized from
            // DocumentSnapshot
            self?.errorMessage =
              "\(error.localizedDescription)"
            return nil
          }
        }
      }
    }
  }
}
```

By conforming BookListViewModel to ObservableObject and marking the books property with the @Published property wrapper, we can connect a SwiftUI List view to the property and make sure the UI updates whenever we receive an update.

```
struct LiveBooksListViewWithClosures: View {
  @StateObject private var viewModel = BookListViewModel()

  var body: some View {
    List(viewModel.books) { book in
      Text(book.title)
    }
    .onAppear {
      viewModel.subscribe()
    }
    .onDisappear {
      viewModel.unsubscribe()
    }
  }
}
```

With just a few lines of code, we've build a UI that will automatically refresh whenever someone makes a change to the data—no matter if this change happens on the frontend or on the backend.

But we can do more! For example, let's say we wanted to display the number of books, making sure this number is updated on the UI as people add new books to the books collection in Cloud Firestore.

Remember that a published property exposes a Combine publisher. We can access this publisher via the property's *projected value*—in this case, $books. This allows us to create a Combine pipeline to determine the number of books. Using the assign(to:) subscriber, we can then assign the result to another publisher which we can connect to the UI to show an always-up-to-date number. A good place to set up Combine pipelines like this is in the view model's initializer.

```
private class BookListViewModel: ObservableObject {
  @Published var books = [Book]()
  @Published var numberOfBooks = 0

  ...

  init() {
    $books.map { books in
      books.count
    }
    .assign(to: &$numberOfBooks)
  }
  ...
}
```

Using Combine to Wrap APIs

This is the most commonly used approach for integrating data sources in SwiftUI apps that make use of Combine, and it works really well. However, it is rather verbose and requires a lot of boilerplate.

Instead of explicitly setting up a snapshot listener, let's see if we can wrap the code in a Combine publisher so we can call it in a more declarative way.

Looking at the code we've discussed so far, we can see we've got two different kinds of calls:

- Fetching a single document, all documents of a collection, or the results of a query are so-called single-shot calls: we make the call to fetch a document (or all documents in a collection/query) and then use the callback handler to receive the result of the call.

- Listening to updates on a single document, a collection, or a query is different: instead of receiving the result of the call just once, we will receive a new snapshot every time there has been an update. We're receiving a stream of updates. This sounds very similar to Combine's definition:

The Combine framework provides a declarative Swift API for processing values over time.[10]

Let's see if we can implement our own publishers to handle these streams of events!

However, Apple actively discourages developers from implementing their own publishers using Combine's low-level primitives (such as Publisher, Subscription, and Subscriber).

---

[10] https://developer.apple.com/documentation/combine

Creating Your Own Publishers

Rather than implementing the Publisher[11] protocol yourself, you can create your own publisher by using one of several types provided by the Combine framework:

- Use a concrete subclass of Subject,[12] such as PassthroughSubject,[13] to publish values on demand by calling its send(_:)[14] method.

- Use a CurrentValueSubject[15] to publish whenever you update the subject's underlying value.

- Add the @Published annotation to a property of one of your own types. In doing so, the property gains a publisher that emits an event whenever the property's value changes. See the Published[16] type for an example of this approach.

So instead of building publishers from scratch, let's follow Apple's advice and create our custom publishers using Combine's higher-level building blocks like PassthroughSubject and Future.

---

[11] https://developer.apple.com/documentation/combine/published

[12] https://developer.apple.com/documentation/combine/subject

[13] https://developer.apple.com/documentation/combine/passthroughsubject

[14] https://bit.ly/3BMDSC6

[15] https://bit.ly/3vDdIOq

[16] https://developer.apple.com/documentation/combine/published

Using `PassthroughSubject` to Wrap Snapshot Listeners

To make integrating with existing code easier, Combine includes the `Subject` protocol. `Subjects` are a special kind of publisher that allow outside callers to inject events into a Combine pipeline. The `Subject` protocol defines a `send(_:)` method that can be used to send specific values to the pipeline.

There are two types of built-in `Subjects` in Combine: `CurrentValueSubject` and `PassthroughSubject`. The main difference between them is that `CurrentValueSubject` remembers the most recently published element, whereas `PassthroughSubject` doesn't keep track of the values it passes on.

`Subjects` are particularly useful for adapting existing imperative code to Combine. In our case, we don't need to keep track of the most recently sent event, so we can use `PassthroughSubject` to create custom publishers for Firebase APIs that send a continuous stream of events, such as a Firestore snapshot listener.

Let's take a look at the steps required to implement a custom Combine publisher for a snapshot listener on a Firestore collection or a Firestore query.

We will implement this as an extension on `Query`. Since `CollectionReference` extends the `Query` interface, the publisher will work for Firestore collections and queries alike:

```
public extension Query {
  func snapshotPublisher(includeMetadataChanges: Bool = false)
    -> AnyPublisher<QuerySnapshot, Error>
  {
    ...
    addSnapshotListener(includeMetadataChanges:
    includeMetadataChanges) { snapshot, error in
```

```
    ...
  }
  ...
 }
}
```

This code fragment adds a method to the Query interface, which returns an AnyPublisher that is generic over a QuerySnapshot and an Error type. Inside the method, we call the original addSnapshotListener method, which takes a closure that we need to implement in order to handle the result of the call. As discussed earlier, the closure will be called whenever the collection or query we're observing is changed (e.g., by adding, changing, or deleting a document). The snapshot parameter of the closure will contain a snapshot of all the documents in the collection or the query. If an error occurs, this will be communicated via the error parameter.

To inject the result of the closure into a Combine pipeline, we need to set up a PassthroughSubject and return it to the caller of snapshotPublisher:

```
public extension Query {
  func snapshotPublisher(includeMetadataChanges: Bool = false)
    -> AnyPublisher<QuerySnapshot, Error>
  {
    let subject = PassthroughSubject<QuerySnapshot, Error>()
    addSnapshotListener(includeMetadataChanges:
    includeMetadataChanges) { snapshot, error in

      ...
    }
    return subject.eraseToAnyPublisher()
  }
}
```

By erasing the type of the subject, we make sure the return type of the snapshotPublisher method stays clean.

Finally, inside the closure, we can use the PassthroughSubject to send events to our subscribers. There are two cases we need to cover: when receiving a snapshot, we can send this to the subject. Should there be an error, we'll have to send a failure to the subject to signal to Combine that the pipeline should be cancelled.

```
public extension Query {
  func snapshotPublisher(includeMetadataChanges: Bool = false)
    -> AnyPublisher<QuerySnapshot, Error>
  {
    let subject = PassthroughSubject<QuerySnapshot, Error>()
    addSnapshotListener(includeMetadataChanges:
    includeMetadataChanges) { snapshot, error in
      if let error = error {
        subject.send(completion: .failure(error))
      } else if let snapshot = snapshot {
        subject.send(snapshot)
      }
    }
    return subject.eraseToAnyPublisher()
  }
}
```

This is looking good so far, but there is one last detail we need to take care of. When calling addSnapshotListener, we receive a handle that we can later use to remove the snapshot listener. You should remove any Firestore snapshot listeners when you're no longer interested in listening to a query or collection.

But how can we store and manage the snapshot listener handle inside the snapshotPublisher method? It turns out, we can make use of Combine's handleEvents operator. This operator allows us to listen to the life-cycle events of a Combine pipeline, for example, when the pipeline is cancelled. So we can store the snapshot listener handle in a local variable and later use it to remove the snapshot listener once the pipeline is cancelled.

```
public extension Query {
  func snapshotPublisher(includeMetadataChanges: Bool = false)
    -> AnyPublisher<QuerySnapshot, Error>
  {
    let subject = PassthroughSubject<QuerySnapshot, Error>()
    let listenerHandle =
      addSnapshotListener(includeMetadataChanges:
      includeMetadataChanges) { snapshot, error in
        if let error = error {
          subject.send(completion: .failure(error))
        } else if let snapshot = snapshot {
          subject.send(snapshot)
        }
      }
    return
      subject
        .handleEvents(receiveCancel: listenerHandle.remove)
        .eraseToAnyPublisher()
  }
}
```

And this is how you can adapt an existing API to Combine!

Let's update the previous code sample to make use of the new publisher:

```
private class BookListViewModel: ObservableObject {
  @Published var books = [Book]()
  @Published var errorMessage: String?

  private var db = Firestore.firestore()
  private var cancellable: AnyCancellable?
```

331

```
func subscribe() {
  cancellable = db.collection("books").snapshotPublisher()
    .tryMap { querySnapshot in
      try querySnapshot.documents.compactMap {
      documentSnapshot in
        try documentSnapshot.data(as: Book.self)
      }
    }
    .replaceError(with: [Book]())
    .handleEvents(receiveCancel: {
      print("Cancelled")
    })
    .assign(to: \.books, on: self)
}

func unsubscribe() {
  cancellable?.cancel()
}
}
```

Using Future to Implement One-Time Fetching from Firestore

Effortless real-time sync is one of the key features of Firestore, but it's not always necessary or appropriate to get real-time updates. Often, it is sufficient to fetch data on demand. Firestore supports fetching data (either a single document, a collection, or a query) once, and you saw an example for this in the beginning of this chapter.

How can this be implemented in Combine? We essentially want to make a request, wait until it is finished, and then send the result into a Combine pipeline.

This is exactly what Futures are there for. A Future is a Publisher that "eventually produces a single value and then finishes or fails."[17]

Let's use a Future to create a single-shot publisher to get a single document from Firestore. This time, we will create an extension on DocumentReference:

```
extension DocumentReference {
  func getDocument(source: FirestoreSource = .default)
    -> Future<DocumentSnapshot, Error>
  {
    ...
      self.getDocument(source: source) { snapshot, error in
        ...
      }
    ...
  }
}
```

Just like every other publisher, Futures are generic over a value and an error type. In our case, the value type is a DocumentSnapshot. You might be wondering why we return a Future instead of an AnyPublisher. Futures have some special properties that set them apart from other publishers. For example, Futures will fire immediately. A normal publisher will only fire if there is a subscriber. To make this transparent to the caller, we explicitly return a Future instead of type erasing to AnyPublisher.

Let's now wrap the call to the closure-based getDocument method inside a Future:

```
extension DocumentReference {
  func getDocument(source: FirestoreSource = .default)
    -> Future<DocumentSnapshot, Error>
```

---

[17] https://developer.apple.com/documentation/combine/future

```
{
  Future { promise in
    self.getDocument(source: source) { snapshot, error in
      ...
    }
  }
}
}
```

The code in the closure will be called when Firestore returns either an error or a document snapshot. The promise parameter of the Future's closure can be used to communicate with the caller:

```
extension DocumentReference {
  func getDocument(source: FirestoreSource = .default)
    -> Future<DocumentSnapshot, Error>
  {
    Future { promise in
      self.getDocument(source: source) { snapshot, error in
        if let error = error {
          promise(.failure(error))
        } else if let snapshot = snapshot {
          promise(.success(snapshot))
        }
      }
    }
  }
}
```

We check to see if we received a snapshot or an error and call the promise accordingly. This might look familiar, as it resembles the code we wrote for snapshotPublisher earlier, but I'd like to call out that the promise expects a Result type, so .failure and .success are cases on the Result type.

And with that, we've successfully adapted the closure-based Firestore API for fetching a single document for Combine by wrapping it in a Future.

Here is how you can call it to fetch a document and map it to a custom Swift struct using our new single-shot Combine publisher:

```
private class BookListViewModel: ObservableObject {
  @Published var book = Book.empty

  private var db = Firestore.firestore()

  func fetchBook() {
    db.collection("books").document("hitchhiker").getDocument()
      .tryMap { documentSnapshot in
        try documentSnapshot.data(as: Book.self)
      }
      .replaceError(with: Book.empty)
      .assign(to: &$book)
  }
}
```

Summary

Apple has done a great job providing Combine publishers for many of their own APIs, but for third-party APIs, we might need to do this work ourselves.

In this chapter, we discussed a couple of approaches we can take to adapt existing imperative code to Combine:

- You saw how you can implement an ObservableObject with a @Published property to expose data via a publisher. This not only allows us to connect SwiftUI views to the published property, but it also enables us to connect a Combine pipeline to the published property.

- It's also possible to create custom publishers using Combine's low-level primitives (such as `Publisher`, `Subscription`, and `Subscriber`). However, Apple explicitly discourages developers from doing so, as this approach requires us to manage back pressure ourselves.

- Instead, Apple recommends using convenience publishers like `PassthroughSubject` and `Future` to implement custom publishers, and we had an in-depth look at how to wrap an existing, closure-based API using this approach.

Which approach you use depends on your use case—using a view model might be the most practical and efficient way in most situations. However, if you're an SDK provider, you should definitely consider implementing Combine publishers for your API. This is what we did at Firebase: we implemented Combine publishers for most of the asynchronous Firebase APIs using `PassthroughSubject` and `Future`.

CHAPTER 13

Combine Schedulers and SwiftUI

By default, any code that you run in response to a UI event in SwiftUI will run on the main thread. Since a lot of our code deals with updating other UI elements in response to some user interaction, this is fine in most cases. For example, you might want to validate the user's input to make sure they filled out all required fields of a multistep form. This is a memory-bound process that runs fast enough to be executed on the main thread without causing any issues.

However, once you want to perform more complex computations or need to access local storage, the network, or any API that has a higher latency than accessing the local memory, you risk blocking the UI if you execute this code on the main thread.

Blocking the UI leads to all sorts of issues: the UI of your application becomes unresponsive, animations will start to stutter, and eventually your users will become unhappy and start leaving negative reviews on the App Store or start complaining about it on Twitter.

This is why you should offload any long-running pieces of code to a background thread. While your code runs in the background, the main thread is free for handling UI events. The user can continue using the app until the background process eventually finishes. Some of these background processes might have a result that you might want to display on the UI. However, since UI updates need to happen on the main thread,

© Peter Friese 2023
P. Friese, *Asynchronous Programming with SwiftUI and Combine*,
https://doi.org/10.1007/978-1-4842-8572-5_13

you will need to switch back to the main thread before you can update the UI with the results you received on the background thread.

Combine provides an elegant and declarative mechanism for controlling where the individual parts of a pipeline run. This mechanism is built on the concept of schedulers, which help us reason about where our code should be executed without having to directly deal with the intricacies of threads.

In this chapter, you will learn how to use this mechanism effectively to help you build apps that make better use of the system's resources so that your apps' UI stays responsive.

What Is a Scheduler

Combine uses Scheduler as an abstraction that allows us to specify *when* and *where* our code is run, so we don't have to work directly with threads. According to Apple's documentation, Scheduler, is *a protocol that defines when and how to execute a closure*[1].

The Scheduler protocol itself defines a number of methods that allow callers to run code immediately, or at a future date and time:

```
public protocol Scheduler {

  /// Describes an instant in time for this scheduler.
  associatedtype SchedulerTimeType : Strideable where
    Self.SchedulerTimeType.Stride :
      SchedulerTimeIntervalConvertible

  /// A type that defines options accepted by the scheduler.
  ///
  /// This type is freely definable by each `Scheduler`.
  /// Typically, operations that take a `Scheduler` parameter
  /// will also take `SchedulerOptions`.
```

---

[1] https://developer.apple.com/documentation/combine/scheduler

```
associatedtype SchedulerOptions

/// This scheduler's definition of the current
/// moment in time.
var now: Self.SchedulerTimeType { get }

/// The minimum tolerance allowed by the scheduler.
var minimumTolerance: Self.SchedulerTimeType.Stride { get }

/// Performs the action at the next possible opportunity.
func schedule(options: Self.SchedulerOptions?,
              _ action: @escaping () -> Void)

/// Performs the action at some time after the specified date.
func schedule(after date: Self.SchedulerTimeType,
              tolerance: Self.SchedulerTimeType.Stride,
              options: Self.SchedulerOptions?,
              _ action: @escaping () -> Void)

/// Performs the action at some time after the specified
/// date, at the specified frequency, optionally taking into
/// account tolerance if possible.
func schedule(after date: Self.SchedulerTimeType,
              interval: Self.SchedulerTimeType.Stride,
              tolerance: Self.SchedulerTimeType.Stride,
              options: Self.SchedulerOptions?,
              _ action: @escaping () -> Void) -> Cancellable
}
```

Different schedulers implement this time-keeping aspect differently, using the associated type SchedulerTimeType. This associated type needs to conform to SchedulerTimeIntervalConvertible, which is a means to express relative time.

Let's look at some of the schedulers that you will run into when using Combine and discuss when to use them.

Types of Schedulers

Here are the schedulers that are most relevant when working with SwiftUI:

- `ImmediateScheduler` is the default scheduler which will be used if you don't specify any other scheduler. It will execute code immediately on the same thread that triggered the pipeline. We will discuss this scheduler in more detail in the next section.

- `RunLoop` is a scheduler which you will see being used quite often. It performs work on a specific run loop.

- `DispatchQueue` allows us to execute code on specific dispatch queues. The most commonly used ones are the main dispatch queue and the background dispatch queues (you can specify different quality of service classes, ranging from `background` to `userInteractive`), but you can create your own dispatch queues as well, and configure them according to your needs.

So which `Scheduler` should you be using?

The most commonly used schedulers that are being used in the context of SwiftUI are `RunLoop` and `DispatchQueue`. Although they seem to be very similar (see Philippe Hausler's answer on the Swift forums[2]), there is one difference that is relevant for any Combine pipeline that needs to schedule code that runs on the main thread for accessing the UI.

As explained in this StackOverflow answer[3], a Combine pipeline will not deliver events while the user is dragging or touching the UI when using `RunLoop`. When using `DispatchQueue` as the scheduler, however, the pipeline will deliver events.

---

[2] https://forums.swift.org/t/runloop-main-or-dispatchqueue-main-when-using-combine-scheduler/26635/2

[3] https://stackoverflow.com/a/61107764/281221

So if you want to make sure your Combine pipelines continue to deliver events even if the user is interacting with the UI of your app (such as scrolling a list, tapping on buttons, or dragging elements across the screen), you should use `DispatchQueue`.

Default Behavior

If you don't explicitly tell Combine how to schedule your code, it will default to running your code on the same thread as the event that triggered the pipeline. When using Combine in SwiftUI, most of your pipelines will subscribe to a published property on one of your view models. SwiftUI runs on the main thread, so any events that originate on the UI will be sent from the main thread.

In the following example, we change the value of a published property in response to a button click. The closure that handles the button click runs on the main thread, so the Combine pipeline in the view model will run on the main thread as well.

```
class ViewModel: ObservableObject {
  @Published var demo = false

  private var cancellables = Set<AnyCancellable>()

  init() {
    $demo
      .sink { value in
        print("Main thread: \(Thread.isMainThread)")
      }
      .store(in: &cancellables)
  }
}
```

```
struct DemoView: View {
  @StateObject var viewModel = ViewModel()

  var body: some View {
    Button("Toggle from main thread") {
      viewModel.demo.toggle()
    }
    .buttonStyle(.action)
  }
}
```

When you run this code[4] and click the button, you will see the following output, which confirms that SwiftUI sends events on the main thread:

```
Main thread: true
```

This scheduling behavior is caused by Combine's default scheduler, ImmediateScheduler. It will execute code immediately on the current thread. So if you send an event from a background thread, the pipeline will run on that specific background thread as well. Let's make a small change to our example and wrap the code that changes the published property in a call to DispatchQueue.global().async { }. As a result, the Combine pipeline will run on the same background thread.

```
class ViewModel: ObservableObject {
  @Published var demo = false

  private var cancellables = Set<AnyCancellable>()

  init() {
```

---

[4] The code (in a slightly enhanced form) is available in UpdatePublishedPropertyView.swift in the source code sample accompanying this chapter in the source code repo for this book.

```
    $demo
      .sink { value in
        print("Main thread: \(Thread.isMainThread)")
      }
      .store(in: &cancellables)
  }
}

struct DemoView: View {
  @StateObject var viewModel = ViewModel()

  var body: some View {
    Button("Toggle from main thread") {
      DispatchQueue.global().async {
        viewModel.demo.toggle()
      }
    }
    .buttonStyle(.action)
  }
}
```

Running this code and clicking the button result in the following output:

```
2022-05-14 12:19:32.093826+0200
SwiftUICombineSchedulers[41912:2513626] [SwiftUI] Publishing
changes from background threads is not allowed; make sure
to publish values from the main thread (via operators like
receive(on:)) on model updates.
Main thread: false
```

This default behavior works well for most cases. For example, if you want to validate the user's input, this can usually run on the main thread, as you'll be combining several pieces of UI state into the `isValid` state of the input form.

However, as soon as you need to access the network (or any other asynchronous data source), things become more complicated, and you will want to run parts of the pipeline on a background thread before coming back to the main thread to update the UI.

One approach for switching threads is to explicitly use `DispatchQueue` and its methods to switch between the main queue (`DispatchQueue.main`) and one of the global background queues (`DispatchQueue.global()`) or a queue you create and manage yourself.

Switching Schedulers

Using explicit calls to switch to the most appropriate `DispatchQueue` certainly works, but this approach will lead to rather verbose code.

Wouldn't it be much nicer if there was a declarative way to make sure the individual parts of your pipelines run on the appropriate thread?

Combine provides a number of operators that allows us to switch between threads by declaring which scheduler to use.

The most important one is `receive(on:)`, which you will find yourself using a lot, especially when accessing the network: it allows us to tell Combine which scheduler to use when receiving events in our subscribers, such as `sink` or `assign`.

Another key operator for scheduling is `subscribe(on:)`—we can use it to specify which scheduler Combine should use when subscribing to an upstream publisher.

Other operators that affect which schedulers are used in our pipelines include `debounce`, `throttle`, and `delay`.

In the following sections, we'll explore how those operators affect the progression of a Combine pipeline that receives an event from a SwiftUI event handler. We'll use the following publisher to simulate a piece of code that performs a long-running computation[5]:

```
func performWork() -> AnyPublisher<Bool, Never> {
  print("[performWork:start] isMainThread: \(Thread.
  isMainThread)")
  return Deferred {
    Future { promise in
      print("[performWork:Future:start] isMainThread:
      \(Thread.isMainThread)")
      sleep(5)
      print("[performWork:Future:finished] isMainThread:
      \(Thread.isMainThread)")
      promise(.success(true))
    }
  }
  .eraseToAnyPublisher()
}
```

Since Futures will run their closure immediately without waiting for a subscriber to be attached, we need to wrap it inside a Deferred publisher. Doing so ensures the code in the closure will only be executed once we connect a subscriber, which allows us to influence which scheduler this publisher will use.

---

[5] See SchedulerDemoViewModel.swift in the sample project for this chapter.

Controlling Upstream Publishers Using subscribe(on:)

By using the subscribe(on:) operator, you can control on which dispatch queue the upstream publisher runs on.

This is useful if you want to make sure the publisher runs on a background thread. Instead of wrapping your code in a call to DispatchQueue.global().async { }, you can add a call to receive(on:). This declarative approach will make your code easier to read and reason about.

The subscribe(on:) operator specifies the scheduler that is used to perform the subscribe, cancel, and request operations of the upstream publisher.

In the following code snippet,[6] we make sure the publisher in performWork() runs on a background thread by adding a call to subscribe(on: DispatchQueue.global(qos: .background) to the pipeline:

```
func start() {
  print("[start:at beginning] isMainThread: \(Thread.
  isMainThread)")

  self.performWork()
    .handleEvents(receiveSubscription: { sub in
      print("[receiveSubscription] isMainThread: \(Thread.
       isMainThread)")
    }, receiveOutput: { value in
      print("[receiveOutput] isMainThread: \(Thread.
      isMainThread)")
    }, receiveCompletion: { completion in
```

---

[6]See LaunchOnBackgroundViewModels.swift in the sample project for this chapter.

```
    print("[receiveCompletion] isMainThread: \(Thread.
    isMainThread)")
}, receiveCancel: {
    print("[receiveCancel] isMainThread: \(Thread.
    isMainThread)")
}, receiveRequest: { demand in
    print("[receiveRequest] isMainThread: \(Thread.
    isMainThread)")
})
.map { value -> Bool in
    print("[map 1] isMainThread: \(Thread.isMainThread)")
    return value
}
.subscribe(on: DispatchQueue.global(qos: .background))
.map { value -> Int in
    print("[map 2] isMainThread: \(Thread.isMainThread)")
    return self.times + 1
}
.sink { value in
    print("[sink] isMainThread: \(Thread.isMainThread)")
    self.times = value
}
.store(in: &self.cancellables)

print("[start:at end] isMainThread: \(Thread.isMainThread)")
}
```

When calling this code from the main thread (e.g., from inside a Button's action handler), you will see the following output on the console:

```
[start:at beginning] isMainThread: true
[performWork:start] isMainThread: true
[start:at end] isMainThread: true
[performWork:Future:start] isMainThread: false

---

[performWork:Future:finished] isMainThread: false
[receiveSubscription] isMainThread: false
[receiveRequest] isMainThread: false
[receiveOutput] isMainThread: false
[map 1] isMainThread: false
[map 2] isMainThread: false
[sink] isMainThread: false
2022-05-10 09:59:07.514607+0200
SwiftUICombineSchedulers[80945:27603444] [SwiftUI] Publishing
changes from background threads is not allowed; make sure
to publish values from the main thread (via operators like
receive(on:)) on model updates.
[receiveCompletion] isMainThread: false
```

As you can see, the call originates on the main thread, but then execution switches to a background thread. As a result, the publisher will be executed on a background thread, freeing the main thread for other UI-related work.

As mentioned before, calling subscribe(on:) will impact the upstream publisher. However, the rest of the pipeline will *also* be executed using the scheduler you specified, which is the reason why SwiftUI issues a runtime warning saying we shouldn't update the UI from a background thread. Remember, all UI updates should be performed from the main thread.

Controlling Downstream Subscribers Using `receive(on:)`

By using the `receive(on:)` operator, you can influence which scheduler Combine will use for all downstream operators and subscribers.

This is useful for making sure the subscribers of a Combine pipeline run on the main thread—for example, when assigning values to a published property that is connected to a SwiftUI view: making any changes to this property will result in a UI update and thus needs to happen on the main thread.

Let's update the previous code snippet by adding a call to `.receive(on: DispatchQueue.main)` right before the `sink` operator:

```
override func start() {
  print("[start:at beginning] isMainThread: \(Thread.
  isMainThread)")

  self.performWork()
    .handleEvents(receiveSubscription: { sub in
      print("[receiveSubscription] isMainThread: \(Thread.
      isMainThread)")
    }, receiveOutput: { value in
      print("[receiveOutput] isMainThread: \(Thread.
      isMainThread)")
    }, receiveCompletion: { completion in
      print("[receiveCompletion] isMainThread: \(Thread.
      isMainThread)")
    }, receiveCancel: {
      print("[receiveCancel] isMainThread: \(Thread.
      isMainThread)")
    }, receiveRequest: { demand in
```

```
    print("[receiveRequest] isMainThread: \(Thread.
    isMainThread)")
  })
  .map { value -> Bool in
    print("[map 1] isMainThread: \(Thread.isMainThread)")
    return value
  }
  .subscribe(on: DispatchQueue.global(qos: .background))
  .map { value -> Int in
    print("[map 2] isMainThread: \(Thread.isMainThread)")
    return self.times + 1
  }
  .receive(on: DispatchQueue.main)
  .sink { value in
    print("[sink] isMainThread: \(Thread.isMainThread)")
    self.times = value
  }
  .store(in: &self.cancellables)

  print("[start:at end] isMainThread: \(Thread.isMainThread)")
}
```

This will tell Combine to use the main dispatch queue for any downstream operators and subscribers. In our case, this means that the sink subscriber will be executed on the main thread, as you can see in the resulting console output. You will also notice that SwiftUI no longer issues a warning about publishing model changes from the background:

```
[start:at beginning] isMainThread: true
[performWork:start] isMainThread: true
[start:at end] isMainThread: true
[performWork:Future:start] isMainThread: false
```

```
[performWork:Future:finished] isMainThread: false
[receiveSubscription] isMainThread: false
[receiveRequest] isMainThread: false
[receiveOutput] isMainThread: false
[map 1] isMainThread: false
[map 2] isMainThread: false
[receiveCompletion] isMainThread: false
[sink] isMainThread: true
```

Other Operators That Influence Scheduling

Combine has a number of operators that affect the timing with which events are passed on to the downstream pipeline:

- debounce publishes elements only after a specified time interval elapses between events.

- throttle publishes either the most recent or the first element published by the upstream publisher in the specified time interval.

- delay delays delivery of all output to the downstream receiver by a specified amount of time on a particular scheduler.

All of these take a time interval and a scheduler on which the operator delivers its output elements. Let's look at a quick example to understand what this means.

A commonly used timing operator in SwiftUI is debounce—it allows us to specify a time interval that needs to elapse between two events that the operator will send to its downstream subscribers. This is particularly useful for search dialogs that call remote APIs to perform a search based on the user's input. To avoid overloading the remote API with too many requests, we typically install a debounce operator on the published property that holds the search term.

Let's look at the code we used in one of the previous chapters about optimizing your network layer:

```
$input
  .debounce(for: 0.8, scheduler: DispatchQueue.main)
  .handleEvents { subscription in
    self.logEvent(tag: "handleEvents")
  } receiveOutput: { value in
    self.logEvent(tag: "receiveOutput - {\(value)}")
  } receiveCompletion: { completion in
    self.logEvent(tag: "receiveCompletion")
  } receiveCancel: {
    self.logEvent(tag: "receiveCancel")
  } receiveRequest: { demand in
    self.logEvent(tag: "receiveRequest")
  }
  .sink { value in
    self.logEvent(tag: "sink - {\(value)}")
    print("Value: \(value)")
    self.output = value
  }
  .store(in: &cancellables)
```

This piece of code takes the input the user types into a text input field and then uses the debounce operator to reduce the number of events that are passed on to downstream subscribers. This means downstream subscribers will only receive the current value of the input property once the user stops typing for 0.8 seconds.

Using DispatchQueue.global(qos: .background) instead will result in all events arriving on a background thread.

This means providing a scheduler to one of the scheduling operators is equivalent to adding a call to subscribe(on:).

Performing Asynchronous Work

Performing computationally intensive work on the main thread is not a good idea—as we saw in the previous examples, running such code on the main thread might result in a janky UI, or even completely blocking the UI.

Just like accessing asynchronous APIs (like the network, a cloud service like Firebase, or even local APIs that process events asynchronously), you should offload any such code to a background thread by subscribing to the respective publisher (or operator) on a background scheduler. When the background process has finished, and the publisher emits an event, you will eventually want to switch to the main thread to update the UI.

Here is the general pattern to use:

```
publisher
  .subscribe(on: DispatchQueue.global())
  .receive(on: DispatchQueue.main)
  .sink { }
```

You can use the overloaded version of `DispatchQueue.global(qos:)` to indicate the quality of service you would like to use for the code that's run in the background

- background: Background tasks have the lowest priority of all tasks. Assign this class to tasks or dispatch queues that you use to perform work while your app is running in the background.

- utility: Utility tasks have a lower priority than default, user-initiated, and user-interactive tasks, but a higher priority than background tasks. Assign this quality-of-service class to tasks that do not prevent the user from continuing to use your app. For example, you might assign this class to long-running tasks whose progress the user does not follow actively.

- `default`: Default tasks have a lower priority than user-initiated and user-interactive tasks, but a higher priority than utility and background tasks. Assign this class to tasks or queues that your app initiates or uses to perform active work on the user's behalf.

- `userInitiated`: User-initiated tasks are second only to user-interactive tasks in their priority on the system. Assign this class to tasks that provide immediate results for something the user is doing, or that would prevent the user from using your app. For example, you might use this quality-of-service class to load the content of an email that you want to display to the user.

- `userInteractive`: User-interactive tasks have the highest priority on the system. Use this class for tasks or queues that interact with the user or actively update your app's user interface. For example, use this for class for animations or for tracking events interactively.

For a sample showing this in action, see `SchedulerDemoView.swift` in the sample project for this chapter.

Integrating with Other APIs

We usually have full control over the code we write ourselves, so we can apply the technique outlined in the previous section to control the scheduling of a pipeline. When consuming code that someone else wrote, we might not always have that luxury. In this section, we will look at a number of examples in which the upstream publisher controls the scheduling—and how we can influence how the rest of the pipeline is scheduled—which is particularly important when assigning the result of a pipeline to a published property that might be connected to the UI.

URLSession

Let's first take a look at accessing the network. We discussed using URLSession in detail in Chapter 9, and you might remember that we ran into some scheduling issues. Here is a typical code snippet that fetches data from a URL and then assigns it to a published property that is connected to a SwiftUI view:

```
URLSession.shared.dataTaskPublisher(for: url)
  .map(\.data)
  .decode(type: UserNameAvailableMessage.self,
          decoder: JSONDecoder())
  .map(\.isAvailable)
  .replaceError(with: false)
  .assign(to: &$isUsernameAvailable)
```

Running this code will result in a warning:

```
[SwiftUI] Publishing changes from background threads is not
allowed; make sure to publish values from the main thread (via
operators like receive(on:)) on model updates.
```

This warning is caused by the fact that URLSession executes on a background thread, and so the rest of the pipeline, including the assign operator, will be executed on the same thread. This means that the UI will be updated form the background thread, which triggers the warning.

To avoid this, all we need to do is add a receive(on:) operator before the assign operator, to make sure we access the UI from the main thread:

```
URLSession.shared.dataTaskPublisher(for: url)
  .map(\.data)
  .decode(type: UserNameAvailableMessage.self,
          decoder: JSONDecoder())
```

```
.map(\.isAvailable)
.replaceError(with: false)
.receive(on: DispatchQueue.main)
.assign(to: &$isUsernameAvailable)
```

Firebase

Another example for an API that managers scheduling on its own is Firebase, Google's app development platform. Most of Firebase's services (like Cloud Firestore, Cloud Storage, Firebase Authentication, etc.) are asynchronous, and that means any calls to Firebase should be executed on a background thread. Let's look at an example and see how Firestore manages this.

The following code snippet shows how you can fetch a single document from Firestore:

```
let docRef = Firestore.firestore()
  .collection("books")
  .document(documentId)

docRef.getDocument(as: Book.self) { result in
  switch result {
  case .success(let book):
    self.book = book
    self.errorMessage = nil
  case .failure(let error):
    self.errorMessage = "\(error.localizedDescription)"
  }
}
```

Firestore creates a serial dispatch queue (see executor_libdispatch. mm, line 362[7]) and uses it to perform all operations that make remote calls to the Cloud Firestore backend:

```
std::unique_ptr<Executor> Executor::CreateSerial(const char*
label) {
  dispatch_queue_t queue =
    dispatch_queue_create(label,
                             DISPATCH_QUEUE_SERIAL);
  return absl::make_unique<ExecutorLibdispatch>(queue);
}
```

Once this call finishes, Firestore will use the main dispatch queue for calling the completion handler. In case you would like to use a different dispatch queue for returning the result, you can use FirestoreSettings. dispatchQueue[8] to set a custom dispatch queue:

```
let settings = Firestore.firestore().settings
settings.dispatchQueue = DispatchQueue.global(qos: .background)
Firestore.firestore().settings = settings
```

This might be useful when you need to perform several dependent operations on a background thread before updating the UI.

In the previous code snippet, we used a completion handler to handle the result of the call to getDocument. Firebase also supports Combine. Here is how the code snippet earlier would look like when using Combine:

---

[7] https://bit.ly/3uVR5Vn
[8] See the documentation at https://bit.ly/3W9FFZS

```
db.collection("books").document("hitchhiker").getDocument()
  .tryMap { documentSnapshot in
    try documentSnapshot.data(as: Book.self)
  }
  .replaceError(with: Book.empty)
  .assign(to: &$book)
```

Since Firestore takes care of dispatching all operations on the most appropriate dispatch queue (a serial background queue for fetching data and the main dispatch queue for returning results), there is usually no need to switch the dispatch queue.

Summary

Traditionally, developers had to handle multithreading manually, often requiring them to switch thread using `DispatchQueue` and other similar mechanisms. On top of requiring an in-depth understanding of thread, this inevitably leads to more verbose code that is difficult to read and maintain.

Combine uses schedulers as a declarative alternative that helps developers abstract away from having to manually wrap your code in calls to `DispatchQueue.main.async { }` etc. Instead, we can use Combine operators like `subscribe(on:)` and `receive(on:)` to declare which scheduling strategy Combine should use.

The key takeaways from this chapter are as follows:

1. If you don't specify a scheduler, Combine will run your code on the same thread as the one you are calling from.

2. For SwiftUI, this will most likely be the main thread.

3. However, asynchronous APIs, such as `URLSession`, might switch to a background thread.

4. In this case, you should use `receive(on:)` to switch back to the main thread before making any updates to the UI.

5. On the other hand, some APIs (like Firebase) might switch back to the main thread before returning a result. You need to be aware of this so you can avoid excessive thread jumping.

6. If you want to offload a long-running process to the background, you can do so using the `subscribe(on:)` operator.

Overall, Combine's schedulers make working with asynchronous code easier and less error prone. Xcode's purple warning messages turn out to be particularly helpful when writing code for SwiftUI.

Part 3

CHAPTER 14

Getting Started
with async/await

We live in an asynchronous world. As users, we have come to expect that interactions with our devices and apps yield almost instant results. But we are pretty much neglecting the fact that more often than not, the systems we interact with are distributed systems: liking a Tweet or an Instagram story, archiving an email, putting an item into your shopping basket—all these actions ultimately result in a network call, an update in a database table, and sometimes even running a piece of business logic on a server.

When dealing with distributed, independently executing systems, asynchronous behavior is the norm, not the exception: anything involving I/O (be it disk or network bound), and even communicating with other processes on the local system happens asynchronously.

The Cambridge Dictionary defines *asynchronous* as *not happening or done at the same time or speed*,[1] and we can observe this kind of behavior in many situations:

- A server needs to handle many clients at the same time, but it might have fewer processors or processor cores than the number of clients it needs this to deal with at the same time.

---

[1] See https://dictionary.cambridge.org/dictionary/english/asynchronous

- Multicore systems run multiple independently executing operations in parallel.

- A client app receives results from a network call it made earlier.

- A local app needs to handle the user's input while at the same time rendering UI updates.

As developers, we are used to most method and function calls to execute and return almost immediately, allowing us to write linear, straight-line code like this example taken from the Swift Programming Language Guide[2]:

```swift
func greet(person: String) -> String {
    let greeting = "Hello, " + person + "!"
    return greeting
}

print(greet(person: "Anna"))
// Prints "Hello, Anna!"
print(greet(person: "Brian"))
// Prints "Hello, Brian!"
```

The calls to the greet function return immediately, and the greetings to Anna and Brian are printed consecutively. Brian will always be greeted after Anna.

The greet function in this example executes *synchronously*. This is possible because it doesn't perform any complex work and doesn't depend on any other (remote) subsystems.

But there are functions that execute *asynchronously*. The most common reasons why functions execute asynchronously are that they require a response from a slow resource (e.g., a server that needs to be

---

[2] See https://docs.swift.org/swift-book/LanguageGuide/Functions.html

accessed via the network, or even a file on the local file system), or they perform expensive work (i.e., a long-running computation).

Computing the thumbnail for an image is an operation that takes a little while—depending on the size of the original image. UIImage has two methods for doing this: the synchronous version (`preparingThumbnail(of:)`[3]) will block the calling thread until the method returns. When using this method in a UI with many thumbnails (such as a collection view), this will inevitably lead to stuttering when the user scrolls quickly. To prevent this, UIImage has a second version of this method that allows developers to call this API asynchronously: `prepareThumbnail(of:completionHandler:)`[4]. This method will not block the main thread, but instead execute asynchronously, so scrolling will be smooth even with a large number of thumbnails being computed in the background.

When calling functions on a slow resource, blocking the caller is not an option in most cases. On most operating systems, the UI runs on the main thread, and blocking a call will result in the UI to become unresponsive and freeze. iOS might event terminate your app if it doesn't respond within a certain amount of time.[5] We've all experienced this, and it is not a great user experience. Blocking calls on a server will result in more threads being spun up to handle any other requests that might come in, resulting in a *thread explosion*,[6] and the server running out of resources quickly. Likewise, if the server isn't able to spin up more threads, it will not be able to handle incoming request, resulting in HTTP 503 (*Service Unavailable*) error messages.

---

[3] See `https://developer.apple.com/documentation/uikit/uiimage/3750835-preparingthumbnail`

[4] See `https://developer.apple.com/documentation/uikit/uiimage/3750845-preparethumbnail`

[5] See Apple's documentation about *Watchdog Terminations* for more details: `https://developer.apple.com/documentation/xcode/addressing-watchdog-terminations`

[6] This is covered in the WWDC 2021 session "Swift concurrency: Behind the scenes". See `https://developer.apple.com/videos/play/wwd-c2021/10254?time=500`

This is why we need a way to handle asynchronicity in our apps. In the following, we will take a look at how to implement asynchronous code using different techniques. The example we will be using is a simple sandwich store that produces artisanal sandwiches.[7]

The general algorithm looks like this:

- Toast the bread.

- Slice the other ingredients (cucumbers, onions, tomatoes).

- Once the bread has been toasted,

    - spread condiments on the bread.

    - layer ingredients on top of one slice of bread.

    - put lettuce on top.

    - put the second slice of bread on top.

- Wrap it all up and hand it to the customer.

You will notice that some of these need to be sequential, while others can be performed in parallel. For example, we don't need to wait idly while the bread is toasted—we can use the time to slice the vegetables in the meantime.

The code for this chapter can be found in the GitHub repository[8] for the book, in the folder Chapter 14. Inside the folder, you will find a .playground file. Open this file in the Swift Playgrounds app,[9] and expand the project navigator (CMD+1) and the debug console (CMD+Shift+Y) to make it easier to navigate between the examples.

---

[7] The code samples for this chapter can be found in a Swift Playground in the folder for this chapter on the book's code repository on GitHub: `https://github.com/peterfriese/SwiftUI-Combine-Book`

[8] `https://github.com/peterfriese/SwiftUI-Combine-Book`

[9] Some of the features used in this playground require the latest version of the Swift Playground app on macOS Ventura. If you're not able to run Version 4.2 of the Swift Playgrounds app on macOS Ventura, you can also open the playground in Xcode.

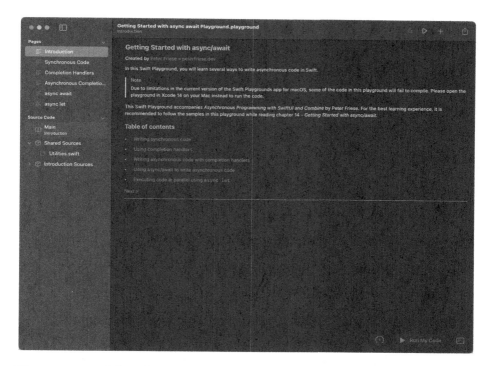

Figure 14-1. *The playground in the Swift Playgrounds app*

Synchronous Programming with Functions

Let's first look at a synchronous implementation of the sandwich-making algorithm:

```
public func customerSays(_ message: String) {
  print("[Customer] \(message)")
}
```

```
public func sandwichMakerSays(_ message: String, waitFor time:
UInt32 = 0) {
  print("[Sandwich maker] \(message)")
  if time > 0 {
    print("                     ... this will take \(time)s")
    sleep(time)
  }
}

func makeSandwich(bread: String, ingredients: [String],
condiments: [String]) -> String {
  sandwichMakerSays("Preparing your sandwich...")

  let toasted = toastBread(bread)
  let sliced = slice(ingredients)

  sandwichMakerSays("Spreading \(condiments.joined(separator:
  ", and ")) on \(toasted)")
  sandwichMakerSays("Layering \(sliced.joined(separator:
  ", "))")
  sandwichMakerSays("Putting lettuce on top")
  sandwichMakerSays("Putting another slice of bread on top")

  return "\(ingredients.joined(separator: ", ")), \(condiments.
  joined(separator: ", ")) on \(toasted)"
}

func toastBread(_ bread: String) -> String {
  sandwichMakerSays("Toasting the bread... Standing by...",
  waitFor: 5)
  return "Crispy \(bread)"
}
```

```
func slice(_ ingredients: [String]) -> [String] {
  let result = ingredients.map { ingredient in
    sandwichMakerSays("Slicing \(ingredient)", waitFor: 1)
    return "sliced \(ingredient)"
  }
  return result
}

//: The main program follows

sandwichMakerSays("Hello to Cafe Synchronous, where we execute
your order serially.")
sandwichMakerSays("Please place your order.")

// We're using a `ContinuousClock` to determine how long it
took to make the sandwich.
let clock = ContinuousClock()
let time = clock.measure {
  let sandwich = makeSandwich(bread: "Rye", ingredients:
["Cucumbers", "Tomatoes"], condiments: ["Mayo", "Mustard"])
  customerSays("Hmmm.... this looks like a delicious \
(sandwich) sandwich!")
}

// This should be roughly 7 seconds (5 for toasting, and 1 for
each ingredient we sliced)
print("Making this sandwich took \(time)")
```

The main work[10] happens in makeSandwich, which takes some parameters that allow the customer to tell us the type of bread, ingredients, and condiments to use.

All steps are executed sequentially, even the ones that take some time, such as toasting the bread. Toasting the bread is simulated by sleeping for a few seconds. This will effectively block the thread, and the toastBread function will only return to the caller once 5 seconds has passed.

The output of this program will look like this:

```
[Sandwich maker] Hello to Cafe Synchronous, where we execute
your order serially.
[Sandwich maker] Please place your order.
[Sandwich maker] Preparing your sandwich...
[Sandwich maker] Toasting the bread... Standing by...
                ... this will take 5s
[Sandwich maker] Slicing Cucumbers
                ... this will take 1s
[Sandwich maker] Slicing Tomatoes
                ... this will take 1s
[Sandwich maker] Spreading Mayo, and Mustard on Crispy Rye
[Sandwich maker] Layering sliced Cucumbers, sliced Tomatoes
[Sandwich maker] Putting lettuce on top
[Sandwich maker] Putting another slice of bread on top
[Customer] Hmmm.... this looks like a delicious Cucumbers,
Tomatoes, Mayo, Mustard on Crispy Rye sandwich!
Making this sandwich took 7.00992275 seconds
```

---

[10] I realize that "work" is a grand word for this simulated sandwich-making algorithm, but bear with me—the principles apply no matter if you're doing real work or just using print statements to simulate the work.

Since we executed all steps serially, the whole program took about 7 seconds (5 seconds for toasting, 1 second each for slicing the tomatoes and cucumbers).

This version of the algorithm was easy to write and understand, since it follows a linear flow—one statement follows the other. When we called a function, we knew that the program will only continue the main flow once the function returns.

This is great for a lot of the code we write, but as soon as we need to deal with asynchronous APIs, using blocking calls won't work anymore for the reasons mentioned earlier.

Asynchronous Programming with Closures

The initial versions of Swift didn't include any language-level, first-class concurrency features. This was in fact a conscious decision by the core team (see the Swift Concurrency Manifesto[11]), so developers had to come up with other ways to deal with asynchronous code.

A common way to implement code that needs to run asynchronously is to use GCD (Grand Central Dispatch) together with closures. *Closures* are self-contained blocks of functionality that can be passed around and used in your code.[12] Closures are typically used to implement callbacks and completion handlers, and this makes them a great fit for handling asynchronous code: once a long-running process has finished, we can use the closure to pass the result back to the caller.

---

[11] https://bit.ly/3PF61k3

[12] See the Swift Language Guide, Closures - https://docs.swift.org/swift-book/LanguageGuide/Closures.html

When using a closure, the toastBread function from the previous section would like this:

```
func toastBread(_ bread: String,
                completion: (String) -> Void) {
  sandwichMakerSays("Toasting the bread... Standing by...",
  waitFor: 5)
  completion("Crispy \(bread)")
}
```

To call this method, you'll have to update the call site like this:

```
toastBread(bread, completion: { toasted in
  print("\(bread) is now \(toasted)")
  // prints "Rye is now Crispy Rye"
})
```

When you compare this to the original version of the function, you will notice a couple of things:

1. The toastBread function no longer has a return value.

2. Instead, there is now an additional parameter completion with a somewhat more complicated looking signature.

3. completion: (String) -> Void) means that the completion parameter takes a function as an input value. This function expects one parameter of type String and does not return any value (i.e., Void).

4. When the toastBread function is ready to return the result of its operation to the caller, it invokes the closure by calling completion and passing in a String.

5. At the call site, we pass in a closure that has the signature expected by the completion parameter.

When dealing with asynchronous code, closures are most commonly used as *trailing closures*. This is a Swift language feature which allows us to simplify the call site:

```
toastBread(bread) { toasted in
  print("\(bread) is now \(toasted)")
}
```

So far, our code isn't really asynchronous yet; the only thing that has changed is how we return the result to the caller.

Let's update the toastBread and slice functions to run asynchronously on the global dispatch queue by wrapping their body inside a call to DispatchQueue.global().async { }:

```
func toastBread(_ bread: String,
                completion: @escaping (String) -> Void)
{
  DispatchQueue.global().async {
    sandwichMakerSays("Toasting the bread... Standing by...",
                      waitFor: 5)
    completion("Crispy \(bread)")
  }
}
func slice(_ ingredients: [String],
           completion: @escaping ([String]) -> Void)
{
  DispatchQueue.global().async {
    let result = ingredients.map { ingredient in
      sandwichMakerSays("Slicing \(ingredient)", waitFor: 1)
      return "sliced \(ingredient)"
    }
    completion(result)
  }
}
```

At the call site, we can now use the completion handler semantics. Since we want to call slice only once the call to toastBread has finished, we need to nest them, like this:

```
toastBread(bread) { toasted in
  slice(ingredients) { sliced in
    sandwichMakerSays("Spreading \(condiments.joined(separator:
    ", and ")) om \(toasted)")
    // ...
  }
}
print("This code will be executed *before* the bread is toasted
and the ingredients are sliced.")
```

One reason why we might want to run toastBread and slice asynchronously on the global thread might be that we're calling separate subsystems of our app to perform those operations, or that we need to access a remote server to fulfill this functionality.

Using closures for handling asynchronous code is a well-established practice, and both Apple's own APIs and many third-party SDKs such as Firebase make use of this approach.

That doesn't mean that it is perfect. In fact, there are many problems with using closures for handling asynchronous behavior in our apps:

It is easy to end up in a pyramid of doom. This refers to the fact that you have to nest any code that depends on the result of a call inside a closure. In our example, we only had to go two levels deep, but have a look at this example from the Swift Concurrency Manifesto[13]:

```
func processImageData1(completionBlock: (result: Image)
-> Void) {
```

---

[13] See https://bit.ly/3WtFOSQ

```
loadWebResource("dataprofile.txt") { dataResource in
  loadWebResource("imagedata.dat") { imageResource in
    decodeImage(dataResource, imageResource) { imageTmp in
      dewarpAndCleanupImage(imageTmp) { imageResult in
        completionBlock(imageResult)
      }
    }
  }
}
}
```

This is a typical example for code that needs to call several asynchronous APIs, passing the result from one call to the next.

If you turn the code sideways, you will see why this is called *pyramid of doom*. Compare this with the linear code from our first example, and you will understand why this kind of code will be much harder to understand.

Error handling will make the code even harder to read. Here is the same code snippet from the Swift Concurrency Manifesto, with error handling added:

```
func processImageData2(completionBlock: (result: Image?, error:
Error?) -> Void) {
  loadWebResource("dataprofile.txt") { dataResource, error in
    guard let dataResource = dataResource else {
      completionBlock(nil, error)
      return
    }
    loadWebResource("imagedata.dat") { imageResource, error in
      guard let imageResource = imageResource else {
        completionBlock(nil, error)
        return
      }
```

```
decodeImage(dataResource, imageResource) { imageTmp,
error in
  guard let imageTmp = imageTmp else {
    completionBlock(nil, error)
    return
  }
  dewarpAndCleanupImage(imageTmp) { imageResult in
    guard let imageResult = imageResult else {
      completionBlock(nil, error)
      return
    }
    completionBlock(imageResult)
  }
}
      }
    }
  }
}
```

Not only is this code a long more verbose, it also requires the caller to check if the callback returned a result or an error. This is easy to forget, and unfortunately, the compiler cannot enforce this kind of error handling at the call site.

It is not always clear which thread a callback is on. Callers of toastBread and slice have no way of telling which thread they will be called back on—unless they have access to the source code, or the documentation of the functions specifically mentions the threading model being used. Callers can solve this by wrapping those invocations inside a call to DispatchQueue.main.async { }, but this might lead to thread hopping if you call several functions that run on different threads.

There is no way to enforce a completion handler be called. This is particularly problematic for callers. Can they expect that the completion handler will be called at all? Will it be called more than once? How will errors be handled? Will the callback receive an error handle? Apple provides some guidelines in their documentation,[14] but it is impossible for the compiler to make any guarantees about them. This makes building good APIs more difficult than it should be.

Overall, using closures will inevitably result in code that is convoluted, hard to read, and error prone.

Asynchronous Programming with async/await

Swift's new concurrency model, introduced with Swift 5.5, makes asynchronous programming a lot easier. It introduces a number of language-level concepts (most prominently the `async/await` keywords) that allow us to make the asynchronous nature of our code explicit. This allows the compiler to perform some compile-time checking, which helps us write better, more error-free programs.

In the remainder of this chapter, we will take a look at some of the new concepts and refactor the closure-based code to an `async/await`–based implementation that is easier to read and maintain.

Defining and Calling Asynchronous Functions

In Swift, an asynchronous function (or an asynchronous method) can be suspended while it is executing. This is particularly useful when the function needs to wait for a slow resource, for example, a network call: instead of blocking the thread while it is waiting for the network call to return, the function can pause execution and give up the thread to other parts of the application. This allows for a better utilization of the system resources and allows for a stutter-free UI.

---

[14] See `https://bit.ly/3W9vQeH`

The places where a function can be suspended are called *suspension points*, and you indicate them by using the `await` keyword when calling an asynchronous function or method:

```
let result = await someAsyncFunction()
```

To define an asynchronous function or method, you use the async keyword:

```
func someAsyncFunction() async -> String {
  let result = // ... async code here
  return result
}
```

Let's take a look at how the code for our sandwich maker would look like when using `async`/`await`.

Let's first update the code for toasting a bread. If you recall, we assume that we will be using some subsystem for toasting the bread (i.e., a toaster) and that this process will take some amount of time. In the code, this is represented by sleeping for 5 seconds:

```
func toastBread(_ bread: String) async -> String {
  sandwichMakerSays("Toasting the bread... Standing by...")
  await Task.sleep(5_000_000_000)
  return "Crispy \(bread)"
}
```

When comparing this code with the completion handler–based version of the code, you will notice a couple of things:

1. We no longer have to provide a parameter for the trailing closure. Instead, we use the `async` keyword to indicate that this is an asynchronous function. This makes the function signature a lot easier to read.

2. We can now specify the return value of this function. Remember, when using the completion handler, the return value had to be part of the completion handler signature. This makes the method signature even easier to read, and as you will see in a minute, it makes the call site cleaner as well.

3. No need to use `DispatchQueue.global().async { }`— SwiftUI's new concurrency model uses a thread pool and will automatically manage threads for us.

The code for the updated `slice` function looks very similar:

```
func slice(_ ingredients: [String]) async -> [String] {
  var result = [String]()
  for ingredient in ingredients {
    sandwichMakerSays("Slicing \(ingredient)")
    await Task.sleep(1_000_000_000)
    result.append("sliced \(ingredient)")

  }
  return result
}
```

Let's now see how we can call those two updated functions. At the call site, we need to use the `await` keyword to indicate that the calls to `toastBread` and `slice` are potential suspension points:

```
func makeSandwich(bread: String, ingredients: [String],
condiments: [String]) async -> String {
  sandwichMakerSays("Preparing your sandwich...")
```

```
let toasted = await toastBread(bread)
let sliced = await slice(ingredients)

sandwichMakerSays("Spreading \(condiments.joined(separator:
  ", and ")) om \(toasted)")
sandwichMakerSays("Layering \(sliced.joined(separator:
", "))")
sandwichMakerSays("Putting lettuce on top")
sandwichMakerSays("Putting another slice of bread on top")

return "\(ingredients.joined(separator: ", ")), \(condiments.
joined(separator: ", ")) on \(toasted)"
}
```

Notice how we can call toastBread and slice without having to use nested closures. This results in straight-line code that almost reads like normal, linear code such as the rest of the sandwich-making algorithm.

Since makeSandwich is now an asynchronous function, just like toastBread and slice, we need to mark it as async as well.

But how can we call asynchronous code from a synchronous context?

Swift provides the Task API, which represents a unit of asynchronous work. By wrapping a call to an asynchronous function inside a Task { }, you can call it from a synchronous context, like an action handler in your UI, or a Swift Playground. Here is how the call to makeSandwich looks like:

```
Task {
  let sandwich = await makeSandwich(bread: "Rye", ingredients:
  ["Cucumbers", "Tomatoes"], condiments: ["Mayo", "Mustard"])
  customerSays("Hmmm.... this looks like a delicious \
(sandwich) sandwich!")
  print("The end.")
}
```

As makeSandwich is now an asynchronous function, we need to use the await keyword to call it. The compiler will issue an error if we forget to do so:

Calling Asynchronous Functions in Parallel

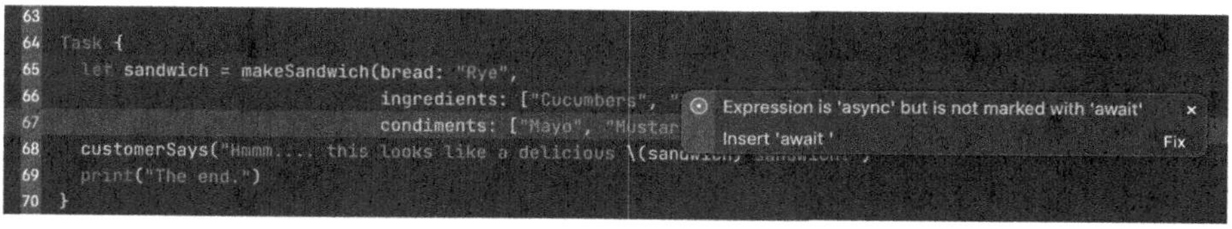

Figure 14-2. *The compiler will issue an error when you call an asynchronous function without the await keyword*

You might have noticed that our sandwich-making process can be optimized.

At the moment, we first call toastBread and wait for it to finish. Then, we call slice to slice the ingredients and wait for it to finish before we move on to assemble the sandwich. There clearly is room for optimization—while the bread is being toasted, we can start slicing the ingredients, reducing the overall waiting time for our customer.

Swift's new concurrency model supports executing several asynchronous functions simultaneously using the async let syntax. To execute code in parallel, prefix a call to one or more asynchronous functions with async let:

```
async let x = someAsyncFunction()
async let y = someAsyncFunction()
async let z = someAsyncFunction()
print("This code will be executed immediately")
```

As long as there are enough resources available, the system will run these at the same time, in parallel. None of these calls will create a suspension point, meaning that any code that comes after will be executed immediately—like the print statement in the code snippet.

To create a suspension point, use await for the constants (x, y, and z in this case):

```
let result = await [x, y, z]
print("The result is \(result)"
```

Let's look at how we can use this to optimize our sandwich-making process:

```
func makeSandwich(bread: String, ingredients: [String],
condiments: [String]) async -> String {
  sandwichMakerSays("Preparing your sandwich...")

  async let toasted = toastBread(bread)
  async let sliced = slice(ingredients)

  sandwichMakerSays("Spreading \(condiments.joined(separator:
  ", and ")) om \(await toasted)")
  sandwichMakerSays("Layering \(await sliced.joined(separator:
  ", "))")
  sandwichMakerSays("Putting lettuce on top")
  sandwichMakerSays("Putting another slice of bread on top")

  return "\(ingredients.joined(separator: ", ")), \(condiments.
  joined(separator: ", ")) on \(await toasted)"
}
```

As you can see, it is possible to use await <constant> at any place in our code—even inside a String interpolation. Using this approach, toastBread and slice will now run in parallel. By instrumenting our code, we can see that this does indeed reduce the waiting time for our customers:

```
let clock = ContinuousClock()
Task {
  let time = await clock.measure {
    let sandwich = await makeSandwich(bread: "Rye",
    ingredients: ["Cucumbers", "Tomatoes"], condiments:
    ["Mayo", "Mustard"])
    customerSays("Hmmm.... this looks like a delicious
    \(sandwich) sandwich!")
    print("The end.")
  }
  print("Making this sandwich took \(time)")
}
```

Instead of waiting 7 seconds, the customer now only has to wait about 5 seconds—that's a nice improvement!

Summary

In this chapter, you learned about concurrency and how Swift's new concurrency model improves the way how we write and consume asynchronous code.

You learned how to use completion handlers to build asynchronous APIs and how to call them. Completion handlers and closures are a very common way to implement asynchronous behavior, and to this day, they are being used in many of Apple's own APIs, and many third-party libraries. They have served the community well, but come with a number of drawbacks, such as the potential to end up in the pyramid of doom, and some uncertainty around which thread you will be called back on. The biggest drawback when using completion handlers for asynchronous code, however, is that they are harder to read than straight-line code, especially for developers new to the concept of asynchronous code.

Swift's new concurrency model (best known as `async/await`) makes both implementing and using asynchronous APIs much easier. In this chapter, you saw how you can use the `async` keyword to declare asynchronous functions and methods and how to use the `await` keyword to call those asynchronous functions. You learned what a suspension point is and that Swift uses a thread pool to manage execution of asynchronous code. We also looked at `async let`, which lets you run several asynchronous functions or methods in parallel, and how to create a suspension point (using `await <constant>` to wait for the result of the call(s).

This was as quick introduction to Swift's new concurrency model. To learn more, I recommend reading the Concurrency chapter in the Swift Programming Language Guide[15] or watching my video series.[16] In the next chapter, we will look at how to use Swift's new concurrency model together with SwiftUI.

---

[15] Available online at `https://bit.ly/3BMEJCO`
[16] See `bit.ly/swift-concurrency-video-series`

CHAPTER 15

Using async/await in SwiftUI

Now that you've got a basic understanding of how Swift's new concurrency model works, let's look at how to use it in a SwiftUI application.

The sample app we're going to build in this chapter makes use of the WordsAPI.[1] This is a fun little API that provides a ton of interesting information about words. You send it a word, such as "Swift", and it will return a bunch of information about this word—for example, "moving very fast," "a small bird that resembles a swallow," or "an English satirist born in Ireland."

The sample app displays a list of suggested words the user can tap on to get more information about them. The app will then fetch the different meanings of the word from WordAPI.com and display them in a details screen.

Throughout the chapter, we will look at how to call this asynchronous code from different situations in the app, for example, when the user taps a button, when they pull to refresh, etc.

---

[1] See www.wordsapi.com

© Peter Friese 2023
P. Friese, *Asynchronous Programming with SwiftUI and Combine*,
https://doi.org/10.1007/978-1-4842-8572-5_15

Fetching Data Asynchronously Using URLSession

URLSession is among the many APIs Apple has upgraded to support async/await, so fetching data using URLSession is now a one liner:

```
let (data, response) =
  try await URLSession.shared.data(for: urlRequest)
```

With some minimal amount of error handling and JSON parsing (using Codable), the code for fetching the details about a word from WordsAPI. com looks like this:

```
private func search(for searchTerm: String) async -> Word {
  // build the request
  let request = buildURLRequest(for: searchTerm)

  do {
    let (data, response) =
      try await URLSession.shared.data(for: request)
    guard let httpResponse = response as? HTTPURLResponse,
            httpResponse.statusCode == 200 else
    {
      throw WordsAPIError.invalidServerResponse
    }
    let word = try JSONDecoder().decode(Word.self, from: data)
    return word
  }
  catch {
    return Word.empty
  }
}
```

By adding the `async` keyword to the signature of the method, we declare that it is asynchronous. The compiler will use this information to make sure this method is called from an asynchronous context and issue compile-time errors if we forget to call the method using the `await` keyword.

Calling an asynchronous method using `await` creates a so-called suspension point. While the function is suspended, the runtime can reuse the thread it was executing on to perform other code in your application.

You can imagine this like being on a call with a call center agent, and being told to "hold the line": while you're listening to some more or less entertaining elevator music, you can continue doing other business, such as drinking a tea, daydreaming about your next vacation, or chatting with other people in your room. Once the call center agent has finished looking up that important information, you'll give them all your attention, essentially resuming the flow of conversation that was suspended when they told you to hang on for a second.

Calling Asynchronous Code

To call asynchronous code, we need to be in an asynchronous context. As we saw in the previous chapter, there are several ways to establish an asynchronous context. Creating a new `Task` is one of them:

```
Task {
  let result = search(for: "Swift")
}
```

While this is easy enough, it would be tedious to have to write this again and again in our UI-facing code. Fortunately, Apple has updated SwiftUI to make calling asynchronous code from inside a UI context as easy as possible. In particular, they've added some APIs that allow us to call asynchronous code:

 – When a view appears (using the `.task` view modifier)

 – When the user pulls to refresh inside a `List` view

For other situations, we will still need to create an asynchronous context ourselves, for example:

 – When the user taps on a `Button`

 – When the user types a search term inside the search bar of a `View`

In the following sections, we will look at some scenarios to see each of these ways to call asynchronous code in action.

The Task View Modifier

One of the most common situations for fetching data is when a view appears on screen. Previously, you might have used the `.onAppear` view modifier to run code when your views appear. When you try to call asynchronous code from within `.onAppear`, the compiler will issue an error saying that it is not permitted to call asynchronous code from a nonasynchronous context:

```
.navigationTitle(word)
.onAppear {                      ⊗  Invalid conversion from 'async' function of type '() async -> ()' to synchronous function type '() -> Void'
    await viewModel.executeQuery(for: word)|
}
```

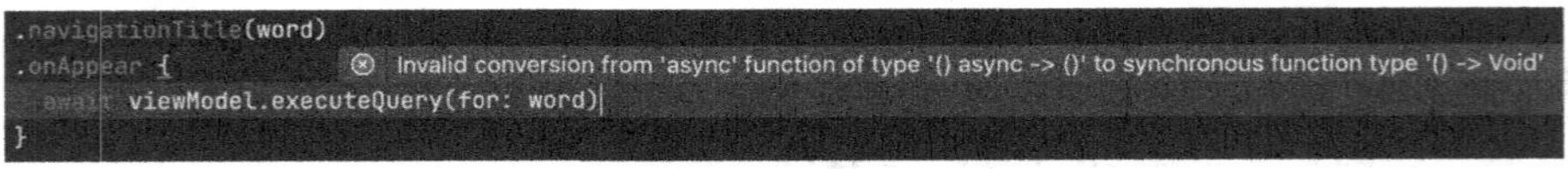

Figure 15-1. *Trying to call an asynchronous function from a non-asynchronous context*

To fix this compile-time error, we could wrap the code in a new `Task`, like this:

```
struct WordDetailsView: View {
  ...
```

```
  var body: some View {
    List {
      ...
    }
    .navigationTitle(word)
    .onAppear {
      Task {
        await viewModel.executeQuery(for: word)
      }
    }
  }
}
```

While this works well, it is a bit verbose, and there is actually a better solution: because fetching data when a view appears is such a common scenario, SwiftUI has a new view modifier that will automatically create a new Task *and* cancel it when the view disappears:

```
struct WordDetailsView: View {
  ...
  var body: some View {
    List {
      ...
    }
    .navigationTitle(word)
    .task {
      await viewModel.executeQuery(for: word)
    }
  }
}
```

This makes our code much more concise and easier to read.

Calling Asynchronous Code When the User Taps a Button

Often, when the user taps a Button, we need to execute code asynchronously—for example, we might want to refresh the data in a list view.

In some beta versions of Xcode 13, a few of Button's initializers supported registering asynchronous event handlers. It seems like this might have been just an experiment, since the public release of Xcode 13.1 no longer contains these initializers. This means we need to use Task to create an asynchronous context inside a Button's event handler if we want to run asynchronous code. Here is an example for a toolbar button that initiates a refresh of the currently displayed data:

```
.toolbar {
  ToolbarItem(placement: .primaryAction) {
    Button("Refresh") {
      async {
        await viewModel.refresh()
      }
    }
  }
}
```

Using Pull-to-Refresh to Update Views Asynchronously

Tapping a button to refresh the UI is great, but have you tried pull-to-refresh? This gesture has been around for several years, and SwiftUI makes it easier than before to implement this in your apps. All you need to do is add the .refreshable view modifier to the view. This view modifier takes a closure that can run code asynchronously. Here is a simple example that triggers a refresh of the data being displayed in a list view:

```
struct LibraryView: View {
  ...
  var body: some View {
    List {
      ...
    }
    .refreshable {
      await viewModel.refresh()
    }
  }
}
```

Searchable Views and async/await

You can add a platform-specific search UI to a SwiftUI view by applying the `.searchable` view modifier. This view modifier takes up to three parameters: the first one is a `Binding` to a `String`, which will contain the search term the user enters. The other parameters allow you to control the placement of the search bar and provide a list of suggested search terms. Since the first parameter is a `Binding`, you can use Combine to drive the search. The following code snippet shows how you can filter the displayed elements in the `List` view by using a Combine pipeline:

```
class LibraryViewModel: ObservableObject {
  @Published var searchText = ""
  @Published var tips: [String] =
    ["Swift", "authentication", "authorization"]
  @Published var favourites: [String] =
    ["stunning", "brilliant", "marvelous"]
```

```
@Published var filteredTips = [String]()
@Published var filteredFavourites = [String]()

init() {
  Publishers.CombineLatest($searchText, $tips)
    .map { filter, items in
      items.filter { item in
        filter.isEmpty ? true : item.contains(filter)
      }
    }
    .assign(to: &$filteredTips)

  Publishers.CombineLatest($searchText, $favourites)
    .map { filter, items in
      items.filter { item in
        filter.isEmpty ? true : item.contains(filter)
      }
    }
    .assign(to: &$filteredFavourites)
}
...
}

struct LibraryView: View {
  @StateObject var viewModel = LibraryViewModel()

  var body: some View {
    List {
      ...
      SectionView("Peter's Tips", words:
      viewModel.filteredTips)
      SectionView("My favourites", words:
      viewModel.filteredFavourites)
    }
```

```
    .searchable(text: $viewModel.searchText)
    .autocapitalization(.none)
    ...
  }
}
```

This is useful for UIs that require immediate feedback, such as filtering a list of results locally, like in the previous example.

However, if you want to kick off the search only when the user has tapped the *Search* button or pressed the *Enter* key, you need to use the .onSubmit(of:) view modifier:

```
struct WordSearchView: View {
  @StateObject var viewModel = WordsAPIViewModel()
  var body: some View {
    List {
      ...
    }
    .searchable(text: $viewModel.searchTerm)
    .autocapitalization(.none)
    .onSubmit(of: .search) {
      Task {
        await viewModel.executeQuery()
      }
    }
    .navigationTitle("Search")
  }
}
```

In this code snippet, the searchTerm property on the viewModel will be continuously updated as the user enters their search term. Only once they hit the *Enter* key on their keyboard or tap the *Search* button will the closure of the onSubmit modifier be executed. Again, as the closure isn't marked `async`, we need to create the required asynchronous context ourselves before we can call the asynchronous `executeQuery` method on the view model.

Updating the UI from the Main Thread

When you run the code we've developed so far, you might notice that Xcode issues runtime warnings for some parts of our code, for example, the following snippet:

Figure 15-2. *Updating the UI from a background thread*

This code asynchronously fetches a random word from WordsAPI and then assigns it to a `@Published` property:

```
class LibraryViewModel: ObservableObject {
  @Published var randomWord = "partially"

  ...

  private func fetchRandomWord() async -> Word {
    let request = buildURLRequest()

    do {
      let (data, response) =
        try await URLSession.shared.data(for: request)
      guard let httpResponse = response as? HTTPURLResponse,
            httpResponse.statusCode == 200 else
      {
        throw WordsAPIError.invalidServerResponse
```

```
    }
    let word = try JSONDecoder().decode(Word.self,
                                          from: data)
    return word
  }
  catch {
    return Word.empty
  }
}

func refresh() async {
  let result = await fetchRandomWord()
  randomWord = result.word
}
}
```

Why is this a problem?

To answer this question, let's first look at the threads our code runs on. There are several ways to do this, and we will look at two:

1. Using the *Debug Inspector*

2. Logging information about the current thread using `Thread.isMainThread`

Let's first instrument the code to log information about the current thread it is executing on:

```
struct LibraryView: View {
  @StateObject var viewModel = LibraryViewModel()
  // ...

  var body: some View {
    List {
      // ...
    }
```

```
   // ...
   .refreshable {
     print("\(#function) is on main thread BEFORE await:
\(Thread.isMainThread)")
     await viewModel.refresh()
     print("\(#function) is on main thread AFTER await:
\(Thread.isMainThread)")
   }
   // ...
  }
}

class LibraryViewModel: ObservableObject {
  // ...
  private func fetchRandomWord() async -> Word {
    print("\(#function) is on main thread:
\(Thread.isMainThread)")

    ...
  }
  func refresh() async {
    print("\(#function) is on main thread BEFORE await:
\(Thread.isMainThread)")
    let result = await fetchRandomWord()
    randomWord = result.word
    print("\(#function) is on main thread AFTER await:
\(Thread.isMainThread)")
  }
  // ...
}
```

When running the app again, we can observe the following output in the console:

```
body is on main thread BEFORE await: true
refresh() is on main thread BEFORE await: false
fetchRandomWord() is on main thread: false
2022-10-01 16:43:10.043735+0200 WordBrowser[44309:2075098]
[SwiftUI] Publishing changes from background threads is not
allowed; make sure to publish values from the main thread (via
operators like receive(on:)) on model updates.
refresh() is on main thread AFTER await: false
body is on main thread AFTER await: true
```

So it seems like the code starts off on the main thread when the user pulls the view down to refresh (after all, this is a user-initiated interaction). However, as soon as refresh() is called, we're no longer on the main thread. All non-UI code is executed on a background thread, and only once the flow of execution returns to the view, will the code resume executing on the main thread (see the last line of the log output).

Let's now use the *Debug Inspector* to take a closer look at this.

Set a breakpoint on the five print statements and launch the app again. When the debugger hits the first breakpoint in the closure of the refreshable view modifier, you can see that this code is actually executed on the main thread:

Figure 15-3. *The closure of the refreshable view modifier is executed on the main thread*

Resume the app, and once it hits the second breakpoint (inside the `refresh()` method of the `LibraryViewModel`, the code now executes on a background thread:

Figure 15-4. *The refresh method is executed on a background thread*

Resume again and continue execution until the debugger hits the first breakpoint inside `fetchRandomWord`, and observe that we're still on a background thread.

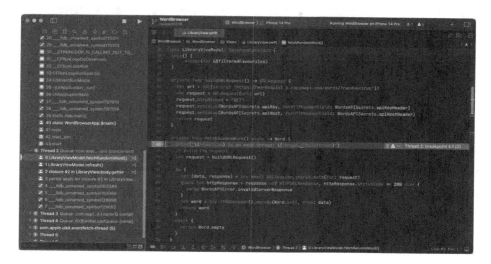

Figure 15-5. *Still executing on the background thread: fetchRandomWord*

Resume again, and after a short while, the third breakpoint is hit—in `refresh()`, just where we called out asynchronously to `fetchRandomWord`. The code still runs on a background thread.

Figure 15-6. *Back in refresh, still on the background thread*

Resume one more time, until the debugger hits the second breakpoint in the closure of the `refreshable` view modifier, and we're back on the main thread!

Figure 15-7. *Back in the closure of the refreshable view modifier, the code continues executing on the main thread*

If you compare the call stacks in Figure 15-3 and Figure 15-7, you will realize that both execute on the same thread (Thread 1), but all the other methods executed on different threads, so what happened here?

As mentioned in the previous chapter, Swift's new concurrency model will use as many threads as your computer/phone has cores, and it will execute your code on any thread from this pool. In particular, when calling await on the man thread, Swift will suspend the current function and continue executing other UI-related code on the main thread (to make sure the app feels responsive to the user). Once the code we're awaiting on resumes, it will be running on a different, non-main, thread.

To get your code back to the main thread, there are a couple of strategies:

- You can wrap any code that updates the UI in a call to `MainActor.run { }`.

- You can mark any functions that update the UI using the `@MainActor` property wrapper.

- You can mark the entire class that contains code updating the UI using the `@MainActor` property wrapper.

Each one of these strategies is more coarse-grained than the previous one, so if you need fine-grained control over which parts of your code run on the main thread, use `MainActor.run { }`. On the other hand, by annotating your entire view model (which usually is a class conforming to `@ObservableObject`) with `@MainActor`, you make sure that all of the code inside runs on the main thread. Unless it is called using `await`, in which case it runs on the concurrent thread pool.

So, to solve the issue in our code, we can annotate the refresh function with @MainActor:

```
@MainActor
func refresh() async {
  print("\(#function) is on main thread BEFORE await:
  \(Thread.isMainThread)")
  let result = await fetchRandomWord()
  randomWord = result.word
  print("\(#function) is on main thread AFTER await:
  \(Thread.isMainThread)")
}
```

This will resolve any issues with accessing the UI from a background thread. Once we add more functions that access the UI to our view model, it might be more efficient to just annotate the entire class, like so:

```
@MainActor
class LibraryViewModel: ObservableObject {
  ...
}
```

Summary

In this chapter, you learned how to use Swift 5.5's new structured concurrency model in SwiftUI. SwiftUI provides well thought-out mechanisms that make calling asynchronous code from the UI as natural as possible.

For example, you can use the .task view modifier to run asynchronous code when a view appears. When using .task instead of .onAppear, SwiftUI will automatically take care of cancelling the task as soon as the view disappears.

Searching and refreshing data are other common situations in which you often need to run asynchronous code. The .refreshable and .searchable view modifiers create an asynchronous context for their closures, so you can easily call asynchronous code inside.

And if you need to call asynchronous code from a nonasynchronous context (such as the action handler of a Button), you can easily create an asynchronous context yourself by wrapping your code in a Task { } block.

You also saw that it might sometimes be more appropriate to use Combine to drive some of the UI instead of using async/await. The .searchable() view modifier is a great example for an API that is more suitable for being used with Combine.

Many of the examples made use of List views. Chapter 5 goes into more detail of how to build simple and advanced List views.

CHAPTER 16

Bringing It All Together: SwiftUI, async/await, and Combine

Mobile applications have to deal with a constant flow of events: user input, network traffic, and callbacks from the operating system are all vying for your app's attention. Building apps that feel snappy is a challenging task, as you have to efficiently handle all those events.

Combine and async/await are some fairly recent addition to the collection of frameworks and language features that aim at making this easier.

In this chapter, we will explore commonalities and differences of Combine and async/await, and I will show you how you can efficiently use both to call asynchronous APIs in your SwiftUI apps.

© Peter Friese 2023
P. Friese, *Asynchronous Programming with SwiftUI and Combine*,
https://doi.org/10.1007/978-1-4842-8572-5_16

To better understand the respective characteristics, we will look at a couple of code snippets taken from a SwiftUI screen that allows users to search for books by title. You will find the source code for this sample app in this book's GitHub repository.[1]

Fetching Data Using Combine

Many of Apple's APIs are Combine-enabled, and `URLSession` is one of them. To fetch data from a URL, we can call `dataTaskPublisher` and then use some of Combine's operators to handle the response and transform it into a data model our application can work with. The following code snippet shows a typical Combine pipeline for fetching data from a remote API, mapping the result, extracting the information we need, and handling errors.

> *Error handling in this code snippet is rather basic. For a more in-depth discussion of error handling in Combine and how to expose error messages to the user in a meaningful way in SwiftUI apps, have a look at Chapter 10, in which this we take a closer look at this important topic.*

```
private func searchBooks(matching searchTerm: String) ->
  AnyPublisher<[Book], Never>
{
  let escapedSearchTerm =
    searchTerm
      .addingPercentEncoding(withAllowedCharacters:
        .urlHostAllowed) ?? ""
  let url =
    URL(string: "https://openlibrary.org/search.json?q=
      \(escapedSearchTerm)")!
```

---

[1] https://github.com/peterfriese/SwiftUI-Combine-Book

```
return URLSession.shared.dataTaskPublisher(for: url)
  .map(\.data)
  .decode(type: OpenLibrarySearchResult.self,
          decoder: JSONDecoder())
  .map(\.books)
  .compactMap { openLibraryBooks in
    openLibraryBooks?.map { Book(from: $0) }
  }
  .replaceError(with: [Book]())
  .eraseToAnyPublisher()
}
```

For someone who is not familiar with Combine, it might not be immediately obvious how this code works, let alone being able to put together a pipeline like this. Getting into a functional reactive mindset probably is one of the biggest hurdles when learning Combine.

Fetching Data Using async/await

Let's now look at how to implement the same method using `async/await`. Apple has made sure that the most important asynchronous APIs can be called using `async/await`. To fetch data from a URL, we can asynchronously call `await URLSession.shared.data(from: url)`. By wrapping this call inside a `try catch` block, we can add the same kind of error handling we implemented in the previous code snippet and return an empty array in case an error occurred.

To make it easier for them (and other SDK providers like Firebase), Apple implemented a concurrency interoperability with Objective-C.[2] In a nutshell, this ensures that the Swift compiler emits an async version

---

[2] See Swift Evolution Proposal SE-0297: `https://bit.ly/3HJIBbg`

of every Objective-C method that has a completion block. To learn more about how this works, check out my video "Using async/await with Firebase,"[3] in which I explain this in more detail.

```
private func searchBooks(matching searchTerm: String) async
  -> [Book]
{
  let escapedSearchTerm =
    searchTerm
      .addingPercentEncoding(withAllowedCharacters:
        .urlHostAllowed) ?? ""
  let url =
    URL(string: "https://openlibrary.org/search.json?q=
      \(escapedSearchTerm)")!

  do {
    let (data, _) = try await URLSession.shared.data(from: url)

    let searchResult =
      try OpenLibrarySearchResult.init(data: data)
    guard let libraryBooks = searchResult.books else {
      return []
    }
    return libraryBooks.compactMap { Book(from: $0) }
  }
  catch {
    return []
  }
}
```

---

[3] https://youtu.be/sEKw2BMcQtQ

If you've got some experience writing and reading Swift code, you will be able to understand what this code does—even if you've got no prior experience with `async/await`: all keywords related to `async/await` blend in with the rest of the code, making it rather natural to read and understand. This is not least due to the fact that the Swift language team modeled Swift's concurrency features similar to how error handling works using `try/catch`.

Of course, to *write* code like this, you need a basic understanding of Swift's concurrency features, so there definitely is a learning curve.

Is This the End of Combine?

Looking at these two code snippets, you might argue that the one making use of `async/await` is easier to understand for developers who might not be familiar with neither Combine nor `async/wait`, mostly due to the fact you can read if from top to bottom in a linear way.

On the contrary, to understand the Combine version of the code, you have to know what a publisher is, why some of the operations are nested (e.g., the code for mapping a book inside the `compactMap/map` structure), and why on earth you need to call `eraseToAnyPublisher`. This can look very confusing if you're new to Combine.

Add to that the lack of sessions about Combine at WWDC 2021—it really seemed like Apple lost their enthusiasm for functional reactive programming.

So, given both code snippets seem to do the same, is this the end of Combine?

Well, I don't think so, and this has to do with the fact SwiftUI is tightly integrated with Combine. In fact, Combine makes a number of things in SwiftUI a lot easier with surprisingly little code.

Connecting the UI...

To better understand this, let's look at how to call the earlier code snippets from SwiftUI. The following code shows a typical way to implement a search screen—we've got a List view to display the results and a .searchable view modifier to set up the search field and connect it to the searchTerm published property on a view model:

```
struct BookSearchCombineView: View {
  @StateObject var viewModel = ViewModel()

  var body: some View {
    List(viewModel.result) { book in
      BookSearchRowView(book: book)
    }
    .searchable(text: $viewModel.searchTerm)
  }
}
```

...to a Combine Pipeline

By making the searchTerm a published property on the view model, it becomes a Combine publisher, allowing us to use it as a starting point for a Combine pipeline. The view model's initializer is a good place to set up this pipeline:

```
fileprivate class ViewModel: ObservableObject {
  @Published var searchTerm: String = ""

  @Published private(set) var result: [Book] = []
  @Published var isSearching = false

  private var cancellables = Set<AnyCancellable>()
```

```
init() {
  $searchTerm
    .debounce(for: 0.8, scheduler: DispatchQueue.main) // (1)
    .map { searchTerm -> AnyPublisher<[Book], Never> in // (2)
      self.isSearching = true
      return self.searchBooks(matching: searchTerm)
    }
    .switchToLatest() // (3)
    .receive(on: DispatchQueue.main) // (4)
    .sink(receiveValue: { books in // (5)
      self.result = books
      self.isSearching = false
    })
    .store(in: &cancellables) // (6)
}

  private func searchBooks(matching searchTerm: String)
    -> AnyPublisher<[Book], Never>
  {
  // ...
  }
```

Here, we subscribe to the searchTerm publisher and then use a couple of Combine operators to take the user's input, call the remote API, receive the results, and assign them to a published property that is connected to the UI:

1.   The debounce operator will only pass on events after there has been a 0.8s pause between event. This way, we will only call the remote API when the user has finished typing or pauses for a brief moment.

2. We use the `map` operator to call the `searchBooks`
    pipeline (which itself is a publisher) and return its
    results into the pipeline.

3. Even though we use the `debounce` operator to
    reduce the number of events, we might run into
    a situation where multiple network requests are
    in flight at the same time. As a consequence, the
    network responses might arrive out of order. To
    prevent this, we use `switchToLatest()`—this
    will switch to the latest output from the upstream
    publisher and discards any other previous events.

4. To make sure we make changes to the UI only
    from the main thread, we call `receive(on:
    DispatchQueue.main)`.

5. To assign the result of the pipeline (an array of `Book`
    instances we receive from `searchBooks`) to the
    published property `result`, we would normally use
    the `assign(to:)` subscriber, but as we also want
    to set the `isSearching` property to `false` (to turn
    off the progress view on our UI), we need to use
    the `sink` subscriber, as this will allow us to perform
    multiple instructions.

6. Using the `sink` subscriber also usually means we
    need to store the subscription in a `Cancellable` or a
    `Set` of `AnyCancellables`.

Notice how easy it is to handle challenging tasks like discarding out-
of-order events or reducing the number of requests being sent by only
sending requests when the user stops typing. As you will see in a moment,
this is slightly more complicated when using `async/await`.

...to an async/await Method

How would the same code look like when using async/await?

To call the async/await-based version of searchBooks, we need to choose a slightly different approach. Instead of subscribing to the $searchTerm publisher, we create an async method named executeQuery and create a Task that calls searchBooks:

```
fileprivate class ViewModel: ObservableObject {
  @Published var searchTerm: String = ""

  @Published private(set) var result: [Book] = []
  @Published private(set) var isSearching = false

  private var searchTask: Task<Void, Never>? // (1)

  @MainActor // (7)
  func executeQuery() async {
    searchTask?.cancel() // (2)
    let currentSearchTerm =
      searchTerm.trimmingCharacters(in: .whitespaces)
    if currentSearchTerm.isEmpty {
      result = []
      isSearching = false
    }
    else {
      searchTask = Task { // (3)
        isSearching = true // (4)
        result = await searchBooks(matching: searchTerm) // (5)
        if !Task.isCancelled {
          isSearching = false // (6)
        }
      }
    }
  }
}
```

413

```
private func searchBooks(matching searchTerm: String)
async -> [Book] {
// ...
}
}
```

Inside the `Task`, we also handle the progress view's state by updating the view model's `isSearching` published property according to the current state of the process.

In the Combine-based version of this part of the app, we used a combination of `map` and `switchToLatest` to make sure we only receive results for the most recent user input. This is particularly important for network requests, as they might return out of order.

To achieve the same using `async/await`, we need to use cooperative task cancellation[4]: we keep a reference to the task in `searchTask` (1) and cancel any potentially running task (2) before starting a new one (3).

Since `searchBooks` is marked as `async`, the Swift runtime can decide to execute it on a non-main thread. However, in `executeQuery`, we want to update the UI by setting published properties `result` (5) and `isSearching` (4, 6). To ensure it runs on the main thread, we have to mark it using the `@MainActor` attribute (7).

As a final step, we need to make a small but important change to the UI: since we cannot subscribe an asynchronous method to a published property, we need to find another way to call `executeQuery` for each character the user types into the search field.

It turns out that Apple added a suitable view modifier to the most recent version of SwiftUI—`onReceive(_ publisher:)`. This view modifier allows us to register a closure that will be called whenever the given publisher emits an event:

---

[4] To learn more about cooperative task cancellation, check out my blog post on this topic: `https://peterfriese.dev/posts/swiftui-concurrency-essentials-part2/`)

```
List(viewModel.result) { book in
  BookSearchRowView(book: book)
}
.searchable(text: $viewModel.searchTerm)
.onReceive(viewModel.$searchTerm) { searchTerm in
  Task {
    await viewModel.executeQuery()
  }
}
}
```

Overall, using `async/await` requires more work on our part, and it is easy to get things like cooperative task cancellation wrong or forget an important step, like cancelling any tasks that might still be running. In terms of developer experience, Combine follows a much more declarative approach than `async/await`: you tell the framework *what* to do, not *how* to do it.

Calling Asynchronous Code from Combine

In the previous section, I claimed that we cannot subscribe to a Combine publisher using `async/await`. But is this actually true? Let's see if we can implement a smart way to combine async/await and Combine.

The following snippet shows a view model that uses a Combine pipeline that calls an asynchronous version of the `searchBooks` method:

```
fileprivate class ViewModel: ObservableObject {
  // MARK: - Input
  @Published var searchTerm: String = ""

  // MARK: - Output
  @Published private(set) var result: [Book] = []
  @Published var isSearching = false
```

```
init() {
  $searchTerm
    .debounce(for: 0.8, scheduler: DispatchQueue.main) // (1)
    .removeDuplicates()                                // (2)
    .handleEvents(receiveOutput: { output in           // (3)
      self.isSearching = true
    })
    .flatMap { value in
      Future { promise in
        Task {
          let result = await self.searchBooks(matching: value)
          promise(.success(result))
        }
      }
    }
    .receive(on: DispatchQueue.main)
    .eraseToAnyPublisher()
    .handleEvents(receiveOutput: { output in           // (4)
      self.isSearching = false
    })
    .assign(to: &$result)                              // (5)
}

private func searchBooks(matching searchTerm: String) async ->
[Book] {
    let escapedSearchTerm = searchTerm
      .addingPercentEncoding(withAllowedCharacters:
        .urlHostAllowed) ?? ""
    let url =
      URL(string: "https://openlibrary.org/search.json?q=
      \(escapedSearchTerm)")!
```

```swift
do {
  let (data, _) =
    try await URLSession.shared.data(from: url)

  let searchResult =
    try OpenLibrarySearchResult.init(data: data)
  guard let libraryBooks = searchResult.books else {
    return []
  }
  return libraryBooks.compactMap { Book(from: $0) }
}
catch {
  return []
}
  }
}
```

This approach allows us to tap into the power of Combine to improve the user experience with just a few lines of code:

- By using the debounce operator (1), we can hold off on sending search requests over the network until the user has stopped typing for a second. This means we will consume less bandwidth (good for the user) and cause fewer API calls (good for us, esp. when calling APIs that might be billed).

- We can further reduce the number of requests by removing any duplicate API calls using the removeDuplicates operator (2).

There are also some advantages on the code level:

- By using the handleEvents operator (3, 4), we can extract the code for handling the progress view from the map and sink operators. This also allows us to replace the sink/store combo by a much simpler and easier to use assign subscriber.

- There is only one place (5) in which we assign the result of the pipeline to the result property, reducing the chances to introduce subtle programming errors.

At the same time, we can use the advantages of async/await when writing network access code: being able to read the code from top to bottom in a linear way makes it a lot easier to understand than code that makes use of callbacks or nested closures.

Let's take a closer look at the code that allows us to call an asynchronous method from a Combine pipeline:

```
somePublisher
  .flatMap { value in
    Future { promise in
      Task {
        let result = await self.searchBooks(matching: value)
        promise(.success(result))
      }
    }
  }
```

To call the asynchronous version of searchBooks, we need to establish an asynchronous context. This is why we wrap the call in a Task. Once searchBook returns, we resolve the promise by sending the result as a .success case value.

We can simplify this code by extracting the relevant part into an extension on Publisher:

```
extension Publisher {
  /// Executes an asynchronous call and returns its result to
  the downstream subscriber.
  ///
  /// - Parameter transform: A closure that takes an element as
  a parameter and returns a publisher that produces elements of
  that type.
  /// - Returns: A publisher that transforms elements from an
  upstream  publisher into a publisher of that element's type.
  func `await`<T>(_ transform: @escaping (Output) async -> T)
  -> AnyPublisher<T, Failure> {
    flatMap { value -> Future<T, Failure> in
      Future { promise in
        Task {
          let result = await transform(value)
          promise(.success(result))
        }
      }
    }
    .eraseToAnyPublisher()
  }
}
```

This allows us to call an asynchronous method using the following code:

```
somePublisher
  .await { searchTerm in
    await self.searchBooks(matching: searchTerm)
  }
```

Summary

The seeming lack of attention Apple paid to Combine at WWDC 2021 resulted in a lot of confusion and uncertainty in the community—should you invest into learning Combine in the light of all the attention Apple put on `async/await`?

To answer this question, we need to take a step back and understand the value propositions of Combine and `async/await`.

At a cursory glance, they seem to address the same use case: asynchronously calling APIs. However, when looking closer, it becomes clear that they are very different indeed:

Combine is a reactive framework, with the notion of a stream of events that you transform using operators before consuming them with a subscriber. This side-effect-free way of programming makes is easier to ensure your app is always in a consistent state. In fact, SwiftUI's state management system makes heavy use of Combine—every `@Published` property is, as the name implies, a publisher, making it easy to connect a Combine pipeline.

`Async/await`, on the other hand, aims at making asynchronous programming and handling concurrency easier to implement and reason about. While this makes it easier to create a linear control flow, it doesn't offer the same guarantees about state as Combine does.

My recommendation is to use whichever of the two makes the most sense in any given situation. For any UI-related task, I personally prefer using Combine, as it gives us unprecedented power and flexibility when implementing otherwise difficult-to-implement aspects like debouncing user input, combining multiple input streams into one, and efficiently handling out-of-order execution of network requests.

Combine and async/await are two different kinds of tools in our tool belt, and it is our responsibility to use them wisely and according to their intended purpose.

My recommendation is to use Combine for UI-related features in your app that needs to deal with handling input from a number of sources. Some examples are as follows:

– Input validation: Validating multiple input fields, making sure the user filled in all the mandatory fields, handling interfield dependencies (e.g., selecting credit card payment requires you to fill out the card number, but pay by invoice requires you to provide an additional address for the invoice)

– Searching and filtering: Making sure to search and filter based on the latest values the user entered in the search bar, along with any filter criteria they selected

– Cleaning up user input before it reaches your data layer: For example, making sure you don't hit your API endpoint for every single character the user types, or to remove duplicate queries, to make your network layer more efficient (and consume less bandwidth)

On the other hand, you might find using `async/await` easier to use than Combine when calling asynchronous APIs, making network requests, or interfacing with BaaS platforms like Firebase.

And finally, as you saw in this chapter, combining async/await and Combine is possible, allowing you to mix and match the best aspects of both approaches.

Index

A

Add Modifiers, 29
AppKit, 5
Apple, 3–5, 8–10, 24, 31, 33, 65, 78,
    80, 117, 123, 154, 158, 167,
    170, 208, 252, 320, 326, 327,
    335, 336, 338, 377, 387, 407,
    409, 414, 420
App Store, 4, 337
Aspect Ratio modifier, 49
Async/await, 412
    APIs, 406
    asynchronous, 387
    characteristics, 406
    code level, 418
    and combine, 130, 415, 420
    combine-based version, 414
    combine's operators, 406
    concurrency model, 385
    cooperative task
        cancellation, 415
    error handling and JSON
        parsing, 386
    frameworks and language, 405
    parameter, 391
    pipeline, 407
    sample app, 385

searchBooks, 413, 414
searching and refreshing
    data, 403
searchTerm property, 393
URLSession, 386
Asynchronous
    algorithm, 366
    APIs, 353
    artisanal sandwiches, 366
    execution, 127
    greet function, 364
    method, 377, 387, 414, 418, 419
    network, 365
    synchronous version, 365
    task, 124
    world, 363
Asynchronous code, 387
    in action, 388
    APIs, 388
    compile-time error, 388
    fetching data, 388
    SwiftUI, 389
    task, 387
    Xcode 13, 390
Asynchronous executeQuery
    method, 394
Asynchronous programming
    APIs, 374, 380

Asynchronous
  programming (*cont.*)
  async/await–based, 377
  behavior, 374
  concepts, 377
  concurrency model, 381, 384
  definition, 378
  functions, 379
  handler–based version, 378
  improvement, 383
  language-level, 371
  makeSandwich, 380, 381
  slice function, 379
  toastBread, 374, 376
    function, 372
    and slice, 380
Attributes inspector, 17, 44
Autocapitalization, 134

B

Backend as a service (BaaS),
  317, 421
@Binding, 95, 97, 98, 123
BookRowView, 121
BookShelfApp.swift, 38
Building techniques, reusable
  SwiftUI components, 70

C

Cambridge Dictionary, 363
Child view, 79, 87, 89
Cloud Firestore, 126, 276, 317, 318,
  356, 357

Code refactoring, 60–62, 64
Code reusable, 60, 313
Combination, 114
Combine, 4, 9, 420
  addSnapshotListener method,
    329, 330
  button click, 341
  callback-driven code, 252
  CollectionReference, 328
  concepts, 307, 308
  create publisher, 271
  CurrentValueSubject, 328
  demo server, 261
  elegant and declarative
    mechanism, 338
  eraseToAnyPublisher
    operator, 260
  fetching data, 255, 256
  flatMap operator, 258
  futures, 345
  handleEvents operator, 330, 331
  isFormValidPublisher, 272
  isUsernameAvailablePublisher,
    260, 261
  lazy computed property, 259
  mapping data, 254
  operators, 308, 344, 345,
    351, 352
    built-in operators, 308
    implementation, 309, 310
    retry operator, 311
  PassthroughSubject, 328, 330
  published property, 258, 341
  publishers, 317

Publishers.
    CombineLatest(), 271
refactoring, 252, 253
retrying, 313, 314
retry operator, 301
send(:) method, 328
server's console output, 261
sign-up form, 256, 257, 259
snapshotPublisher, 329, 330
subjects, 328
subscribers, 259
tuples, key paths, 254
updation, 331
username, 275
username publisher, 258
UserNameValid enum, 272
user's input, 275
view model, 257, 260
wrapping APIs, 325
Combine framework
  features, 99
  ObservableObject, 99
  @Publishedturns, 99
  SwiftUI's relation, 106
CombineLatest, 133
Combine pipeline, 133, 163, 410
Combine-specific—filter, 134
Complex list rows, 116
Complex views, 92
Concurrency model, 123, 125–127,
    377, 379, 381, 383–385,
    401, 402
Consumer-facing platforms, 5
Container views

categories, 78
complex UI, 79
grouping, 73
return type, 73
ContentView, 23, 39, 56, 64
ContentView.swift, 15
Cross-platform UIs, 82
Custom list rows, 113
CustomRowView, 116

D

Data binding, 7, 8, 56–58
Developers, 275
Device/network offline errors
  APIError, 286, 287
  connectivity, 286
  isUsernameAvailable
    Publisher, 288
  mapError, 286
  mobile devices, 286
  network error, 289
  usernameMessage, 289
  view model, 287, 288
DispatchQueue.global(qos:), 353
Displaying book details,
    view, 53–55
Domain-specific language (DSL),
    6, 7, 9, 92, 140, 204, 223
Drill-down navigation
  App struct, 185
  BookDetailsView, 188, 189
  BookEditView, 189, 190
  BookRowView, 187, 188

Drill-down navigation (*cont.*)
 Book struct, 185
 Contacts app, 184
 Edit button, 184
 initializer injection, 186
 list bindings, 187
 NavigationLink, 188
 ObservableObject, 185
 root view, 186
 @StateObject, 186
 static list of books, 185
 updation, 190
 view model, 185
Dynamic lists
 Apple, 117
 asynchronous data
  fetching, 123–125
 bindings, 121, 123
 displaying elements, 117,
  119, 120
 pull-to-refresh, 126, 127,
  129, 130
 searching, 130, 132–134

E

Editor placeholder, 23, 28
enum, 95, 155, 156
@EnvironmentObject, 98, 103–106
Error handling, 275
 checkUserName
  AvailablePublisher, 284
 Chrome Dino game, 277
 error conditions, 278

error message, 277
extensions, 284
flatMap, 282
ignoring error, 276
inline error, 278
isUsernameAvailable
 Publisher, 285
network API
 APIError, 281, 282
 checkUserNamer
  AvailablePublisher, 280
 concerns, 279
 network errors, 280, 281
 sign-up form, 279, 280
requirements,
 solution, 283, 284
retrying, 276, 277
typealias, 284
view model, 283
Expanding, 80
ExtractedView, 61
Extract Subview, 60, 62, 65

F

Firebase
 asynchronous, 318
 BookListViewModel, 324
 Combine, 357
 Combine pipeline, 325
 definition, 317
 published properties, 325
 services, 318, 356
 view model, 322, 324

Firestore
cloud firestore, 318
collections/queries, 328, 329
combine, 321
data, 318
dispatch queue, 357, 358
documents, 318
fetching data, 318, 319, 332, 356
Future, 333
DocumentReference, 333
DocumentSnapshot, 333
getDocument method, 333
promise parameter, 334
properties, 333
single-shot Combine
publisher, 335
snapshot/error, 334
real-time live sync, 319, 332
SDK, 318
snapshot listener, 319, 328, 330
updatation, 319, 320
Flat lists, 117
FocusableListView view, 161
FocusedReminder property, 157,
160, 163
@FocusState, 154, 162
Forms, 167
BookDetailsView, 180
Boolean property, 183
buttons, 177, 178
data model, 179
display data, 179
dynamic data, 181
headline text, 170

Hello World, 168, 169
images, 170, 172
input elements, 168
label, 173, 174
NumberFormatter, 183
preview provider, 184
sign-up form
JSON document, 249
username, 248, 249
static data, 168, 170, 179
static forms, 204
TextField, 182
theme, 168
toggle, 175, 176, 180
UI elements, 168, 179, 180
UITableView, 170
version, 182
Frame modifier, 49
Full swipe, 147, 153
Functional reactive
frameworks, 4, 8
Functional reactive programming,
99, 207–209, 409

G

GitHub repository, 36, 56, 154, 251,
366, 406

H

Headers and footers, 137, 138
Hierarchical lists, 117
Horizontal stacks and spacers, 65

HStack, 48, 53, 67, 148
Hug, 65
Hugging, 80

I, J, K

Image and Text views, 67
Imperative UI toolkits, 93
IndexSet, 145
Input forms, 167
Input validation
  binding, 200
  BookEditViewModel, 197
  Book property, 198
  BookShelfApp, 197
  Bool value, 203
  combine pipelines, 236, 237
  completion handler, 198
  contacts app, 191
  dismiss action, 200
  events, 227
  flow of information, 196
  form validation, 192, 193
  functionality, 199, 200
  binding, 198
  initializer, 203
  ISBN, 191
  isISBNValid, 202
  isValid property, 241
  map closure, 203
  @ObservableObject, 196
  password, 238, 240, 241
  Publishers.CombineLatest, 242

save function, 201
sign up form, 191, 227–229
social features, 226
source of truth, 197, 198, 201
steps, 191
SwiftUI, 202
user account, 227
username, 232, 233
users' data, 226, 227
validation message, 234, 235
view model, 193, 194, 196, 202,
  229, 231, 242
wrappedValue, 201
Interface Builder, 7
Internal server errors
  APIError enum, 299, 300
  dataTaskPublisher, 302, 303
  demo server, 304
  error message, 300, 301
  HTTP status code, 298
  implementation, 302
  pressure, 301
  retry operator, 301
  Sound breakpoint, 304
  tryCatch operator, 302
  username, 304
  verification errors, 301
International Standard Book
  Number (ISBN), 66,
  191–193, 202, 203, 225
Internet, 8, 247, 263
iPad Simulator, 190
iPhone, 182

L

Layout behavior
    expanding, 80
    hugging, 80
    SwiftUI layout process, 79
Library, 66, 67
List cells, 139
.listSectionSeparator(), 141
.listSectionSeparatorTint(), 141
.listStyle view modifier, 135
List views
    complex list rows, 114, 116
    custom list rows, 111, 112, 114
    dynamic, 117
    lines of code, 107
    static text, 108
    SwiftUI view creation, 108
    SwiftUI Views inside list rows,
        109, 111
    UI structures, 107

M

@MainActor, 125, 129
Managing focus
    Apple's documentation, 154
    editing, 154
    eliminating empty elements,
        163, 164
    faster navigation, 154
    @FocusState, 154, 156
    handling the enter key, 158, 159
    in List views, 156, 157
    MVVM approach, 159, 160,
        162, 163
    SwiftUI, 154
Mark as read/unread action, 148
Memory-bound process, 337
Mobile applications, 405
Model View Controller (MVC), 10
Model View Presenter (MVP), 10
Model, View, ViewModel (MVVM),
    10, 159, 160, 162, 163
Multiple swipe actions, 150, 152
Multithreading, 262–263, 358

N

Nested lists, 117
Network access
    API endpoints, 264
    Apple's documentation, 266
    CPU cycles, 263
    debounce operator, 269
    edge connection, 263
    removeDuplicates, 270, 271
    root cause, 264, 265
    share() operator
        events, 268
        print() operator, 267
        subscribers, 266
        subscriptions, 268
        $username publisher, 267
    subscribers, 266
    test server, 263

New SwiftUI app creation
  Canvas, 16
  iOS section selection, 12
  naming the project, 13
  two-way tooling, 17
  Xcode, 11, 12, 15, 18

O

Objective-C method, 408
ObservableObject, 98, 99, 106, 123
@ObservedObject, 98, 101, 103
@ObservedObject view model, 121
onDelete modifier, 144, 148
onDelete's closure, 146
onDelete view modifier, 150
onMove view modifier, 145
.onSubmit view modifier, 158
Opaque return type, 39
Opaque type, 74
Operators, 308
  .addTopping, 216
  combine, 214
  CompactMap, 214, 215, 217
  filter operator, 217, 218
  map, 213, 214
  names, 213
  parameters, 218, 219
  pipelines, 215
  .prefix operator, 219
  publisher, 215
  toppings, 219

P, Q

Parent view, 79
Placeholder, 28
Preview canvas, 51, 59, 67
Preview configuration, 58
PreviewProvider, 40, 71, 72
Property wrappers, 94, 95, 106
@Publishedturns, 99
Publishers, 308
  CombineLatest, 221
  creation, 327
  errors, 209
  events, 353
  long-running
    computation, 345
  pizza delivery service
    address, 220
    .eraseToAnyPublisher()
      operator, 220
    order status, 220
    pipelines, 220
  pizza ordering app, 210
  pizza toppings, 209
  place order button, 210
  .print() operator, 222, 223
  subscribe(on:)
    operator, 346–348
  types, 221
  values, 209, 210
Publishers.CombineLatest, 133
Pull-to-refresh, 126, 127, 129, 130
Pyramid of doom, 36, 60

R

RandomAccessCollection, 56, 117
Reactive programming, 248
ReactiveX, 208
Rendering process, 83
Response parsing errors
    alert, 295, 296
    data, 293
    decode operator, 293
    decoding errors, 294
    error message, 293–295
    events, 297
    guidance, 293
    isUsernameAvailable
        Publisher, 298
    network request, 298
    situations, 293
    view model, 296, 297
Retry operator
    code, 311
    exponential backoff, 314–316
    extension, 311
    implementation, 312
    parameters, 312
    Publishers.TryCatch, 312
RxSwift, 4

S

SampleBooks, 37
Sandwich-making process,
        381, 382
Schedulers
    access network, 344
    combine pipeline, 342
    default behavior, 344
    definition, 338
    ImmediateScheduler, 342
    output, 343
    protocol, 338, 339
    receive(on), 344
    SchedulerTimeType, 339
    subscribe (on), 344
    threads, 344
    types, 340
Scrolling views, 9
Searchable
        BooksListView, 134
SearchTerm publisher, 411
Separators, 140, 141
Single View, 72
Smalltalk-esque call semantics, 4
Source of truth, 93, 248
Spacer, 67
Spacer view, 51
@State, 95–98, 121
@StateObject, 98, 99, 101, 119
StateStepper, 100
String interpolation, 28
Struct, 95, 96
Styling
    headers and footers, 137, 138
    list cells, 139
    list styles, 135
    separators, 140, 141
    SwiftUI 3, 134
Subscribers, 211, 212, 308
    receive(on:) operator, 349, 350

Swift Concurrency Manifesto, 375

Swift language, 6

    feature, 373

    team, 409

Swift Package Index, 70

Swift Playgrounds, 4, 366, 367

Swift programming

    language, 4, 364

Swift's new concurrency model,

    123, 125–127

SwiftUI, 390, 402, 410

    application, 385

    Apple's investment, 5

    async/await, 247, 248

    attributes, 6

    bugs, 6

    callbacks, 247

    collaboration, UI designers and

        developers, 6

    combine, 247, 248

    cross-platform UI toolkit, 5

    declarative syntax, 129

    flexible stack-based layout

        system, 139

    input elements, 182

    inspector, 29

    interactivity, 19, 21–24

    key components, 69

    network-driven Combine

        pipeline, 248

    property wrappers, 248

    reactive state management

        system, 207, 248

    reusable UI components, 33

software development, 6

text and image, 33

traditional application, 11

tutorial, 11

UIs, 207

user interface elements, 75

"write once, run everywhere"

    paradigm, 5

Xcode's preview canvas, 6

SwiftUI properties

    composition over inheritance, 9

    declarative *vs.* imperative, 7

    state function, 10, 11

    state management, 8, 9

    views, 10

SwiftUI's state management,

    27–29, 31

    applications data model, 93

    binding objects, 98

    binding value types, 95–98

    @EnvironmentObject, 103–106

    live preview button, 30

    ObservableObject protocol, 99

    property wrappers, 94, 95

    @StateObject, 99, 101

    user greeting, 25, 26

    views and data model sync, 69

SwiftUI View file, 64

    code editor, 41

    complex UIs, 40

    container components, 40

    image scaling, 49

    preview, 46

    source code update, 46

text view, 41, 48
VStack and Image view, 48
VStack container, 47
Xcode tooling, 40
swipeActions modifier, 147,
148, 151
Swipe actions
adding, 150–152
Apple's Mail app, 143
controls, 147
easy-to-use UI affordance, 143
features, 143
full swipe, 153
list row, 147
modifiers, 148
moving and deleting, 145, 146
onDelete, 150
styling, 153
swipe-to-delete, 144, 145
trailing edge, 148–150
UIKit, 143
Swipe-to-delete, 144, 145
Synchronous programming
makeSandwich, 370
sandwich-making algorithm,
367, 370
toastBread function, 370

T

TextField view, 96
Text Field, 27
ToastBread function, 372

U

UIKit, 5, 9, 67, 143, 182
UI-related task, 420
UITextField, 82
UI views
controls and indicators, 76
elements, 74
images, 75
shapes, 77
URLSession, 386
fetching data, 249, 250, 355
issues, 250, 251
publishing, 355
receive(on:) operator, 355
thread, 355
User interface (UI), 74, 78
aspects, 34
blocking, 337
elements, 337
events, 337
framework, 33
updates, 338, 353
Users, 247

V

Validation errors
backend implementation, 289
URLErrors, 289–291
username, 289
view model, 292, 293
Value, 28
View composing, 36, 37, 39, 40

View, Interactor, Presenter, Entity,
    and Routing (VIPER), 10
View modifiers
    app customization, 83
    child views, 87, 89
    configuring views, 84–86
    registering action
        handlers, 89–92
    Swift methods, 84
View modifiers, 19, 65–66, 83–92, 123,
    127, 130, 132, 134, 135, 141,
    145, 147, 150, 158, 162, 170,
    388–389, 400, 403, 410, 414
View protocol, 39, 72, 73, 84
Views, 10, 65
    composing, 74
    ContentView, 72
    custom types, 74
    decomposing, 80
    hierarchy, 81, 82
    just descriptions, 80, 92
    PreviewProvider, 71, 72
    primitives, 82, 83
    structs, View protocol, 72, 73

structure, 71
Swift package, 70
SwiftUI documentation, 80
SwiftUI's building UIs, 70
UI (*see* UI views)
Views library, 20, 21
VStack, 54, 67, 73, 148

W

Worldwide Developers Conference
    (WWDC), 3, 66

X, Y, Z

Xcode, 11, 18, 21, 22
    editor, 17
    graphical tooling, 41
    Library, 19
    New File dialog, 64
    preview canvas, 72
    refactoring tools, 120
    source editor, 16
    two-way tooling, 31

Printed in the United States
by Baker & Taylor Publisher Services